TEACHER DEVELOPMENT AND THE STRUGGLE FOR AUTHENTICITY

Professional Growth and Restructuring in the Context of Change

Edited by

Peter P. Grimmett
Jonathan Neufeld

Foreword by Michael Fullan

Teachers College, Columbia University
New York and London

133885

Published by Teachers College Press, 1234 Amsterdam Avenue
New York, NY 10027

Chapter 3 is adapted from "Restructuring Restructuring: Postmodernity and the
Prospects for Educational Change," Andy Hargreaves, 1994. Reprinted by permission of *The Journal of Education Policy.*

Portions of Chapter 6 are from *Realms of Knowledge,* Leslie Santee Siskin, Falmer
Press, 1994. Used by permission of the publisher.

Library of Congress Cataloging-in-Publication Data

Teacher development and the struggle for authentiticy : professional
    growth and restructuring in the context of change / edited by Peter
    P. Grimmett, Jonathan Neufeld ; foreword by Michael Fullan.
        p.   cm.—(Professional development and practice series)
    Includes papers given at a conference sponsored by the British
Columbia Steering Committee for Teacher Development, held at
Vancouver in February 1991.
    Includes bibliographical references and index.
    ISBN 0-8077-3351-2.—ISBN 0-8077-3350-4 (pbk.)
    1. Teachers—In-service training—Congresses. 2. Teachers—
Vocational guidance—Congresses.   I. Grimmett, Peter Philip.
II. Neufeld, Jonathan.   III. Series.
LB1731.T38   1994
371.1'46—dc20   94-9673

ISBN 0-8077-3351-2
ISBN 0-8077-3350-4 (pbk.)

Printed on acid-free paper
Manufactured in the United States of America
98 97 96 95 94 8 7 6 5 4 3 2 1

In Memory of
Thomas B. Greenfield
1930–1992
Teacher, Scholar, Philosopher, Visionary

From the Series Editor

The central task of the current reform movement in education is to build and transform schools that aspire to achieve democratic ideals. The purpose of the Professional Development and Practice Series is to contribute to this historic transformation by presenting a variety of descriptions of practice-oriented research-narratives, stories, and case studies of innovative work that can lead to a deeper understanding of educational practice and ways to improve it. At this time of important educational change, we need to be informed by the special knowledge of university- and school-based educators who, working in and with the schools, are illuminating the ways change can take place, and what it looks like.

As new organizational arrangements and collaborative relationships are forged and studied, enduring organizational and pedagogical problems are being seen in fresh ways, leading us in new and promising directions. For example, even as the views of how teachers and students develop and learn change, more actively engaging them in their own constructions of knowledge, the connections between teaching, learning, and assessment are being reexamined. The authors in this series, having undertaken to struggle with the problems of practice and the challenge of rethinking the future of our nation's schools, are seeking to involve us in this most important and ongoing process.

The continuous growth and development of teachers, although accepted by most educators as a necessity for real change in schools, may be the area which is most misunderstood. Teachers, it is assumed, can be "taught" new techniques, programs, or curricula, unrelated to the students they teach or the school within which they work; short-term workshops or staff-development days commonly serve as the means by which teachers learn new pedagogy or curriculum. Teachers' differences in knowledge, skill, ability, or motivation, in this way of thinking, are nonexistent.

Fortunately, there is a growing recognition that this set of assumptions about teaching as solely technical work needs serious reconsideration. In *Teacher Development and the Struggle for Authenticity*, Grimmett and Neufeld and the contributors to this volume recognize that teachers are affected not only by the context that exists within their own classroom, but by the larger context of the school and the society within which they are embedded. An understanding of how teachers develop and change involves more than the cataloging of new methods and techniques, it involves an analysis of this complex connection. As part of this analysis, the authors involve the reader in the "struggle for authenticity" in teacher learning. They see this struggle as taking place between those who advocate a behaviorist view of teaching and those who take a constructivist view.

Although advocating that teachers have a greater voice in their own development, the authors are not romantic about teaching or teachers. They recognize that we are developing a new way of thinking about teacher growth, but that the road to fuller understanding of this process has many detours and wrong turns. This book pushes us further along in "the struggle" to understand what practical conditions are needed to create a new view of teacher development and with it, a new conceptualization of school change.

Ann Lieberman

Contents

PART III: Authentic Development: Some Possibilities

Foreword

Teacher development receives a great deal of lip-service these days, but there is depressingly little fundamental analysis of what the concept means. *Teacher Development and the Struggle for Authenticity* represents a multi-faceted, deep contribution to our understanding of the nature and dilemmas of teacher development.

The strength of the book is its exceptionally strong conceptual base, yet it is grounded in the reality of countless cases and situations. Teaching as a profession is at a crossroads in the 1990s. There is much fanfare about the importance of developing teacher professionalism, and about the critical role of teachers in educational reform. Yet many approaches to reform treat the teacher as the problem rather than the solution. Others speak of teacher development in glowing but vague terms assuming that its virtues will flourish merely by giving teacher development a chance to unfold. The urgency of the situation notwithstanding, the debate is largely superficial. There is a need to push deeper into the meaning, complexities and dilemmas involved in pursuing teacher development.

Teacher Development and the Struggle for Authenticity provides both the big picture and a series of focussed pictures on the many faces of teacher development. Grimmett and Neufeld in the first and last chapters lay out a framework for understanding the "settings, conditions, and criteria" of teacher development. In a creative and insightful way, they display the context and contours of understanding the key issues in teacher development. In addition to identifying a number of specific issues and lessons, they draw the convincing conclusion that "the struggle for authenticity in a changing educational context is constituted and continually reconstituted around the negotiation of perplexing dilemmas and vexing contradictions."

The agenda then, by definition, will be perpetually unfinished and in need of action and reflection. The series of chapters in the book, however, provide us with a variety of lenses and tools for struggling productively with the many dilemmas. The three chapters in Part I contribute new perspectives for redefining teacher development in more fundamental terms. We are left with a greater appreciation of the power of teacher develop-

ment when it is understood as a life-long pursuit of sorting out and addressing the dilemmas of teaching in a context of constant change.

The four chapters of Part II examine particular conditions. Here we
see the dilemmas in action. Are national reform policies opportunities or
constraints, and how can teacher development influence the possibilities?
How can internal school development and external contexts be reconciled?
What are the hidden dilemmas behind the empowerment movement, such
as do new forms of apparent collegiality create new hierarchies?

The third part identifies some different possibilities. New ways of looking at teacher development are pursued with insightful results.

In short, the chapters in *Teacher Development and the Struggle for Authen-*
ticity take us to a new plane. A crucial step has been taken in redefining
the field of teacher development.

Michael Fullan

Preface

This book is one of the outcomes of a highly successful international conference on teacher development held in Vancouver, British Columbia, Canada, in February 1991. This conference took place at a time when the province of British Columbia had introduced changes to the educational programs in the schools. The new programs, contained in *Year 2000: A Framework for Learning*, were designed to respond to a combination of societal (e.g., increasing cultural diversity, changing family patterns, rapid technological advancement) and educational (e.g., promoting thinking, cooperative learning, case study teaching, whole language, etc.) changes. For some teachers, this systemwide attempt at innovation generated much excitement and many opportunities to develop their practice by building a learner-focused curriculum. For others, it led to a period of questioning and self-doubt as they grappled with the change from a fairly traditional approach to educational programming to a progressive one in which the curriculum was no longer viewed as "ground to be covered" but as a broader concept framed around students' needs, interests, and choices.

The conference was framed around four themes: (1) The uncertainty / opportunity of change; (2) the purpose of change; (3) rethinking change and the conditions of change; and (4) changes in society and their impact on education. Each theme had a set of questions. For example, the theme of the uncertainty / opportunity of change was instantiated by the following questions:

- How do teachers handle / transcend the uncertainty, pressures, and contradictions of teaching and the accompanying press for improvement?
- How do I, as a teacher, change when I have taught successfully all these years and continue to grow with integrity and authenticity?
- How do teachers *know* they are developing? How do they know when they have changed their practice?
- How do teachers transform mandated change into opportunities for professional renewal?

Over 700 delegates (state / province, district, and school-based practitioners as well as university faculty, but mostly teachers) grappled with these questions. Out of their deliberations emerged the sense that teacher development in a changing educational context is neither simple nor straightforward. Indeed, it was conceived of as a struggle, sometimes sisyphean and disconcerting, sometimes felicitous and effectual. This struggle comes about as teachers wrestle with changes in the larger societal context as they affect learning in schools and also with the changes taking place in the educational context designed to accommodate educational responses to changes in the broader social context. For teachers rooted in this period of tumultuous change, however, the question of what is genuine and authentic arises. Change for the sake of change is ultimately demoralizing. Recalcitrance in the wake of needed change is ultimately stultifying. What, then, are they to do? How are they to make sense of mandated educational change in a context that is, itself, constantly changing?

Teacher Development and the Struggle for Authenticity explores these questions and issues. It examines how teachers learn through struggle and how that struggle is marked by an earnest search for authentic professional development and classroom action. This book, international in scope, is specifically designed to stimulate interest and debate in the rapidly developing field of teacher development. We offer it as a beginning characterization of such a field and as a suggested point of departure for future attempts at conceptualizing teacher development.

While it is of value for participants in all branches of the educational enterprise to be increasingly sensitive to the conditions that encourage teacher development, this volume is aimed specifically at teacher educators, educational researchers, and practitioners in the school setting. The purpose of the book is fourfold.

First, it attempts to respond to the diverse needs of its primary audience by developing a theoretical grounding in the field so that the expression of teachers' voices raises a practical consciousness, not a series of extraneous issues disconnected from student learning. The aim here is to provide a basis for dialogue between and among teachers, educational researchers, teacher educators, and educational administrators so that "giving voice" does not become a euphemism for "giving vent" when one or more parties attempt to impose their agenda on others, thereby creating a monologue.

Second, it attempts to provide clarification and illumination so that teachers can derive and articulate their own criteria for development by describing how varied sets of conditions and associated settings connect with different forms of teacher development. Third, and closely related to the second purpose, it sets out to frame teacher development within the broader social context of the postmodern world. In so doing, the book shows how the conditions that foster and/or constrain teacher development are connected in important ways to the larger social context. It also illustrates how teachers derive their criteria for development in a postmodern context, documenting how these criteria do not comprise a technical formula based on some "grand narrative" but constitute indicators representative of the diversity and complexity that characterize current practice.

Fourth, the book is not a vehicle for expressing the voice of marginalized teachers on their own behalf; rather it is an attempt at articulating the conditions under which teachers can speak for themselves. The collected pieces in this volume cannot, then, be consolidated as an interpretive voice for teachers; nor can the book be used as a sourcebook for advising teachers. Rather, this collection clarifies crucial points of intersection between and among the settings, conditions, and evolving criteria of teacher development. The relationships produced by these intersections deserve reader attention. This volume examines some of these relationships by focusing on the social and economic conditions in which teachers develop—or are thereby hindered—and then discusses how these relationships are important to the development of teachers.

As such, the book has two intended audiences, namely practitioners and academics. The practitioner audience would consist of those persons who work in cross-role ways to nurture teacher development and the renewal of schools. This would include classroom teachers, school and district administrators; district and state consultants; policy makers at the local, state, and national levels; and parental and community groups interested in the reframing of schooling as a societal means for educating children. The academic audience would consist of university-based scholars and researchers who work with teachers collaboratively in the pursuit and study of teacher development and who integrate the knowledge and understandings generated from this focus into teacher education programs.

Special thanks are due to the British Columbia Steering Committee for Teacher Development for organizing the original conference and generously making limited resources available for the preparation of this book. This committee, a consortium representing the various stakeholder groups in the province of British Columbia, consisted of the following membership:

Alf Clinton (British Columbia Association of School Superintendents)
Peter Ellis (British Columbia College of Teachers)
Gaalen Erickson (University of British Columbia)

Peter Grimmett (Chair—Simon Fraser University)
Robin Hansby (Delta School District Teacher, British Columbia)
Linda Kaser (British Columbia Principals' and Vice-Principals' Association)
Ted Riecken (University of Victoria)
Mohammed Shamsher (British Columbia Teachers' Federation)
Marvin Wideen (Simon Fraser University)

Special thanks are also due to Maureen Woodward at Simon Fraser University for typing parts of the manuscript; and to Susan Liddicoat, Acquisitions Editor at Teachers College Press, and Cathy McClure, Developmental Editor at Teachers College Press, for their help in bringing this project to completion.

The Struggle for Authenticity in a Changing Educational Context

PETER P. GRIMMETT
JONATHAN NEUFELD

We live in a world that is increasingly characterized by the widespread disintegration of social and personal relationships, rampant uncertainty, and a discrediting of "grand theories," such as rationalism, capitalism, Marxism, and so forth, which previously had been regarded as capable of making sense of life's phenomena and experiences. At the same time, there has been a shift from the use of industrial assembly-line production techniques to more flexible ways of producing goods and accumulating wealth. These new ways have led to the dispersion of manufacturing bases from traditionally recognized locations to places of cheaper labor costs and easier control, thereby creating considerable human displacement. These changing conditions have led to two broad competing trends in society: a neoconservative reaction and the gaining of voice by previously marginalized individuals and groups. The neoconservative reaction welcomes the information age, with the compression of time and space and the globalization of world economies that it has brought. The gaining of voice by previously marginalized groups celebrates grass-roots uprisings of ordinary people against so-called experts and brings attention to the rights and interests of those who are disenfranchised in policy making and the allocation of resources.

This chapter is based, in part, on the research project "Teacher Development through Administrative or Collegial Processes of Instructional Consultation" (Peter P. Grimmett, Principal Investigator), funded by the Social Sciences and Humanities Research Council of Canada (Grants #410–85–0339, #410–86–2014 and #410–88–0747). It is gratefully acknowledged that this work could not have been carried out without this funding. The opinions expressed in this chapter do not necessarily reflect the policy, position, or endorsement of SSHRCC.

THE CHANGING EDUCATIONAL CONTEXT

These two societal trends have made deep inroads into the educational context, essentially foreshadowing the kinds of changes taking place in schools and classrooms. There is currently considerable pressure for the reform of schools. This pressure is both political and economic and is usually applied from arenas of knowledge and social control, which are perceived as being outside particular school settings. It typically leads to a reactionary stance emphasizing centralized policy making and control of resources, a concern with the delivery of subject-centered core knowledge and skills and an accompanying preoccupation with external assessment of outcomes relative to national standards, and ultimately a reiteration of the teacher's role as "curriculum-deliverer" in classrooms characterized by Firestone (1992) as reflecting the metaphor of students-as-workers. Marshall (1992) maintains that these reform efforts are steeped in behaviorist views of learning and consistent with the factory model of the classroom as a workplace. "Teachers/managers reward students/workers with praise or grades for producing worksheets/products as evidence that they have acquired the basic facts and skills that teachers have provided" (pp. 1–2).

At the same time, there is a call for the restructuring of schools from within as student-centered places of learning. This is based on constructivist (Bruner, 1986; Newman, Griffith, & Cole, 1989; Vygotsky, 1978) and social constructivist (Chandler, 1992; Collins & Green, 1992; Cook-Gumperz, 1986; Edwards & Mercer, 1987; Santa Barbara Classroom Discourse Group, 1992; Weade, 1992) views of learning and is framed around "the need to redefine learning, to rethink the purposes of learning and the consequences for learners of different conceptualizations of learning, and to reconsider elements essential to educational reform" (Marshall, 1992, p. 3). The emphasis here is on students-as-learners (Firestone, 1992) in classrooms-as-learning-places (Marshall, 1992) where learning requires the active participation of the learner, taps into individual and social processes, assumes students to be constructors (as well as recipients) of knowledge, and ultimately views teachers as curriculum-makers.

Marshall (1992) elaborates on these two trends as they support and constrain meaningful learning for students in schools. She describes certain factors that constrain teachers' attempts to implement opportunities for multiply connected meaningful understandings of the world. These she associates with the behaviorist reform efforts. They include an emphasis on factual and procedural knowledge; pressures of content, coverage, time, and assessment; and beliefs about the effectiveness of controlling strategies. She contrasts these with those factors associated with constructivist and social constructivist epistemologies that support teachers' attempts to implement opportunities for multiply connected meaningful understandings of the world. These include teachers' knowledge of how students construct meaningful understanding; opportunities for learning that focus on understanding key ideas and their interrelationships; teachers' expectations and press for understanding; and sharing responsibility for the generation of knowledge and the assessment of learning.

The Notion of Struggle

For teachers, their work context is constantly in a state of flux and subject to competing emphases that, in the final analysis, may be on a collision course. Within this changing and conflictual educational context, teachers search for conditions in which to develop as professional educators. Pursuing this search, however, is problematic; it frequently involves them in a struggle. Teachers struggle because the conditions of the practical setting in which they do their work frequently prevent their professionalism from obtaining its rightful recognition; these conditions also present teachers with great difficulties. These difficulties may take the form of obstacles or constraints hindering development, of temptations for teachers to do the contractual minimum,[1] or of the need to contend with others who are opposed to educational changes. Dealing with these difficulties requires great effort and exertion for teachers who are concerned with the enhancement of student learning (as distinct from the work comfort of school practitioners), such as the ones suggested by Marshall (1992) and by the *Year 2000* (British Columbia Ministry of Education, 1990) educational program in British Columbia. Teachers take pains to stretch themselves dutifully to address the vexing questions and perplexing dilemmas inherent in the daily messiness of practice. In doing so, they sometimes enjoin the fight (with themselves, with colleagues, with superordinates and curriculum policy, and with parents and students) over what is pedagogically appropriate for a particular set of students with specific learning needs in a particular set of classroom conditions and circumstances. Teachers may view their engaging in conflict in a negative or constructive way. Viewed negatively, conflict becomes a source of subversion of one's professional autonomy, a stressful imbroglio rather than a meaningful pursuit. Viewed constructively, conflict becomes a point of frustration and perplexity potentially capable of disrupting or transforming the purposes of teaching and teacher development. The struggle lies in ensuring that the potential for the transformation of practice is, in fact, central to the interests of teachers, students, and their learning. Conflict, then, is viewed as a normal aspect of struggle when practitioners engage in the mutual negotiation of professional purpose and task. It is

> a struggle over assigned meaning, a struggle over discourse as the expression of both form and content, a struggle over interpretation of experience, and a struggle over "self." . . . It is a struggle that makes possible new knowledge that expands beyond individual experience and hence redefines our identities and the real possibilities we see in the daily conditions of our lives. . . . It is the struggle through which new knowledge, identities, and possibilities are introduced that may lead to the alteration simultaneously of circumstances and selves. (Lewis & Simon, 1986, p. 469)

Such a struggle over assigned meaning—that is, the interpretation of experience—and over "self" inevitably involves a grappling with what is genuine and not artificial for any one individual or group. It resonates with Kincaid's (1990) *Lucy*, the story of a young woman on the island of Antigua who was forced by circumstances to be two-faced, "outside false, inside true" (p. 18). It is a struggle for authenticity in which teachers attempt to discover both their true selves as responsible professionals and the new knowledge that enables them to see possibilities in teaching that will lead to a redefinition of classroom realities and roles and an enhancement of student learning. Ultimately, it is a struggle for teachers to find what Sergiovanni (1992) has characterized as the motivational and inspiring forces of moral leadership in a constantly changing educational context.

The Notion of Authenticity

Teachers are motivated and inspired in different ways. Figure Intro. 1 shows how motivation can be conceived of in traditional, alternative, and authentic forms. Traditionally, teachers do what is rewarded. Their motivation is extrinsic and their involvement calculated. When teachers strive to be less controlled by external factors and less dependent on extrinsic gain, they do what they find rewarding. This alternative form of motivation is intrinsic and the involvement is personal. But traditional and alternative forms of motivation do not stamp teachers out as autonomous agents. The difference for Sergiovanni (1992) lies in moral forms of motivation and involvement. We choose to call this *authentic motivation*. This occurs when teachers strive to do not what the organization rewards, nor what they themselves find intrinsically and professionally satisfying, but what is good and important for learners in any given context and set of circumstances. Whereas traditional motivation can lead to a sense of being bound by the agendas of others, alternative forms of motivation can be equally bound by self-oriented agendas. Whereas the former can cultivate feelings of helplessness and powerlessness, the latter could foster feelings of narcissism, hedonism, and irresponsibility. Authentic motivation, by contrast, is essen-

Figure Intro 1. Traditional, alternative, and authentic forms of motivation

RULE	MOTIVATION	INVOLVEMENT
Traditional What gets rewarded gets done	Extrinsic gain	Calculated
Alternative What is rewarding gets done	Intrinsic gain	Personal
Authentic What is good gets done	Moral aim	Moral

From *Moral Leadership* by T. J. Sergiovanni: San Francisco, Jossey-Bass, p. 27. Copyright 1992 by Jossey-Bass. Adapted with permission.

tially moral; it is caught up in a struggle to do what is necessary and of value, not just for the organization nor just for oneself, but ultimately in the important interests of learners. As Taylor (1991) suggests:

> Authenticity . . . involves (i) creation and construction as well as discovery, (ii) originality, and frequently (iii) opposition to the rules of society and even potentially to what we recognize as morality. But it is also true . . . that it . . . requires (i) openness to horizons of significance (for otherwise the creation loses the background that can save it from insignificance) and (ii) a self-definition in dialogue. (p. 66)

The struggle for authenticity,[2] then, is a moral quest requiring teachers to transcend traditional and alternative forms of motivation to engage in the pursuit of moral aims, questions, and interpretations of teaching. Ultimately, it involves teachers in negotiating the necessary tension between creative originality and self-definition through dialogue around horizons of significance.

TEACHERS' STRUGGLE FOR AUTHENTICITY

The struggle for authenticity takes place in a world increasingly composed of groups that have been previously marginalized and who are now engaged in a struggle to ensure that their voices are heard and their messages taken seriously. The ideal of a "grand theory" or a "totalizing project" is being replaced by the expression of contesting views that challenge existing power structures and relationships. Among those of previously marginalized groups, we hear the voices of teachers. Their struggle for authenticity represents a daily grappling with dilemmas of practice and is continually reconstituting itself. Understanding how teachers develop the practice of teaching requires increased knowledge of the settings in which their diverse development takes place and of the macro- and micro-level conditions that influence it. It also requires some illumination of the criteria that teachers use in judging whether their practice has undergone positive change.

The Settings, Conditions, and Criteria of Teacher Development

The development of teachers emerges in two distinct but connected settings. In the practical setting, teachers struggle to maintain their integrity in a changing workplace that is frequently destabilized by an explosion of innovative teaching and learning strategies. In a theoretical setting, they are conceived of as practicing a craft within a burgeoning but as yet theoretically young field of study. These two distinct but connected settings, the practical and the theoretical, function within varied layers of macro-level social and economic conditions that influence, but are not always conducive to, the derivation of criteria for teacher development. This book attempts to examine the relationship between the conditions of the larger social context and the settings of teacher development and, within each setting, between the micro-level conditions or development processes and teachers' understandings of changed practice, with a view to articulating the evolving criteria for teacher development from the diverse and increasingly complex perspectives of teachers. The aim of such an examination is to provide all constituents of the educational enterprise with an opportunity to formulate their own coherent grasp of how and when teacher development takes place within a broader, social context.

Recent sociological research exploring the practical setting has increased our knowledge of the conditions under which teachers gain a sense of professional identity and integrity. These conditions include collaborative working arrangements and restructured roles and responsibilities. Less research has been undertaken, however, that articulates criteria for development in this setting and that connects these criteria to the conditions that support teacher development. Increased knowledge of this relationship would expand our theoretical understanding of teacher development and would also be of value to teachers, educational researchers, teacher educators, and educational administrators.

The Relationship Between Criteria of Teacher Development and Supportive Conditions in the Practical Setting

This book sets out to raise important issues for both practitioners and academics to address. For teachers and educational researchers, there is a need to

- Be conscious of the practical setting of teacher development and of the criteria that teachers view and value as being indicative of their development
- Be more aware of and skilled in strategies of reciprocal exchange through which theoretical formulations can be brought into the dialogue of teachers who, in turn, reconstruct such formulations in light of the specifics of their practical situation

For teacher educators, there is a need to

- Be more astutely aware of the social context of the school into which teachers are occupationally socialized
- Evaluate the possible discrepancy between preservice preparation programs fostering collaborative conditions for novice teachers and the potentially conflicting conditions of constraint or contention, which typically characterize the practical setting of the workforce

For educational administrators, there is a need to

- Consider how the growing field of teacher development fits into a broader social, economic, and intellectual context and to understand that the expanding practice and theory in this field is, in large part, a consequence of these larger social changes
- Understand how certain processes (e.g., the mentoring of new teachers, collegiality between and among experienced practitioners) may be useful for occupational socialization but are incomplete solutions to the challenge of nurturing meaningful conditions for the personal and professional development of teachers
- Discriminate between superficial adoptions of technical discourse based on innovative strategies in the teacher development literature and genuine attempts at experimenting with a learner-focused approach to teaching. When examined critically, the former may serve only to fortify existing unequal relationships of centralized control rather than furthering the student-oriented ends of teacher development

• Explore how the conditions and evolving criteria of teacher development might restructure the current practice of administering
schools and their personnel

OVERVIEW OF THE BOOK

The book opens with the optimistic tone characteristic of much of the
teacher development literature. Some current conditions and evolving
criteria are presented by both Lieberman and McLaughlin, along with the
redefinitions and reformed assumptions that permeate the theoretical and
practical settings of teacher development. The discussion is then extended
to focus on professional discourse as a way of creating new conditions for
teacher development. It is shown how the practical setting is becoming conceptually delineated into distinctive discourse communities framed around
organizational units such as the department, the school, or the district as
well as around recently formed collaborative networks that transcend traditional organizational boundaries. A theoretical relationship is introduced
between teachers' personal and professional microdevelopment as adult
learners in the specific occupational context and the broader social and cultural macrochanges taking place in the world at large.

This mood of optimism then takes an ironic turn by showing how the
hopes and aims of teacher development may be systematically thwarted,
not necessarily by external interventions but rather through the manipulation of the very discourse and conditions evolving within the communities of the practical setting. Readers are prepared for this critical commentary by Hargreaves's chapter arguing how restructuring may alternatively
be conceived as a reformulation of organizational arrangements within the
existing power relations. In this manner, some of the ideas and terminology of restructuring have been co-opted by a corporate mentality, thereby
undermining the purposes for which restructuring originally came into
being. This chapter presents a contrasting framework that challenges the
reader to reconsider familiar definitions and assumptions central to the current teacher development theory. The purpose is to dispel the common
misconceptions that teachers are indiscriminately interested in the forces
of freedom and choice while administrators are more interested in consolidating and maintaining control over teachers.

Woods, Chard, and Siskin then move the discussion beyond the practical setting of the school to investigate the broader social and economic
contexts that have a direct effect on the conditions of teacher development.
Two main features of the context are regarded as potentially hindering the
furtherance of teacher development. First, an inhospitable political and

economic climate can negatively influence the conditions required for teacher development to become a healthy force in the practical setting. Second, the lack of a coherent direction for teacher development in the theoretical setting may be partly the result of misunderstanding and mis-interpretation of the definitions and assumptions of teacher development in the practical setting. The reader is thus left with a warning to take heed of current economic and political trends that influence, positively or nega-tively, the conditions, the criteria, and the settings of teacher development. These contextual trends have a bearing on the nature and degree of teacher development and may even determine how it will be defined as a field of study and as a practical endeavor.

Ceroni and Garman examine conditions in which criteria often cate-gorized by theoreticians and teachers as "growth enhancing" (e.g., collabo-ration, teacher empowerment) are more accurately thought of as manipu-lated versions of teacher development intended to further the ends of centralized control. If not as veiled methods of externally rooted control, they may be seen as reborn hierarchies actually peopled by teachers but disguised as enabling or empowering processes. It is pointed out that the underlying reasons for these mutations of teacher development are situ-ated in the assumptions and interests of some political players (who are not teachers) being deeply embedded in visible criteria for productivity and effectiveness, which these same political players have selected, imposed, and deemed appropriate.

The last section of the book returns the reader to the optimistic mood of the initial chapters. Through presentation and examination of exemplars of those conditions that led to initial feelings of hope, the authors reaffirm the challenge for commitment and connection in practical and theoretical communities. MacKinnon and Grunau provide a detailed account of a highly successful and experimental teacher education program in which preservice teachers were prepared for their practical setting under con-ditions that allowed them to construct highly supportive communities through mutual interaction. Socialization into the profession took place, in these cases, through the forming of relationships and the construction of discourse communities. Central to this process is a conscious shift away from educating teachers along individualistic lines toward one that pivots on a view of self arising from social interaction and connection within a social community of diverse but sharing individuals. A discussion of the polyvocal forms of discourse arising from this innovative preservice pro-gram is included.

Commitments and challenges, which had seemed to be stifled by a hostile context and conditions dominated by oppositional forces, are now revisited by the concluding chapter, which illustrates how teaching efficacy in the practical setting is enhanced when healthy conditions for teacher development are present. Egan's chapter focuses on the individual teacher working quietly for the students in the classroom. Here the author examines the individual aspect of teaching and argues that a developing teacher is one who is imaginative and transfers this imagination into the planning of learning activities that are meaningful for the educational development of students. Imagination was similarly noted in the previous, less optimistic section of the book. There the practical conditions of teacher development were continually undermined by a hostile political environment but imaginative teachers ingeniously found ways of creating "opportunities to teach." Thus the optimistic and less optimistic sections of the book combine to demonstrate how reflection and creative imagination come about when teachers work in ways not unlike those that are conducive for their students' educational development.

In summary, this book contributes to our knowledge by identifying and elaborating on four critical categories that are necessary components in a theoretical understanding of teacher development. These are the social and economic context in which the theoretical and practical settings are situated; the conditions that influence the nature, scope, and direction of teacher development; the settings, theoretical and practical, in which teacher development constitutes itself; and the evolving criteria that indicate how teachers determine that their practice is developing. The criteria, be they imaginative thought and action, an emerging professional discourse, or restructured power relationships, are formed within settings linked to conditions that define and determine their evolution. This book expands the challenges of teacher development beyond our common understandings by situating them among much broader social and economic movements occurring in the contemporary world. In doing so, it may have the potential to extend the theoretical resources that connect with teachers' discourse of hope in their practical setting. It also emphasizes the urgency of teacher development in the practical setting and increases the reader's understanding of the important relationships of conditions within context and criteria within setting.

NOTES

1. March (1984) elaborates on how calculated involvement around a narrowed focus can lead to this kind of performance:

> Long before reaching the top, an intelligent manager learns that some of the more effective ways of improving measured performance have little to do with improving product, service or technology. A system of rewards linked to precise measures is not an incentive to perform well; it is an incentive to obtain a good score. (pp. 27–28)

2. The life of Nietzsche provides one example of a struggle for authenticity. Richard Blunck, who devoted himself to Nietzsche's life and work for 40 years only to find that much of the material he had collected was destroyed in World War II, penned these words about Nietzsche in the introduction to Curt-Paul Janz's (1978) major biography of the German philologist and philosopher:

> Despite the contradictory character of his views and positions, a more profound and elevated intellectual force is communicated that is not confined to positions and truths but constantly both ignores and transcends them in the service of an authenticity that knows no law other than itself and the eternal flux of life with all its transformations and creativity.
>
> Such authenticity, however, does not consist in collecting knowledge and ordering things in a rational manner, little as it can do without these processes, but is a feature of the ethical personality, of the heart's courage, and the dauntless and indefatigable nature of the mind. . . . Spurred on by this authenticity, he [Nietzsche] waged a single-minded, unwearying struggle against an age that was sinking deeper and deeper into hopeless dishonesty, a struggle against his own happiness, against fame, and even against his tender heart. (cited in Miller, 1988/1990, pp. 88–89)

REFERENCES

British Columbia Ministry of Education. (1990). *Year 2000: A framework for learning*. Victoria, BC: Queen's Printer.

Bruner, J. (1986). *Actual minds, possible worlds*. Cambridge, MA: Harvard University Press.

Chandler, S. (1992). Learning for what purpose? Questions when viewing classroom learning from a sociocultural curriculum perspective. In H. H. Marshall (Ed.), *Redefining student learning: Roots of educational change* (pp. 33–58). Norwood, NJ: Ablex.

Collins, E., & Green, J. L. (1992). Learning in classroom settings: Making or breaking a culture. In H. H. Marshall (Ed.), *Redefining student learning: Roots of educational change* (pp. 59–85). Norwood, NJ: Ablex.

Cook-Gumperz, J. (Ed.). (1986). *The social construction of literacy*. Cambridge, UK: Cambridge University Press.

Edwards, D., & Mercer, N. (1987). *Common knowledge*. London: Methuen.

Firestone, W. A. (1992). Organizational design and teaching for student learning. In H. H. Marshall (Ed.), *Redefining student learning: Roots of educational change* (pp. 265–291). Norwood, NJ: Ablex.

Janz, C-P. (1978). *Friedrich Nietzsche* (3 Vols). Munich: Hanser.

Kincaid, J. (1990). *Lucy*. New York: Farrar, Straus & Giroux.

Lewis, M., & Simon, R. I. (1986). A discourse not intended for her: Learning and teaching within patriarchy. *Harvard Educational Review, 56,* 457–472.

March, J.G. (1984). How we talk and how we act: Administrative theory and administrative life. In T. J. Sergiovanni & J. E. Corbally (Eds.), *Leadership and organizational culture* (pp. 23–32). Urbana: University of Illinois Press.

Marshall, H. H. (1992). Seeing, redeeming, and support student learning. In H. H. Marshall (Ed.), *Redefining student learning: Roots of educational change* (pp. 1–32). Norwood, NJ: Ablex.

Miller, A. (1990). *The untouched key: Tracing childhood trauma in creativity and destructiveness* (H. Hannum & H. Hannum, trans.). New York: Doubleday. (Original work published 1988)

Newman, D., Griffith, P., & Cole, M. (1989). *The construction zone: Working for cognitive change in school.* Cambridge, UK: Cambridge University Press.

Santa Barbara Classroom Discourse Group. (1992). Constructing literacy in classrooms: Literate action as social accomplishment. In H. H. Marshall (Ed.), *Redefining student learning: Roots of educational change* (pp. 119–150). Norwood, NJ: Ablex.

Sergiovanni, T. J. (1992). *Moral leadership: Getting to the heart of school improvement.* San Francisco: Jossey-Bass.

Taylor, C. (1991). *The malaise of modernity.* Toronto: Anansi.

Vygotsky, L. (1978). *Mind in society: The development of higher psychological processes.* Cambridge, MA: Harvard University Press.

Weade, G. (1992). Locating learning in the times and spaces of teaching. In H. H. Marshall (Ed.), *Redefining student learning: Roots of educational change* (pp. 87–118). Norwood, NJ: Ablex.

TEACHERS' STRUGGLE FOR AUTHENTIC DEVELOPMENT: EMERGING THEORETICAL PATTERNS

Part I introduces the reader to the emerging theoretical patterns of teacher development conceived of as a struggle for authenticity. Many of the ideas contained in this section possess a freshness that is both captivating and exciting. Indeed, the attempt to honor and validate the knowledge and practice of teachers has become a central tenet in recent efforts at systemic education reform.

Lieberman begins by broadening the definition of teacher development around teacher inquiry and the need to build a culture of support. Such a culture would involve norms of collegiality, openness and trust, and the provision of opportunities and time for disciplined inquiry where teachers could learn new content in the context of their work. To achieve this would inevitably call for a rethinking of leadership functions and the building of networks and coalitions. The commitment and challenge of teacher development, then, lies in providing opportunities and support for teachers to become leaders and learners in the context of teaching.

McLaughlin elaborates on the notion of context. She shows how teacher development is inextricably bound up with contexts that she characterizes as "professional discourse communities." Reporting on a series of studies undertaken by the Center for Research on the Context of Secondary School Teaching (CRC) at Stanford University, she documents how discourse communities manifested themselves in the different work contexts of departments, schools, districts, and collaborative networks associated with secondary school teaching. The studies also show relationships between the presence or absence of such discourse communities in these various contexts and teachers' sense of efficacy as practicing professionals. Accordingly, McLaughlin concludes that tending and supporting the presence of healthy professional communities in the different contexts of secondary school teaching should become an important priority in the current restructuring efforts.

Hargreaves takes up the notion of restructuring to suggest that it is not as straightforward as some advocates have made it out to be. He suggests that the very notion itself may indeed be in need of some restructuring. His chapter, then, examines some of the meanings of restructuring, along with a number of key choices and dilemmas that restructuring poses for teacher development. He begins by distinguishing restructuring from its antecedent of educational reform. Against this backdrop, he depicts two different scenarios of educational restructuring. These two scenarios are used to highlight tensions in restructuring between bureaucracy and professionalism. He goes on to show how these tensions are not just endemic to education but are rooted in the wider tensions of contemporary society. Hargreaves ends by exploring the implications of these tensions in restructuring in the form of four fundamental dilemmas: vision and voice, mandates and menus, trust in persons or processes, and structure and culture. The challenge of restructuring, for Hargreaves, is to move school structures away from premodern and modern models to ones that help teachers work together more effectively as a community in collaborative cultures of positive risk and continuous improvement.

CHAPTER 1

Teacher Development

Commitment and Challenge

ANN LIEBERMAN

A major commitment for all of us in the coming decade is to build the kind of conditions that make possible teachers' continuous growth by providing ongoing opportunities for inquiry into their own practice. The challenge of how to do this, though seemingly obvious, has been historically elusive. Virtually the entire educational establishment has been set up to accept quick fixes—single-shot workshops, or even week-long summer seminars and "good presenters"—rather than developing a set of mutually reinforcing conditions that would need to be considered, understood, and built over time. What we are learning about these conditions, what they look like in practice, and what research knowledge has accumulated about them is the focus of this chapter.[1]

TEACHER DEVELOPMENT: A BROADER CONCEPT

The concept of teacher development redefines the old idea of in-service education or staff development since it concerns itself with teachers' continuous inquiry into practice, viewing teachers as adult learners. The concept of teacher development assumes that the teacher is a "reflective practitioner," someone with a tacit knowledge base, who continuously builds on that base through ongoing inquiry into practice, constantly rethinking and reevaluating his or her own values and practices in concert with others. In the past staff development or in-service education meant a workshop aimed at individual teachers, often carrying with it the assumption that presentation and knowledge of a topic were sufficient for teachers actually to use such ideas in their own classrooms. But the concept of teacher development represents a much broader idea. It is not only the means by which teachers improve and work on their practice with their students, but it also means building a more collaborative culture in the school, one in which teachers are encouraged and supported to lead and learn from one another. What follows is a framework for developing such a culture of inquiry in schools, providing examples of how schools are accomplishing this in different ways. Also included is a discussion of the problems and dilemmas, an inevitable part of the change process, that must be worked on and worked through to create and sustain such a culture.

TEACHER INQUIRY: BUILDING A CULTURE OF SUPPORT

In the last decade both research and practice have provided us with some important insights into how a culture of support could be constituted. Five important elements created from research and practice serve as the organizing themes for this chapter: (1) norms of collegiality, openness, and trust; (2) opportunities and time for disciplined inquiry; (3) teacher learning of content in context; (4) rethinking the functions of leadership; and (5) networks, collaborations, and coalitions. Each of these elements will be discussed, along with examples of how they combine to create a culture of support for teachers engaged in continuous inquiry.

Building Norms of Collegiality, Openness, and Trust

What has become the classic contemporary study of staff development also gives us the clearest description of collegiality in practice. Little's (1986) study of six schools involved in staff development in a medium-sized urban environment ascribed the critical importance of successful implementation of an innovative program to the building of norms of collegiality and experimentation. In schools where the principal was actively engaged *with* teachers and consistently announced expectations for and modeled behaviors of collegiality, there was increased support for self-examination, risk taking, and collective reflection on practice. When principal and teachers observed each other in classrooms, had time to talk about what they were doing, and worked to find solutions to commonly defined problems, the lives of the teachers and the principal were transformed. Traditions of practicality, privacy, and isolation were replaced by shared ownership of issues and problems of practice, a willingness to consider alternative explanations, and a desire to work together as colleagues. The staff was building a new set of norms for work and thus a new culture that encouraged and supported inquiry.

Although the success of the program rested on long-term habits of shared work and shared problem solving among teachers, such patterns of mutual assistance, together with mechanisms by which teachers can emerge as leaders on matters of curriculum and instruction, are not typi-cal of schools in general (Little, 1986). It is important to recognize that these ideas of shared work, shared problem solving, mutual assistance, and teacher leadership in curriculum and instruction form the centerpiece for the building of a school culture that expects, encourages, and supports continuous inquiry into practice.

Little's work was followed by that of Rosenholtz (1989), who focused on the workplace conditions for teachers and examined how teachers socially construct their beliefs about schools, schooling, and teaching. She found that there was a strong relationship between the structures, norms, and pattern of interactions in school cultures and the potential for teacher growth and development. Four variables influencing teachers' perceptions of opportunities to learn were identified: goal setting, teacher evaluation, shared goals, and teacher collaboration. In more collaborative settings teachers reported that teaching is a complex craft with professional learn-ing as an unending process. In isolated settings with little principal support, barriers to collaboration, and limited collective goals, teachers reported that their professional learning was limited to the first two years of teaching. A new line of research has been developing to investigate workplace condi-tions that affect not only the culture of the school but also the way teach-ers engage in learning (see, for example, Louis, 1992). Current research at Stanford by McLaughlin and her associates (1990) has conceptualized, through research on secondary schools, three elements that build norms of collegiality: the building of a professional community (which is differ-ent in each school and dependent, in part, on agreement on goals for the school), some structure for problem solving (how this is accomplished also differs, depending on teachers' definitions of how they think about prob-lems of practice), and teachers' influence and control over their work.

Examples of opportunities for collegiality. But what are some examples of how this collegiality is built and enacted? For schools recently engaged in building a structure for school site management and shared decision making, the team has become a forum for the building of collegiality (see Lieberman, Darling-Hammond, & Zuckerman, 1991). Particularly in urban areas where there have been few, if any, structures for public discussion, the school site team has become a significant place where teachers, prin-cipals, and parents have begun to discuss larger visions for the school, important differences in values concerning child development, learning styles, approaches to curriculum and instruction, and more. People hold-ing different values and coming from varying ethnic and racial backgrounds have a place and a structure that can be used to work on the complex prob-lems involved in changing urban schools. Without some structure for this kind of discourse to take place, we cannot seriously expect to change the schools.

Although numerous examples of teacher isolation have been documented by researchers (Jackson, 1986; Lieberman & Miller, 1984; Lortie, 1975), few have documented the effects of structures that deliberately promote public dialogue and the building of collegiality. However, there are some schools that have created formal structures for engaging teachers in working together around a focus on students, thereby helping to create the conditions for continuous inquiry into practice in a collaborative setting (see, for example, Louis & Smith, 1992).

In Central Park East elementary school in New York City, a structure and a process for student and curriculum review has become a permanent part of the school (child and curriculum review). For example, one day a week a teacher volunteers to discuss a particular child, displaying the student's work and giving information about the academic, social, and emotional makeup of the child—a means of gaining insights into and a better understanding of how to work more effectively with the child. Although one teacher presents knowledge about one child, the entire staff works through (in a go-round fashion) central understandings about the child *before* anyone discusses additional strategies for working with him or her. What is learned along the way is not only how to help this particular student, but a way of sharing, teaching, and learning from one another. In this case such a formal structure builds the expectation that all teachers have responsibility for the students in the school and that all share equally in working together to learn from and contribute to better practice and more informed knowledge about their collective responsibilities to students and to one another as professionals.

Other formal mechanisms, which include grade-level meetings, department meetings, and new committees formed to take on different tasks such as rethinking curriculum and instructional strategies, also serve to provide the means for greater collegiality. But there are informal structures as well, both deliberate and casual, that help to build a culture of continuous inquiry: teacher centers, networks, coalitions organized for particular subject areas, and so on. In fact, any group, small or large, formal or informal, provides the means for building participation that is more collegial, particularly when student learning and teacher work are the focus. Some schools have always tied their schoolwide goals to what happens in the classroom, but many have not. What distinguishes the kind of collegiality here is that there is opportunity for sharing and growing professionally in the form of structures for teacher learning that are legitimated by one's peers.

Opportunities and Time for Disciplined Inquiry

In schools where teachers begin to assume leadership roles in curriculum and instruction, and to think about individual and collective strategies for working more successfully with students, we need to think through how opportunities and time for such pursuits can be made available. Elementary and secondary schools have not been structured to permit or encourage teachers to spend time on thinking and planning. But serious efforts to restructure schools to serve students better inevitably raise the problem of how and when teachers can accomplish this work. Some schools have begun to stretch the margins of time in planning how to do this.

The retreat. Across the country, the notion of a retreat, a full day or more spent away from school, has come to be accepted in many places as an important way to get school faculty to work together on schoolwide issues. For some it is the beginning of real discussion *for the first time* of deep and important differences in the values teachers hold about students, in pedagogical practices, in assumptions about how students learn as well as differences in child development practices. In a recent study of schools in the process of restructuring, the retreat (as well as the school site team) were found to be significant forums for teachers confronting both their differences and their similarities in pedagogical practice (Louis, 1992).

School level groups that promote collegiality. One secondary school in New York City, Central Park East, has totally reorganized the curriculum and the structure of the high school. Teachers are members of one of two teams, which serve as the major organizing structures in the school. There is a humanities team and a math/science team. Each of these teams is responsible for creating curriculum, drawing on their colleagues' resources in the planning. The humanities team, for example, plans on the basis of themes. Team meetings are spent working through how a particular theme can manifest itself in the curriculum. "What experiences will students have?" and "How will we know when they know?" are the kinds of questions asked and worked through by the team. The team's work is to plan together, to help make sure that there is a consistency of theme throughout everyone's teaching and learning experiences, and to promote public discussion about problems and practices as they occur. While students are participating in community service once a week, the team spends two and one-half hours on planning curriculum, alternative assessments, and means to ensure that learning and teaching are integrated in such a way that the experiences that students have provide the means for them to "exhibit" what they know.

The content of the curriculum is organized around themes that cut across subject matter, encouraging a richer diversity of learning experiences. Teachers work hard to make connections across subject areas, discussing how their work and focus in individual classrooms can be connected to an integrating idea. The vision of the school—expressing the shared values of the staff—is to "help students use their minds well." Each team is led by a teacher–facilitator who teaches in the school but who is given time and responsibility for facilitating the team meeting.

There are some schools that divide the "work" to be accomplished by the teachers into task forces, thus sharing responsibility for the complex task of rethinking the school. In one school, Stephen Day, the responsibilities are divided into (1) academic success, (2) professionalism, and (3) student life and discipline. Representatives of each task force then meet in a "steering committee," whose function is to coordinate the work of the school. Such innovative structures create opportunities for dialogue even as the team members continually struggle with the greatest resource problem of all—time.[2]

Teacher Learning of Content in Context

We have been looking at a variety of ways to enable teachers to work together. Let us consider the content of these new restructuring efforts and examine whether providing mechanisms for teachers to work together has direct and important consequences for student learning. An integral part of rethinking schools is confronting how teachers learn in the context of their classrooms. This learning of content in context, acknowledging the complexity of teaching and learning, provides for flexibility and diversity, emphasizing the importance of the content areas and the teacher's responsibility to teach children something of value.

Teacher learning and student learning can be seen as sharing a common developmental ideology (Elkind, 1989). Viewed from this perspective, all learners have developing abilities. The task of the school, then, is to match learning opportunities to these developing abilities. Such a viewpoint sees the student as creative, active, and continuously engaged in constructing his or her own understandings of subject matter. Recent research on cognition further supports this developmentalist view and, by extension, the content-in-context position. It recognizes the complexity of learning in school: the necessity, for example, for children to construct problems that may be poorly defined and conceived so that they can learn from their mistakes, learn the importance of prior knowledge, and appreciate the mix of social and cognitive skills that help define problems (Devaney & Sykes, 1988). Contradicting the assumptions about the necessity for teachers to control both the content of the classroom and the students themselves, this line of research dramatically shifts the focus from the traditional teacher-centered to the learner-centered classroom. Teaching is in the process of being reconceptualized. Teaching and learning are not seen as separate functions, but rather as interdependent parts of the whole. Teachers are learners, too. They pose questions, help solve problems in their own practice, and think deeply about understanding the learning process for themselves and their students. Learning is no longer consumption or memorization, but rather engagement in knowledge production. Teaching is not performance, but facilitative leadership. Curriculum is not given and prescribed, but constructed on the basis of the needs of the learners. All this requires deemphasizing lecture, drill and practice, worksheets and seatwork, and adding dialogue, discussion, and cooperative and independent research to the teacher's repertoire.

Examples of content-in-context approaches. But what does this look like in practice? The whole-language approach to reading, learning math through manipulatives, a problem-solving approach to science, the process approach to writing—all of these are content-in-context approaches to curriculum, and all of them shift responsibility to the learner to do the work and the teacher to help set up the environment and facilitate the process. Foxfire, an approach to student experiential learning, is a case in point. Wigginton (1991), high school teacher and founder of Foxfire, has created 11 principles that exemplify both a developmental and constructivist approach to student learning. In abbreviated form, the 11 principles are:

- All work teachers and students do together must flow from student desire.
- The role of the teacher is that of collaborator and team leader and guide, rather than boss or the repository of all knowledge.
- The academic integrity of the work must be absolutely clear.
- The work is characterized by student action rather than passive reception of processed information.
- A constant feature of the process is its emphasis on peer teaching, small-group work, and teamwork.
- Connections of the work to the surrounding community and the real world outside the classroom are clear.
- There must be an audience beyond the teacher for student work.
- As the year progresses, new activities should grow out of the old.
- As teachers, we must acknowledge the worth of aesthetic experience and help students derive the principles we employ to create beautiful work.

- As the students become more thoughtful participants in their own education, our goal must be to help them increasingly and willingly guide their own learning, fearlessly, for the rest of their lives.
- The work must include honest, ongoing evaluation for skills and/or content as well as changes in student attitudes.

These principles, born and constructed out of practice, represent what the researchers on cognition are talking about, but they also imply what classroom practice might look like if trust, openness, and collaboration were valued and disciplined inquiry encouraged. The teacher outreach networks, organized by Foxfire to model principle-based practices with teachers who then use these practices with their students, have been successful precisely because teachers attempt to integrate these principles into their classrooms and then work collaboratively in their networks. In this way they get support and are able to share their problems and their practices with other teachers going through similar learning experiences.

Observing and being engaged in the way teachers learn the writing process approach, rethinking their role in encouraging student writing, is another case in point. Fletcher (1991) documents a year as a teacher educator trying to introduce the writing process in elementary schools in New York City. One teacher he worked with used 179 dittos as the central organizing structure for her class—there are 179 teaching days in the school year—while another teacher insisted on reading stories with happy endings as a means of motivating her inner-city students to write. Both teachers dramatize the complexity of understanding content-in-context learnings for teachers. For the former, no amount of modeling student choice and participation in writing their own stories could break the habit of teacher control. For the latter, however, the big insight came one day when the teacher read a story with a sad ending. Students cried as a young boy died of a bee sting. So moved were the students by this ending—death being a not uncommon happening in their own lives—that they began to pour out their own stories of death, divorce, violence, friendship, and concern. For the teacher who had always controlled her own feelings as well as those of the students, this major insight came in the context of her own classroom (encouraged by a teacher educator) and led to a major transformation in her facilitation of student work (see Fletcher, 1991).

There is much still to be learned and understood about teachers' learning of content in context. We cannot, and should not, romanticize process approaches to student or adult learning. These approaches must be continuously studied and examined. Student products must grow in complexity and thought. Teachers' understanding of student learning and development must grow as a result of their continuous inquiry into classroom practice. We are not seeking the final answer to successful classroom practice, but rather the development of habits of mind that make it legitimate to ask questions continuously about learning, about students, and about the content of the curriculum. Such engagement encourages new and more open relationships with one another, creating an acceptance and acknowledgment of teacher and student differences and a broader understanding of strategies that promote learning within continuously growing diverse student populations. It also legitimates teaching and learning as part science and part craft, with both parts continuously interacting and changing as a result of teachers' professional learning from their students and their colleagues.

Rethinking the Functions of Leadership

For the most part, schools have been organized hierarchically: Principals are leaders and teachers are followers. However, schools in the process of restructuring are coming to understand that this conception of leadership restricts the building of a culture of inquiry. Sergiovanni (1989) makes an important distinction between technical and managerial conceptions of leadership and cultural leadership:

> Transformative leaders practice the principle of power investment. They distribute power among others in an effort to get more power in return. They know it is not power over people and events that counts, but power over accomplishments and the achievement of organizational purposes. To gain control over the latter, they recognize that they need to delegate or surrender control over the former. (p. 220)

What is being proposed here is a different view of the roles of the principal and the teacher. Principals have power in this view, but it is "power to accomplish" rather than "power over people and events." In such a definition, principals practice the concept of "leadership density," that is, leadership is shared and broadly exercised. When talked about in this way, leadership becomes something that both administrators and teachers can have and use; and leadership becomes an essential ingredient in transforming schools into centers of inquiry. Some studies have begun to document the kinds of changes that principals are making as they move from conventional to more transformational forms of leadership. For example, Derrington (1989) documented the bumpy move from traditional to transitional to transformational in a study of three high school principals attempting to change and broaden their views of leadership. Movement from adversarial to competitive to collegial was also accompanied by a change of the principals' view of the teachers, who were seen first as objects to be improved and eventually as partners. In all cases, the principals spoke of the difficulties of relinquishing control—sometimes because it was difficult for them, but sometimes because teachers had difficulty taking leadership.

In studying the expanding role of the teacher, Wasley (1989) and Smylie and Denny (1989) reveal the tensions and dilemmas faced by practitioners as new and unfamiliar leadership roles are being created. Teacher leaders are often confused about the primary purpose of their positions: Are they to support teachers or to support administrators? They also have difficulty filling a role beyond that of classroom teacher, especially where no clear expectations exist.[3] In part, these difficulties stem from the fact that other supportive organizational conditions or expectations for change have not existed. In fact, teacher leadership roles are often created without the organizational conditions to support them. New and innovative leadership roles, whether formal or informal, must have organizational and cultural supports to sustain them.

Teacher leadership: formal and informal roles. In spite of these difficulties, a number of teachers are in leadership positions and the numbers are growing. In Maine, formal roles of team leader have been created in an elementary school in Narraganset. These teachers deal with budget and schedules, organize field trips, and serve as mentors. But the more powerful and influential positions have arisen informally from the faculty's participation in working to restructure their school as a center of inquiry (Miller, 1990). Informal roles of the teacher as scholar, researcher, visionary, and expert have arisen as a result of the reexamination of the kindergarten program, working on alternate assessment strategies, and participation in staff development workshops on the meaning of intelligence. Through these activities and numerous discussions, various teachers have emerged with strengths in different areas. One teacher, who enjoys doing research, has become the resident researcher on assessment, intelligence, and metacognition and has gained respect from her colleagues as a "teacher scholar." Another, who has emerged as the resident "visionary," is working on the uses of technology in the classroom. Others, through long years of good teaching, have been recognized for their respect for and success with students.

In Santa Fe, New Mexico, a school with a short history of restructuring is carrying out another experiment in teacher leadership. The principal, having taken a job at the state level, was replaced by a management team made up of five teachers (see Wasley, 1992). In the beginning, all these teachers taught students and shared the administrative functions. As of this writing, one is now a facilitator for the staff while the others are sharing responsibilities for budget, programming, schedules, staff development, and so forth.

In the Puget Sound Educational Consortium, a school–university partnership between 12 school districts in the Puget Sound area and the University of Washington, teachers are participating in rethinking the pre-service program at the university (Grossman, 1992). They are also expanding their leadership roles from teaching associate (team teaching at the university) to roles involving restructuring the schools from which they come. In some cases, this has put teachers at the forefront of planning and executing new designs for restructured schools. Although none of these changes has come about without conflict, tension, or battles over turf—which seem to be an inevitable part of the change process—they are none-theless important attempts at creating and using a broader range of talent in the school in the service of students and faculty.

Building Networks, Coalitions, and Collaborations

Emphasizing the school site as the focus for building a culture of inquiry is important, but it is also necessary to develop support outside the school. Schools in the process of change need to build or be a part of larger net-works whose norms and activities are concerned with similar types of change efforts. In this way they can avoid becoming isolated and, at the least, have some buffer against criticism from other schools resistant to change. Most important, perhaps, they can at the same time continue to gain support and knowledge from like-minded groups.

In this period of intense reform, a variety of different kinds of networks and collaboratives have been formed. In some cases they may be informal, made up of loosely connected individuals; others may be more formalized partnerships among institutions; and some may be organized with a par-ticular content focus as their theme. Whatever the case, such groups share some common characteristics: They are alternative in nature, share a com-mon purpose, exchange information and psychological support, are vol-untary, and are based on equal participation of all members (Parker, 1979).

Examples of networks and coalitions. Two well-known school–university partnerships, the Puget Sound Educational Consortium and the South Maine Partnership, are both members of the National Network for Edu-cational Renewal. Both networks have organized groups of teachers who come together regularly to discuss and act on matters of common concern. Teacher groups have dealt with issues of equity, teacher leadership, restruc-turing schools, grouping practices, early childhood education, and at-risk students. The power of these groups is that they are self-directed, define their own agendas, and provide opportunities for teachers to teach one another, exchange experiences, do action research across districts, create new roles—and all in an atmosphere of support and common understanding. These networks develop supportive innovative norms providing the extra encouragement that these teachers need to return to their schools with renewed energy, vision, and commitment.

The Coalition of Essential Schools is an example of collaboration at the national level, drawing schools together to share a common purpose and a clearly defined mission. The coalition, based on the work and leadership of Ted Sizer, is comprised of more than 40 high schools who subscribe to a common set of principles. These include conceptualizing the roles of teachers as "generalists" and students as "workers" within the framework of re-created high school curricula. "Less is more," the credo of the group, suggests that students better develop their minds and abilities by studying fewer subjects but studying them in depth. A coalition of this kind, which provides support for a new vision of the high school along with a set of guidelines for change, allows for individual contextual differences, even as its principles bind the schools together in common cause.

Both major teacher unions in the United States are heavily engaged in building networks for restructuring schools. In these networks they are organizing specific teachers to work on restructuring their schools while providing supportive conditions that help to keep them bound together within a flexible set of guidelines. A recent documentation of a 12-school network created by the New York City Teachers' Centers Consortium of the United Federation of Teachers points to some significant lessons being learned about restructuring schools in a large urban setting. These include further learning about the change process, new and promising organizational strategies, and the kinds of external supports needed for school restructuring (for further discussion, see Lieberman et al., 1991).

Networks, collaborations, or coalitions are not always formally constructed organizations. There are loosely connected groups made up of people who come together informally on a voluntary basis. Some of these networks develop around specific subject-matter areas, while others are organized around resource or teacher centers. They bring people together in flexible ways that are more closely aligned with the kinds of support, encouragement, and informality needed to make changes in schools than are typically provided in bureaucratic settings.

Schools, like teachers, can become isolated and feel estranged from the mainstream. Schools, like teachers, must learn to reach out beyond their traditional borders and create sources of support, challenge, and legitimacy for themselves. Teachers who see themselves as part of a school in the process of change must also see themselves as part of a profession in the process of change. In that way, the norms and values of the school become part of a larger social system, one that sustains and encourages improvement.

Networks, collaborations, and coalitions, whether they offer a broad vision of school change or are formed to work on particular subject-matter content, have become powerful means to build professional community for teachers engaging in creating new visions and possibilities for education. They make available a form of teacher development that attends to the learning of new content in the context of one's own classroom, and they offer nonhierarchical relationships that often provide for genuine learning communities. Many of these networks are now being systematically documented and evaluated, giving us unprecedented opportunities for increasing our knowledge of how they really work (see, for example, Bascia, 1991; Carter, 1991; Lichtenstein, McLaughlin, & Knudsen, 1991; Lord, 1991; Smith, 1991). Along with their positive qualities and contributions, we are finding out that they are not without their problems.

When professional networks are formed outside the school, how do teachers find support inside the school? When networks deal with teachers as individuals, how do they move to reaching teachers in organizations? In growing school–university partnerships, who owns the agenda? And how does this get worked on and worked out over time? How does learning outside the school find support inside? Although teacher involvement in networks enhances professional community, how do we deal with questions of quality? Does becoming involved in looking for new ways to understand and think about one's classroom practices automatically transform them into new ways of engaging students? And how do we deal with the inevitable criticism and tension that comes when teachers spend time with their colleagues that may be perceived as taking time away from students?

CONCLUSION

The growth of networks, collaborations, and coalitions fostering norms of collegiality, openness, and trust, opportunities for inquiry, the learning of content in context, and the reconstruction of leadership roles is being accompanied by the growth of a new language, a language that is trying to explain and describe new ideas, such as teacher research, expanded teacher roles, peer coaching and peer learning, problem posing, problem finding, authentic assessment, shared decision making, and collaborative networks and coalitions. Apparent contradictions and tensions are synthesized in terms such as *systematic ad-hocism* (coined by Lynne Miller to describe the realities of planning for serious change efforts) or my own oxymoron, *collaborative entrepreneurship* (which links working collectively to entrepreneurial drive and creativity). But perhaps more importantly, we are developing a language of hope, commitment, and connection. When seen in this way, teacher development becomes central to the process of education— not just a new course or project or a different way of teaching reading, but a set of interrelated conditions to be built, nurtured, and supported over time.

NOTES

1. See Lieberman and Miller (1990). Portions of this article have been adapted for inclusion here.
2. This school was part of a larger study reported in Lieberman et al., (1991).
3. For a detailed explication of some of the tensions and dilemmas facing practitioners in lead teacher roles, see Chapter 7 of this volume.

REFERENCES

Bascia, N. (1991, April). *The trust agreement projects: Establishing local professional cultures for teachers*. Paper presented at the symposium "What are collaboratives and teacher networks all about?" at the annual meeting of the American Educational Research Association, Chicago.

Carter, B. (1991, April). *The Stanford/schools collaborative: Building an inquiring community of practitioners and scholars*. Paper presented at the symposium "What are collaboratives and teacher networks all about?" at the annual meeting of the American Educational Research Association, Chicago.

Derrington, M. L. (1989). *The role of the principal: Tradition, transition, and transformation*. Unpublished doctoral dissertation, University of Washington, Seattle.

Devaney, K., & Sykes, G. (1988). Making the case for professionalism. In A. Lieberman (Ed.), *Building a professional culture in schools* (pp. 3–22). New York: Teachers College Press.

Elkind, D. (1989). Developmentally appropriate practice: Philosophical and practical applications. *Phi Delta Kappan, 71*(2), 113–117.

Fletcher, R. (1991). *Walking trees: Teaching teachers in the New York city schools*. Portsmouth, NH: Heinemann.

Grossman, P. (1992). Teaching to learn. In A. Lieberman (Ed.), *The changing context of teaching* (Ninety-first yearbook of the National Society for the Study of Education, part I) (pp. 179–196). Chicago: University of Chicago Press.

Jackson, P. (1986). *The practice of teaching*. New York: Teachers College Press.

Lichtenstein, G., McLaughlin, M., & Knudsen, J. (1991, April). *Teacher empowerment and professional knowledge.* Paper presented at the annual meeting of the American Educational Research Association, Chicago.

Lieberman, A., Darling-Hammond, L., & Zuckerman, D. (1991). *Early lessons in urban school restructuring.* New York: National Center for Restructuring Schools, Education and Teaching.

Lieberman, A., & Miller, L. (1984). *Teachers: Their world and their work.* Alexandria, VA: Association for Supervision and Curriculum Development.

Lieberman, A., & Miller, L. (1990). Teacher development in professional practice schools. *Teachers College Record, 92*(1), 105–122.

Little, J. W. (1986). Seductive images and organizational realities in professional development. In A. Lieberman (Ed.), *Rethinking school improvement: Research, craft and concept* (pp. 26–44). New York: Teachers College Press.

Lord, B. (1991, April). *Subject area collaboratives, teacher professionalism and staff development.* Paper presented at the symposium "What are collaboratives and teacher networks all about?"at the annual meeting of the American Educational Research Association, Chicago.

Lortie, D. C. (1975). *Schoolteacher: A sociological study.* Chicago: University of Chicago Press.

Louis, K. S. (1992). Restructuring and the problem of teachers' work. In A. Lieberman (Ed.), *The changing context of teaching* (Ninety-first yearbook of the National Society for the Study of Education, part I) (pp. 138–156). Chicago: University of Chicago Press.

Louis, K. S., & Smith, B. (1992). Cultivating teachers' engagement: Breaking the iron law of social class. In F. M. Newmann (Ed.), *Student engagement and achievement in American secondary schools.* New York: Teachers College Press.

McLaughlin, M. (1990, April). *Strategic dimensions of teachers' workplace context.* Paper presented at the symposium "Tensions in teachers' culture, career and context" at the annual meeting of the American Educational Research Association, Boston.

Miller, L. (1990, April). *Teacher leadership in a culture of inquiry.* Paper presented at the annual meeting of the American Educational Research Association, Boston.

Parker, A. (1979). *Networks for innovation and problem solving and their use for improving education: A comparative view.* Dissemination Process Seminar, IV. Washington, DC: National Institute of Education.

Rosenholtz, S. J. (1989). *Teachers' workplace.* New York: Longman.

Sergiovanni, T. J. (1989). Leadership needed for quality schooling. In Thomas J. Sergiovanni and John H. Moore (Eds.), *Schooling for tomorrow: Directing reforms to issues that count* (pp. 213–226). Boston: Allyn & Bacon.

Smith, H. (1991, April). *Foxfire affiliated teacher networks.* Paper presented at the symposium "What are collaboratives and teacher networks all about?" at the annual meeting of the American Educational Research Association, Chicago.

Smylie, M. A., & Denny, J. W. (1989, March). *Teacher leadership: Tensions and ambiguities in organizational perspective.* Paper presented at the annual meeting of the American Educational Research Association, San Francisco.

Wasley, P. (1989). *Reform rhetoric and real practice: A study of lead teachers.* Unpublished doctoral dissertation, University of Washington, Seattle.

Wasley, P. (1992). A teacher run school: Teacher leadership revisited. In A. Lieberman (Ed.), *The changing context of teaching* (Ninety-first yearbook of the National Society for the Study of Education, part I) (pp. 212–235). Chicago: University of Chicago Press.

Wigginton, E. (1991). *The Foxfire approach: Perspectives and core practices.* Rabun Gap, GA: Foxfire Fund.

CHAPTER 2

Strategic Sites for Teachers' Professional Development

MILBREY WALLIN MCLAUGHLIN

Probably nothing within a school has more impact on students in terms of skills development, self-confidence, or classroom behavior than the personal and professional growth of their teachers. (Barth, 1990, p. 49)

Teachers and researchers roundly criticize traditional approaches to teachers' professional development as a waste of time and ill suited to either teachers' needs or society's interests (Little et al., 1987; McLaughlin, 1990; Smylie, 1990). But what takes the place of the usual in-service activities and workshop-style presentations as staff development strategies? What kinds of activities or environments support the kinds of personal and professional growth to which Roland Barth refers?

This chapter draws on three years of field work in diverse secondary school settings to argue for and illustrate a different way of thinking about teachers' professional development.[1] It sees professional development not as a special project or scheduled event but as a locally constructed product of an active professional community that is responsive to teachers' immediate professional concerns as well as their professional identity.

My analysis is based on the view that teachers' professional development of the most meaningful sort takes place not in a workshop or in discrete, bounded convocations but in the context of professional communities—discourse communities, learning communities. Further, I show that teachers can and typically do belong to multiple professional communities, each of which functions somewhat differently as a strategic site for professional growth. Thus the argument is made that enabling professional growth is, at root, about enabling professional community.

DISCOURSE COMMUNITIES
AND PROFESSIONAL DEVELOPMENT

Teachers' professional development needs are urgent and extend far beyond the boundaries of the "special projects" or focused reforms that have typically provided the impetus for staff development. The demand for professional development arises from the "typical" teachers' classroom and day-to-day responsibilities. Today's students present teachers with challenges that many teachers say they are unprepared to meet (McLaughlin, Talbert, & Phelan, 1990). Today's students bring cultural perspectives, languages, family circumstances, values, and mores to the classroom that differ significantly from those of yesterday's students.

By teachers' reports, today's students comprise the single most salient and problematic "context for teaching" (McLaughlin et al., 1990; Metz, 1993; Nias, 1985). Many teachers say that they simply do not know how to help these students, who are unlike the students they were trained to teach or those whom they have taught in the past.[2]

Teachers' concerns about their ability to respond effectively to today's students or in students' disappointing performance show up in their reported sense of personal and professional efficacy (Ashton & Webb, 1986; Smylie, 1990). For example, more than one-third of the teachers responding to Center for Research on the Context of Secondary School Teaching (CRC) surveys believe they are unsuccessful in teaching the students in their classrooms (McLaughlin et al., 1990).

Teachers make different adaptations in response to the challenges presented by contemporary students. Not all of these responses are positive ones from the perspective of students, society, or the teachers themselves. Table 2.1 sketches the diversity of teachers' responses we observed across different domains of classroom activities: authority relations, pedagogy, and instructional content.

Two of the three instructional responses—enforcing traditional standards and change (or lowering) of expectations—diminish the school experience of both teachers and students. Teachers feel frustrated, burned out, and disconnected from teaching (see also Farber, 1991). Students unable to adapt to traditional content or pedagogy feel unsuccessful; students whose teachers have reduced expectations are exposed to "dumbed-down" curricula, with few challenges or opportunities for authentic accomplishment.

Many teachers who have made an effort to change their practices in response to the needs and demands of today's students—teachers who engage in what Woods (see Chapter 4) calls "creative teaching"—also report fatigue, low morale, and professional isolation. But we also find

Table 2.1. Teachers' adaptations and responses to "Today's Students"

| Adaptations to "new" students | Domains of Adaptation | | | Teachers' affective responses |
	Authority Relations	Pedagogy	Content Emphasis	
Maintain/ enforce trad'tnl standards	More rules More sanctions	More worksheets and tests	Fail more addtn'l make-up, remedial	Burn-out; frustration
Change expectations	Tolerate "disrespect" disorder	Tolerate inattention and incompletes	lower standards for coverage/ achievement	Disengagement
Change practices	Construct group norms Rule consensus	Group work Cooperative learning	Process emphasis; broaden defn'tn of achievement	Efficacy fatigue

another, smaller group of teachers who have changed their practices to accommodate the different learning styles, needs, and backgrounds of today's students and who report feeling neither burned out nor disillusioned, but rather efficacious and energized by the process of responding to the challenges of diverse students in their classrooms.

As we looked across our sites at teachers who report a high sense of efficacy, who feel successful with today's students, we noticed that while these teachers differ along a number of dimensions—age and experience, subject area, track assignment, and even conceptions of pedagogy—all shared this one characteristic: membership in some kind of a strong professional community. Further, almost without exception, these teachers singled out their professional discourse community as the reason that they have been successful in adapting to today's students, the source of their professional motivation and support, and the reason that they did not burn out in the face of some exceedingly demanding teaching situations.[3]

We found active, positive discourse communities at different locations in teachers' professional domain—at the department level, at the school level, at the district level, and within teachers' professional networks. Each occasion for community arose for a different reason, functioned in a different structural and cultural context, took a different form, and served a somewhat different purpose. Each also made a somewhat different contribution to teachers' professional development, dignity, competence, and efficacy. Each community was important in its own right to teachers' growth and professional learning. Each describes a different "story," told below.

Professional Discourse Community at the Department Level

The department, high school teachers say, comprises the workplace of greatest salience (Siskin, 1994).[4] The secondary school department collects teachers of like subject-area interests, expertise, and professional language.[5] The department comprises the natural location for teachers to consider issues of practice and professional growth, providing opportunities for up-close professional reflection and learning.

However, most departments fall far short of this image of learning communities for teachers (Johnson, 1990; Siskin, 1991). Most departments are fragmented, providing no cohesive sense of community for teachers; others are segmented, comprised of warring factions (Siskin, 1994). Moreover, and importantly, we found that those unusual departments that were characterized by strong professional collegiality and mutual support were not school-level creations, but rather communities constructed at the department level. We found that even within the same school, departments can and do vary significantly in the kind of professional community they constitute and the support they give to teachers' professional lives. Figure 2.1 illustrates the variation in departmental collegiality within a single school, Oak Valley High (CRC Site 10).

Figure 2.1 illustrates two important points about departmental variation in collegiality.[6] First, it shows that variation in collegiality is not a product of differences among subject areas. The lower line plots collegiality by subject area as reported by teachers responding to the national Administrator and Teachers Survey (ATS). These data show that there is nothing inherent in the structure or organization of a subject area that suppresses or promotes collegiality on a systematic basis. Social studies teachers, for example, are not just "naturally" more collegial than are math teachers.

Second, while Oak Valley's school level score on a collegiality index is above the national average, department measures within Oak Valley swing from well above the national average (e.g., departments 01 and 03) to significantly below (e.g., departments 02 and 05).[7]

What, then, makes for a vital professional community at the department level? How is it created and sustained? Characteristics of Oak Valley's department 01 suggest a number of important factors and lessons.

Strong, active leadership. Teachers see strong, active leadership that furnishes vision as creating a strong professional community. Oak Valley teachers carefully distinguish between a vision that unifies and integrates departmental practice and one that perceives "one right way" of practice:

Figure 2.1. Department variation in collegiality

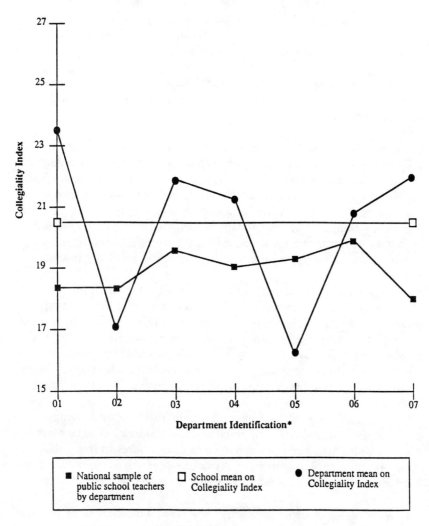

* Departments are represented by codes to protect the anonymity of teachers' responses to collegiality questionnaire items. Means are plotted only for department with ≥5 teacher scores.

> Morale in our department is the highest it has been in 23 years because of
> the quality of the department chair. An insecure administrator or chair
> comes in to "shape things up" in the department or to require people to
> "do things my way." A good department chair has to know how to de-
> velop and build consensus. That's what we have.

The strong commitment of department 01's chair to writing provides that
integrating conception around which consensus can be forged and practice examined.

A common meeting area.   A large department office provides space for the
daily lunches at which faculty gather to discuss practice and classroom
issues. Professional interactions among faculty reflect strong *norms of sharing*. Faculty in department 01 say that "it is important not to hide ideas. In
our department when anyone comes up with a new idea or way to think
about something, they automatically run off 10 dittos." This view stands
in contrast to the sentiment we heard in other settings in which "sharing"
was seen as essentially synonymous with stealing another's intellectual
property.

   Sharing and a strong sense of collective responsibility for instruction
extend to teachers' assignments. Within department 01, assignments are
rotated. No teacher, regardless of tenure, is "entitled" to specific courses
(e.g., Advanced Placement courses), and difficult assignments are shared
among the faculty. They maintain that this policy of course rotation is
essential to teachers' sense of equity. "At the basic level, what impacts teachers most is the equitable distribution of resources and fair teaching assignments."

   In addition, the rotation of course assignments provides important
opportunities for discussion of practice and consideration of new strategies. A faculty member from department 03 attributes to this policy the
transformation of his department over a one-year period from one of isolated and defensive teachers to a vital, lively professional community:

> What's going on in our department now is awesome. Nine or 12 of us are
> actually sitting around the lunch table and talking about practice. All of
> this came about because our assignments changed. Because people had
> new assignments, they were open to looking at what they were doing, hear-
> ing about new ideas. The advanced classes require greater innovative-
> ness, but the lower level classes are more demanding to teach. . . . You
> really have to create it all yourself. The new assignments created a greater
> interdependence among the faculty. We now feel we are being treated
> fairly.

Along with these norms of sharing and openness about practice come *high standards and expectations*. Mutual support in department 01 and mutual obligation for high professional standards go hand in hand. Advice at lunch meetings has to do with ways to get better, rather than to "cope"; colleagues push one another to examine what they are doing and improve.

Not surprisingly, this departmental climate has produced leaders in local, state, and national professional organizations and at least four of the faculty have published in professional journals. Teachers are proud and excited about their accomplishments and credit their chair for enabling them to think harder and take risks through constant support and feedback, development of high standards for practice and norms of sharing, and his style of "coaching" and prompting of teachers.

A vital professional community at the departmental level also pays attention to the *signs and symbols* of community and membership. Weekly celebrations recognize birthdays and other important personal events for members. The department chair has taken pains to build some sort of social life for the department, whether based in professional activities such as conferences or in purely social activities such as potluck dinners or occasional Sunday afternoon barbecues.

Department 02 at Oak Valley underscores the importance of these factors by their absence. This department, teachers say, has community "only in common mailboxes." "Faculty is out there floating; there is no agreement on what is important, no agreement on standards." In contrast to the policy of rotating assignments in departments 01 and 03, teachers in department 02 compete for classes and students.

The department 02 chair also leads with an iron hand. A teacher commented, " In our department, there is just one right way to do things . . . her way." Teacher-talk about the profession and the future contrasts vividly in these two departments, located only a breezeway from each other. Department 01 teachers excitedly examine and debate new curricula and ideas for practice without worry of appearing inadequate; future plans include more publications, curricula development, ideas to be tested. Teachers in department 02 are discouraged, weary, and describe themselves as "just putting in time." They feel isolated, misunderstood, undersupported, and flat. Whereas faculty in department 01 teach one another what they know, their colleagues in department 02 hide both their good ideas and their uncertainties.

Barth highlights the importance of the school principal in creating and nurturing a "community of learners" (Barth, 1990). The principal, he maintains, is the most important reason why teachers grow stale or are stifled on the job. The section that follows affirms and elaborates Barth's conclusion. However, our experience in secondary schools leads us to amend

Barth's comment to include department chairs. As Oak Valley demonstrates, department chairs create "microcultures" that determine the character and contribution of a teachers' professional community and the concomitant opportunities for stimulation and growth.[8]

Further, these departmental communities comprise a most important opportunity because they enable professional development that is constant, ongoing, tied to the classroom, and embedded in current practice. Evidence about teachers' diminished sense of efficacy and variously effective adaptations to today's students underscores the importance of this "up-close" community. Because it is rooted in the everyday realities of classrooms and of department life, the department is the strategic site for referential support and advice and counterpoint to the emotional oscillations of the classroom. The very strong department-level communities we encountered were the exceptions; they supported not only learning and growth for teachers, but also for all students, regardless of their academic ability, cultural background, or academic motivation. Strong departmental communities enabled faculty to develop effective responses to today's students.

Professional Community at the School Level

For teachers for whom department- or subject-area affiliation were especially salient, school-level community was important but served a different purpose, one of professional identity, institutional pride, and supportive context for department efforts. Unlike what we saw in departments, the school level was not typically a site for growth. "Mission" schools and smaller secondary schools with a clear sense of purpose and charter, however, constitute exceptions to this general statement. Teachers in these schools obtained low "departmentalization" scores on the CRC survey and framed their professional affiliation primarily in terms of the school as a whole. In these schools, identification with department or subject area was superseded by membership in a strong, chartered school community.

In the five such schools in our sample, we found consistent and strong teacher efficacy. Figure 2.2 shows teachers' sense of efficacy plotted by subsamples of schools. The five schools that comprise a pattern of teachers' efficacy that departs from that reported for "regular" urban high schools are all mission schools.

Two of these schools are independent academic, college preparatory schools whose students in a sense resemble "yesterday's students" (or at least an idealized version) in terms of academic interests and motivation, family supports, and participation in the cultural mainstream. Teachers' sense of efficacy in these schools is defined largely in terms of the academic

Figure 2.2. Teacher efficacy by age cohort and teaching context

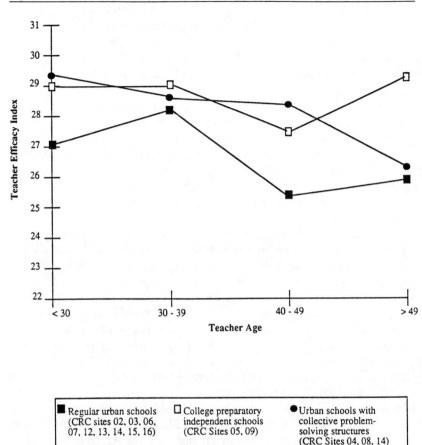

achievements of their students as indicated by college acceptances, academic honors, and scores on standardized tests.

The other three schools serve urban populations or especially problematic adolescents. One of the schools, a performing arts magnet, Ibsen, has a high minority enrollment (within its large, urban district, it is second only to an essentially all-black high school in the number of black male students) and serves youngsters from impoverished neighborhoods as well as youngsters from more affluent addresses who participate in the magnet program. Despite its magnet status, it ranks below the district average in funding for its programs. Yet it ranks at the very top of the district's secondary schools in reading and writing scores, and its students score in the top quartile in mathematics. And whereas students from other schools in the district with similar demographic and socioeconomic status (SES) characteristics drop out at high rates, Ibsen has one of the lowest dropout rates in the district and one of the highest rates of college attendance—80% of its graduates go to college.

The other two schools, Greenfield (an independent school) and Prospect (a public school), are alternative schools serving youth alienated from school and education. These schools are "last-chance" institutions and extraordinarily successful in putting their students squarely on the road to responsible adulthood. With few exceptions, students who attend Greenfield and Prospect not only graduate from high school but more than 50% go directly on to higher education; others find jobs or other kinds of productive activity.

These five very different schools share elements that contribute to and sustain school-level professional community. *Strong norms and beliefs* about purpose and practice are supported and reinforced by *active school leadership*. Vision, energy, and involvement are as critical at the school level as they are at the department level. In each of these schools, administrators have made a clear and personal commitment to what the school stands for and norms of practice. To advance that commitment, school leaders, most particularly the principal, have instituted proactive strategies to maintain and enforce these school-level norms and values.[9] Leaders in these schools make developing a strong, cohesive community an express priority and monitor its "health" on a regular basis.

School leaders have also developed school-level *problem-solving structures,* which enable issues of practice to be addressed, student problems to be discussed, and differences among faculty (or students) to be aired and resolved. Problem-solving structures comprise ways for teachers to receive feedback about their performance and information about their students, to have opportunities to communicate with colleagues, and to move outside their classrooms to address issues as a faculty.

The ways in which school leadership has created these structures and opportunities vary by school. Effective problem solving corresponds closely to school mission. Problem solving in both the public and the independent alternative schools serving disaffected youngsters involves intense student-focused discussion for several hours each Wednesday. In the academic preparatory schools, problem solving centers around faculty meetings in which students' college achievements, test performance, and the like are reviewed and suggestions for ways to enhance academic performance are debated. Greenfield also uses a semiannual faculty retreat to reaffirm school values and mission and to conduct a critical examination of practice.

Problem solving at Ibsen generally revolves around discussion of problems and strategies of coordinating academics and the arts. Moreover, as part of their school improvement program, the faculty established a Faculty Assistance and Support Team (FAST) expressly to bring consistency to teachers' interactions with students both in and out of the classroom and to provide whatever support is needed to enable a teacher to develop practices consistent with the school's priorities. Faculty meetings at Ibsen, like those at Prospect and Greenfield, minimize administrative issues and focus on teachers' concerns with instruction and managing the school environment.

As with the department chairs in the highly collegial settings discussed earlier, administrators in these schools also stimulate a climate of *risk taking and reflection*. Teachers visit one another's classes, and team assignments or cross-disciplinary projects are encouraged. At Ibsen, teachers have developed a number of interdisciplinary activities, such as a recent project combining social studies, English, and science. At Greenfield, teachers comment that "we are never criticized for trying something new, even when it doesn't work out as intended. We are criticized only for unexamined practices and failure to construct new practices in the face of problems with a student or a class."

Prospect's faculty has collectively built a highly innovative curriculum combining what they see as the best of vocational and academic instruction; they see their charge as experimentation with and invention of more effective ways to work with their special student population. Mutually reinforcing conditions exist within each of these schools to bind the faculty together into an active professional community characterized by trust, openness, and norms of professional problem solving and growth.

By teachers' reports, the consequences of these different school-level professional communities for teachers' sense of efficacy are major. Teachers working within a vital, positive professional community feel they belong to a team or collective effort, that the faculty as a whole (rather than each as an individual) are responsible for the accomplishments (and the disappointments). Teachers in schools with strong professional community report feeling invigorated, challenged, professionally engaged, and empowered in the most fundamental sense.

In schools like Ibsen, Greenfield, and Prospect, which serve challenging, nontraditional students, we see the strong school-level community as essential. These communities enable awareness of shared goals, shared challenges, and collective responsibility. In so doing, these school-level communities have vanquished the isolation, sense of relative impotence, and demoralization described by teachers in other settings as the struggle to adapt to the changed realities of urban classrooms unfolded.

Parallels between strong, positive professional community at the school level and the department level are evident. Just as the department chair is key to a lively department community, so is the principal critical to a vigorous, effective school-level community. Each of these schools has a leader committed to problem solving as opposed to problem hiding, to ongoing affirmation of school goals and values, and to maintaining a climate of trust in which risks can be taken and values enacted, a climate in which one need not be ashamed of failure. Each of these schools has a leader who recognizes that individual teachers cannot do it alone and who accordingly establishes and persistently monitors norms of mutual support and obligation.

Especially important at the school level are the ways in which leaders manage differences between and among faculty in terms of professional interests and perspectives, assignments and responsibilities, and needs and involvements. Most critical is their attention to and respect for classroom needs and demands, different instructional preferences, and the development of strategies that embrace rather than ignore that diversity. School-level planning committees, or attention in faculty meetings to issues of resource allocation or of student and teacher assignments, all bring issues of equity and support for differences to the table, enabling the construction of policies that integrate these varied needs and preferences within school diversity and maintain strong community (see also Barth, 1990).

Professional Community at the District Level

Similar themes and essential differences emerge when we examine professional community at the district level. Figure 2.3 shows clear district influence on teachers' sense of efficacy (a finding that surprised us). Once again, analogous to the department and school levels, the differences lie primarily in the ways in which district-level administrators construct, support, and maintain professional community at the district level (Miller [1988] supports this finding).

This significant role that the district can play in creating professional community is especially important to understand given the current enthusiasm for restructuring or site-based decision making and the dismantling or disenfranchisement of district offices that often accompanies such efforts.

Districts affect how teachers feel about themselves as professionals. Professional community at the district level is primarily ideational. It comprises the norms, rules, codes of conduct, and work culture that influence

Figure 2.3. Faculty efficacy by school, district, state, and sector

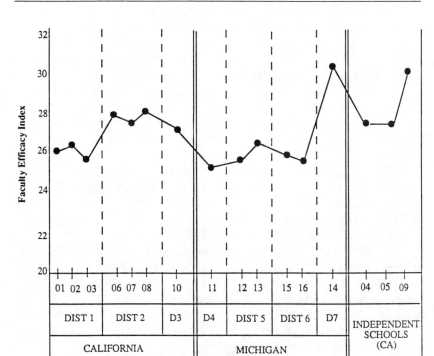

Faculty Efficacy Index = Mean Teacher Efficacy Score for the School

teachers' conception of task and professional identity, broadly conceived in terms of value and worth. Its power and significance lie in its daily influence in teachers' lives as they adapt the norms, codes, and beliefs of the larger community to particular school, department, and classroom practices and actions.

While they are similar conceptually, professional communities at the district and school levels differ in important respects. District-level community is both more fragile and more difficult to achieve because of the physical and functional distance between district offices and schools.

Yet district-level professional community makes an important and particular contribution to teachers' work lives, one distinct from that at the school or department level. The relevance of district-level professional community lies in the overarching sense of professional identity, influence, and pride it fosters in teachers and in the associated congruence of district goals, organizational mission, and individual practice.

In our sample, teachers' judgments of professional community in their district ranged from effectively nonexistent to strong and integrated. We saw that, independent of school-level culture and community, different district professional communities have very different meanings to teachers' lives in the workplace. Further, we found that both positive and negative perceptions of district-level professional community function independently of those at the site level because they establish the broad boundaries for present workplace conditions as well as future prospects, broadly conceived.

To this point, consider these very different district workplace contexts contained in Figure 2.3. Teachers in Oak Valley (district 3) speak of themselves as respected professionals, underscoring the trust and authority they perceive vested in them by district policies and practices. Oak Valley teachers emphasize the pride they feel as Oak Valley teachers.

Teachers in another district, Mostaza (district 1), use fundamentally different terms when they talk about their district. They talk of being "infantilized" by district actions and policies, of not being trusted and respected, and of being treated as "automatons, not professionals." They would not recommend Mostaza as a place to work and take little pride in their district affiliation, even though their particular departments or schools may be a source of professional self-esteem.

How did these positive district-level professional communities come to be? How are they reinforced? Professional community at the district level requires not only positive values and norms, but a self-conscious acceptance of the many disparate elements that comprise "district." District officials face a greater challenge than school administrators in finding ways simultaneously to embrace the diversity of the district's classrooms and professionals and to forge a coherent, positive district identity. And it requires visible, credible, consistent messages from district administration and leadership that teachers are valued, respected professionals.

Oak Valley and Adobe Viejo (district 2) have a number of strategies to integrate school- and classroom-level diversity. One is a strategy of curriculum development that brings teachers together on district subject-area committees to review and develop curriculum policies. This committee structure is designed specifically to give voice to multiple perspectives and enable consensus among teachers about instructional goals and content. This centralized strategy permits teachers to make choices for their classrooms within this agreed-upon structure. Similarly, teachers play a key role in identifying professional development needs and activities. The district frames staff development activities primarily in terms of a "menu" from which teachers can select activities. The opportunities for any given year are identified by a teacher-led professional development committee. The district's role is one of broker, facilitator, convener, and manager.

Oak Valley also pays explicit attention to the symbolic and ceremonial aspects of district-level professional community. As part of a process of "socialization" to district norms, practices, and expectations, teachers new to the district are brought together for one month before school begins and on three occasions each month during their first year. District administrators and teacher leaders meet with new teachers to explain and elaborate what it means to teach in Oak Valley.[10]

District leadership style generally exhibits the presence or absence of a vital, cohesive professional community. Officials in districts such as Oak Valley, with its strong professional community, use *cultural authority* to communicate, reinforce, and monitor district goals and norms of professional conduct. "The way we do things around here" is powerful motivation and correction in Oak Valley.

By contrast, Mostaza's leadership has had to invoke *coercive authority* to implement district directives, bring a measure of cohesion to instructional practices in the district, and control centripetal forces in the organization. The pervasive feeling among Mostaza teachers of "them/us" is a predictable consequence and leads to fragmentation rather than integration of community, work culture, and effective authority. Even well-regarded and effective principals have been unable to overcome Mostaza teachers' feelings of distrust, pessimism, and professional indignity.

Strong and supportive professional community does not just "happen" at the district level any more than it does at the school or department levels. It requires active, ongoing attention by district officials—heed to the messages conveyed to teachers by district policies and practices, care for the quality and availability of communication channels, respect for the diversity inevitable in any district, and attention to the form and nature of professional development activities. Communication in large districts is especially important when "communication up and down the hierarchy may be Kafkaesque" (Brown, 1991, p. 247). Managing and nurturing professional community at the district level is, at heart, a problem of managing district-level norms and values and of providing the material and moral support that motivate and enable teachers to do their best. It is about enabling the creation and vitality of professional communities at multiple sites.

The relationships between teachers and district that are powerful influences on teachers and teaching have less to do with hierarchical structures and controls and everything to do with the norms, expectations, and values that shape district professional community. Leadership affects the quality and quantity of discourse in departments, schools, and districts. With Rex Brown (1991), we found that "again and again, we saw that the difference between a school or a district that offered conditions hospitable to thoughtfulness and a school or district that did not was a difference in the kind, quality, and coherence of the conversations that were taking place there" (p. 246).

Leaders at the district, school, or department level have the strategic opportunity to collect people, foster the conditions of talk and reflection, and enable critical examination of assumptions and practice.

Teachers' Networks and Collaboratives

We have also encountered instances in which teachers' networks or collaboratives provided the site for critical and particular forms of professional community and growth. A powerful example of the strategic role of teachers' collaboratives is provided by an urban mathematics collaborative, in which math teachers participate in a demanding, intense, and professionally challenging professional community created to enhance practice and forge new relationships for teachers (Lichtenstein, McLaughlin, & Knudsen, 1992; Little & McLaughlin, 1991).

The collaborative provides opportunities for professional development that differ critically from even the best of district and local university offerings for important structural reasons. Members of the collaborative meet regularly to examine new ideas, experiment, and discuss the demands of their classrooms. District-offered workshops tend more to generic pedagogies and have limited appeal to subject-area specialists; the university subject-specific offerings fall short because they are divorced from the concrete context of the classroom and local knowledge of school, classrooms, and faculty. Teachers do not leave their classrooms behind when they participate in collaborative activities.

The collaborative also engages teachers in the larger policy arena affecting the subject—the shaping and testing of National Council of Teachers of Mathematics standards and the California Mathematics framework, for example. The collaborative thus provides multiple and different opportunities for leadership, inside the school and classroom, in the district or in the broader policy system.

The high level of trust and candor established in the collaborative promotes a high rate of experimentation and innovation in mathematics instruction. Through its support of field-tested ideas, teacher-designed workshops, classroom demonstrations, and insistence on achievement for all children, the collaborative has created a norm of informed experimentation and risk taking in classroom practices.

Because of its support of professional reflection and change, a collaborative network offers a safe and effective way to enhance the expertise and capacity of mathematics teachers. By organizing mutual support among teachers and creating mechanisms for sharing methods and materials within and across departments, the collaborative provides ongoing support for teachers who have inadequate or outdated preparation in math. This support appears particularly important in the context of these urban districts, with large number of crossover teachers assigned to math classes. Teachers report that the collaborative has provided especially important support of their efforts to adapt their practices to the needs of the low-achieving students who now fill their algebra 1 classes as a consequence of state law discontinuing consumer math and other nonacademic math classes.

Teachers' sense of ownership is vital to the success and effectiveness of the math collaborative, as is the message inherent in the collaborative's philosophy and operations: Teachers are valued professionals. So, too, is the flexibility with which collaborative staff can respond to teachers' requests and their success in brokering access to a broad base of professionally relevant knowledge.

SUMMARY AND CONCLUSION

These department, school, district, and collaborative communities illustrate the extent to which professional development is not a special project activity or only an in-service problem. Issues of and opportunities for professional development occur in assorted forms, formats, and forums in the daily lives of teachers.

Because multiple professional communities exist in any teachers' professional "map," there are multiple strategic sites for professional growth. Teachers' professional development may occur (or not) at different locations within the educational policy system—district, department, school, professional organizations. Each professional community, and the professional development opportunities it provides, takes a different form and function and makes a different and important contribution to teachers' lives. Each matters fundamentally and particularly to teachers' motivation, commitment, and sense of professional efficacy.

While professional communities developed at different sites in the educational policy system make different contributions to teachers' lives and careers, healthy communities also share common characteristics:

• Healthy professional communities at all levels embrace diversity. They acknowledge and integrate the tension between individual and group, and they possess effective strategies of conflict resolution that enable individual preferences and needs to coexist within the context of shared beliefs, goals, and values.

• Healthy professional communities maintain problem-solving structures that enable individuals to examine the problems they face and enlist the advice and perspectives of colleagues. Learning and professional growth requires ongoing problem solving. Learning occurs at all levels of professional community when individuals challenge one another, evaluate their own thinking, and construct practice and principles together.

• Healthy professional communities at all levels maintain strategies for critical review and reflection. They recognize that shared beliefs can be shared delusions and open themselves to scrutiny and feedback from others on a regular basis.

• Healthy professional communities exhibit high levels of trust and teamwork. They are safe places in which to examine practice, try new ideas, and admit disappointment. They provide a setting of collective endeavor and reliable alliance, rather than isolated, individual effort; they create and foster interdependence. Healthy communities achieve the difficult combination of low anxiety and high standards essential to learning (see also Barth, 1990).

• Healthy professional communities of all varieties pay active attention to the ongoing renewal of community. As John Gardner (1991) advises, passive allegiance is insufficient. Individuals must see themselves as having a positive, ongoing duty to nurture and reconstruct community. An important part of this reconstruction is affirmation. A healthy community continually validates itself through ceremonies, symbols, and celebrations. Each of the professional communities we examined here—department, school, district, and collaborative—developed ways to reward itself, celebrate itself, and strengthen bonds, whether through lunchtime rituals or through ceremonies recognizing individual achievement.

Enabling professional development is about enabling professional communities characterized by candor, sharing, mutual dependence and support, trust, and high standards. Such professional communities are created and sustained only if they are valued and nurtured by leaders throughout the system. The only way to make professional development an ongoing, satisfying, challenging part of teachers' lives is to make the tending and support of teachers' professional community a number-one priority. Indeed, all else is arguably of secondary importance.

NOTES

1. The research on which this analysis draws was carried out by the Center for Research on the Context of Secondary School Teaching, located at Stanford University and funded by the U.S. Education Department, Office of Educational Research and Improvement, Grant # G0087C0235.

2. See also, Brown (1991) for a discussion of constraints on teachers' abilities to move from traditional lecture-type teaching to active, hands-on learning as a response to different learning styles and interests of the students in their urban classrooms. In another context, Anderson's (1990) description of the frustrations and concerns of the "old heads" suggests that today's youth in urban communities differ in critical ways from youth of just a few years ago. The "old heads," like many teachers with whom we spoke, complain that they do not understand "kids today" and are unable to communicate effectively with them.

3. Our observation is consistent with a well-established stream of psychological literature that highlights the role of community in promoting positive adaptation to professional work and the importance of the continued availability of intellectual challenge, stimulating collegial discourse, and opportunities to share social realities. See literature cited in Farber (1991) for a useful analysis of this point.

4. This statement is not intended to reify the secondary school department or to suggest that it comprises a necessary (or even desirable) organizational arrangement. It simply represents what is typical in most American high schools.

5. Nias (1985) comments about the importance of shared language and the fact that most teachers do not have it. Subject-area differences confound the problem. Nias points out that the language particular subject areas use to attach meaning to their work differs in fundamental ways. See also Siskin (1994) for discussion of teacher language specific to content areas.

6. "Collegiality" as shown here is an index (30-point scale) constructed from teachers' responses to multiple questions about collegial relations:

Using the scale provided, please indicate the extent to which you agree or disagree with each of the following statements:

> You can count on most staff members to help out anywhere, anytime— even though it may not be part of their official assignment.
> Teachers in this school are continually learning and seeking new ideas.
> There is a great deal of cooperative effort among staff members.
> Staff members maintain high standards.
> This school seems like a big family, everyone is so close and cordial.

7. "Oak Valley" and all other proper names used in this chapter are pseudonyms. The departments are identified only by number to protect the anonymity and confidentiality of respondents.

8. Hill and Bussey (1993) provide a rich description of the department chair's role and outline concrete strategies to enhance the professional life and practice of a department community.

9. For example, in ethnically diverse Ibsen, success for all students is the express priority of the principal, who monitors and supports that focus for faculty efforts in multiple ways. She has developed a grade-reporting scheme that reports students grades for each teacher's class by ethnicity. Both she and teachers are thus able to see if all the students in a teacher's class are performing well and at the same level. The principal has used these reports to point out instances in which students of one ethnic group are not performing as well as those of another in the same class and to provide whatever assistance is needed until all students are performing well.

10. Another district with a strong professional community has used a different strategy to build and maintain that community. Training in conflict resolution for the entire district brought teachers, administrators, staff, and aides together in groups. According to participants, these opportunities for interaction and discussion provided valuable opportunities for district employees to understand the perspectives of others and, especially for people generally excluded from district meetings—secretaries, maintenance personnel, aides—to feel a sense of belonging to a district community.

REFERENCES

Anderson, E. (1990). *Streetwise: Race, class, and change in an urban community.* Chicago: University of Chicago Press.

Ashton, P. T., & Webb, R. B. (1986). *Making a difference: Teachers' sense of efficacy and student achievement.* New York: Longman.

Barth, R. S. (1990). *Improving schools from within.* San Francisco: Jossey-Bass.

Brown, R. G. (1991). *Schools of thought: How the politics of literacy shape thinking in the classroom.* San Francisco: Jossey-Bass.

Farber, B. A. (1991). *Crisis in education: Stress and burnout in the American teacher.* San Francisco: Jossey-Bass.

Gardner, J. W. (1991, January). *Community.* Unpublished manuscript, Stanford University.

Hill, D., & Bussey, B. (1993). *Building a learning community.* Stanford University: Center for Research on the Context of Secondary School Teaching.

Johnson, S. M. (1990). *Teachers at work: Achieving schools.* New York: Basic Books.

Lichtenstein, G., McLaughlin, M. W., & Knudsen, J. L. (1992). Teacher empowerment and professional knowledge. In A. Lieberman (Ed.), *The changing contexts of teaching* (Ninety-first yearbook of the National Society for the Study of Education, part I) (pp. 37–58). Chicago: University of Chicago Press.

Little, J. W., Gerritz, W. H., Stern, D. S., Guthrie, J. W., Kirst, M. W., & Marsh, D. D. (1987). *Staff development in California.* Joint publication of the Far West Laboratory for Educational Research and Development (San Francisco) and Policy Analysis for California Education (University of California at Berkeley and Stanford School of Education).

Little, J. W., & McLaughlin, M. W. (1991). *Urban math collaborative: As the teachers tell it.* Stanford University: Center for Research on the Context of Secondary School Teaching.

McLaughlin, M. W. (1990). *Enabling professional development: What have we learned?* Stanford University: Center for Research on the Context of Secondary School Teaching.

McLaughlin, M. W., Talbert, J. E., & Phelan, P. K. (1990). CRC *Report to the field sites.* Stanford University: Center for Research on the Context of Secondary School Teaching.

Metz, M. H. (1993, April). Teachers' ultimate dependence on their students. In J. W. Little & M. W. McLaughlin (Eds.), *Teachers' work: Individuals, colleagues, and contexts* (pp. 104–136).

Miller, L. (1988). Unlikely beginnings: The district office as a starting point for developing a professional culture of teaching. In A. Lieberman (Ed.), *Building a professional culture in schools* (pp. 167–184). New York: Teachers College Press.

Nias, J. (1985). Reference groups in primary teaching. In S. Ball & I. Goodson (Eds.), *Teachers' lives and careers* (pp. 105–119). London: Falmer.

Siskin, L. S. (1991). Departments as different worlds: Subject subcultures in secondary schools. *Educational Administration Quarterly, 27*(2), 134–160.

Siskin, L. S. (1994). *Realms of knowledge: The academic department.* Philadelphia: Falmer.

Smylie, M. (1990). Teacher efficacy at work. In P. Reyes (Ed.), *Teachers and their workplace* (pp. 48–66). Newbury Park, CA: Sage.

CHAPTER 3

Restructuring Restructuring

*Postmodernity and the Prospects
for Educational Change*

ANDY HARGREAVES

In its report, *A Nation Prepared*, the Carnegie Forum on Education and the Economy (1986) announced the need to "restructure schools." This restructuring, it was thought, would respect and support the professional autonomy of teachers to make decisions in their own classrooms that best met local and state goals, while also holding teachers accountable for how they did that.

In this chapter,[1] I examine some of the meanings of restructuring, along with a number of key choices and dilemmas that restructuring poses for educators, particularly with regard to teacher development and professional growth. I begin by distinguishing restructuring from its antecedent of educational reform. Two different scenarios of restructuring, as represented by the writings of Sarason and Schlechty, are then explored. I argue that these scenarios together highlight tensions in restructuring between bureaucracy and professionalism. Such tensions are not peculiar to education but are rooted in wider tensions in society as a whole as it moves into the restructured era of postmodernity. Finally, the implications of these tensions in restructuring for educators are explored in the form of four fundamental dilemmas between

- Vision and voice
- Mandates and menus
- Trust in persons and trust in processes
- Structure and culture

THE CONTEXT AND MEANING OF RESTRUCTURING

Change by *restructuring* has followed quickly on the heels of change by *reform*. Change by *reform* sought to mandate improvement upon teachers by bureaucratic control and compliance, rather than by supporting teachers in improving themselves and creating restructured opportunities for them to exercise their professionalism. In the era of *reform*, the United States placed substantial emphasis on teacher certification and on basic competency tests for teachers. In many states and school districts, initiatives to motivate the teaching force included such measures as merit pay, career ladders, and differentiated staffing. In the United Kingdom, central controls over teacher preparation were exerted at the national level through procedures of accreditation for teacher education programs. These accredited programs devoted more attention to practical teaching experience and subject-matter mastery and, by implication, less attention to critical reflection on the purposes, ethics, and social consequences of different versions of teaching (see Rudduck, 1989). In 1988, a newly legislated teacher contract also enumerated the number of hours for which teachers would be minimally contracted, including what was termed *directed time* out of class: to be directed according to the wishes of the head teacher or principal.

Within the context of change by reform, measures designed to motivate teachers were paralleled by ones aimed at improving curriculum and instruction. In the United Kingdom, the increased prominence given to subject-matter knowledge in teacher education and the governmental imposition of a subject-based National Curriculum betrayed a shift from broad sponsorship of teachers through self-education, self-evaluation, and critical reflection at the school level to training and induction in contents and principles already determined elsewhere—at the national level.[2] In the United States, many career ladder and teacher leadership programs selected, rewarded, and evaluated teachers not according to multiple criteria of excellence and professional growth, but according to those teachers' adherence to approved models of instruction, often ones that placed a premium on mastery of basic skills.[3] In these cases, the reform of teaching and the reform of instruction went together. Teacher development was not self-development. It was development directed toward the goals of others within a bureaucratic context of regulation and control.

It did not take long for problems in the reform paradigm to surface. It underestimated the divisive effects of career ladders among teachers, misunderstood the basis of teacher motivation as one rooted not in extrinsic career "carrots" but in intrinsic work rewards, and did not appreciate that, because of teachers' control over the sanctuaries of their own classrooms, teacher improvement could not be mandated by bureaucratic regulation. More than this, as the U.S. debt crisis mounted and the responsiveness of the corporate world to global competitiveness became sluggish, there were growing concerns that young people leaving high school needed more than

the traditional minimum competences and basic skills that had preoccu-
pied reformers' thinking hitherto. Problem solving, higher-order thinking
skills, risk taking, teamwork, and cooperation: These were emerging as the
skills and competencies that young people would require as America en-
tered the global information society. Tinkering and quick fixes within the
bounds of the existing system, it seemed, could not bring about significant
improvements even in terms of the basic skills and academic achievements
that comprised the traditional goals of schooling. Certainly, they could not
meet the still greater educational challenges now being posed by the new
information society. Reform within the bounds of the existing system was
apparently not enough. Something more fundamental was called for: nothing short of a complete *restructuring* of the organization of teaching and
learning to meet the challenges of the twenty-first century.

In the space of just a few years, restructuring has become common
currency in educational policy vocabulary, right up to the office of president in the United States and among ministers and civil servants in other
national and regional policy contexts (O'Neil, 1990). Yet its meanings are
various, conflicting, and often ill defined. As Tyack (1990) observes, where
restructuring is concerned, vague is vogue.

The possible components of restructuring are many and various.
According to Murphy and Evertson (1991), they comprise school-based
management, increased consumer choice, teacher empowerment, and
teaching for understanding. For the National Governors' Association (1989),
they include curriculum and instruction redesigned to promote higher-
order thinking skills, the decentralization of authority and decision making to site level, more diverse and differentiated roles for teachers, and
broadened systems of accountability. While the specific components of
restructuring vary from one writer to another, most seem to agree that
what is centrally involved is a fundamental redefinition of rules, roles, responsibilities, and relationships for teachers and leaders in our schools (see,
for example, Schlechty, 1990). Beyond this point, though, the desire for
consensus about and commitment to restructuring in general has left its
specific meaning undefined.

But the broader meanings of restructuring are not infinite. While the
particulars vary from scheme to scheme, certain general patterns of restructuring, which embody quite distinct principles of power and control and
which serve very different purposes, are becoming evident. Two scenarios
of restructuring offer an initial flavor of some of the important contrasts
here.

The first is drawn from Sarason's (1990) account of *The Predictable
Failure of Educational Reform*. Sarason argues that by the criterion of classroom impact, most educational reform has failed. This failure, he says, is

predictable. He identifies two factors as responsible for this. First, he notes that the different components of educational reform have been neither conceived nor addressed as a whole in their interrelationships as a complex system. If components such as curriculum change, professional development, or new teaching strategies are tackled in isolation while others are left unchanged, the success of the reforms will almost certainly be undermined. Sarason supplies numerous historical examples of such failed reforms. That such patterns are not merely a matter of historical record but persist as a chronic feature of our present systems is strikingly revealed in recent studies of the implementation of manipulative problem-solving approaches to mathematics teaching in California.[4] These evaluations show that teachers commonly fail to implement the programs because of the persistence of other programs that emphasize direct instruction in basic skills and because the dominant forms of evaluation and testing continue to be of a conventional paper-and-pencil kind. Sarason's argument has two important implications. First, significant change in curriculum, assessment, or any other domain is unlikely to be successful unless serious attention is also paid to teacher development and the principles of professional judgment and discretion contained within it. Second, teacher development and enhanced professionalism must also be undertaken in conjunction with developments in curriculum, assessment, leadership, and school organization.

Sarason's (1990) second, and arguably more radical, contention is that major educational change is unlikely to be successful unless it addresses school power relationships. "Schools . . . remain intractable to desired reform as long as we avoid confronting their existing power relationships" (p. 5). These include relationships between administrators and teachers, between teachers and parents, and between teachers and students. Sarason argues for a radical rethinking of how schools and classrooms are run. His vision of restructuring entails change that is comprehensive in scope, accompanied by significant, not superficial, redistributions of existing power relationships between and among principals, teachers, parents, and students. It is a vision that is rooted in a sociopsychological understanding of human motivation and commitment and in a sociopolitical understanding of schools as places not only devoted to teaching and learning but also defined through relationships of power and control. Restructuring, for Sarason, means redefining these relationships in fundamental ways.

In the second scenario, Schlechty (1990) also sets out a comprehensive restructuring agenda. Like Sarason, Schlechty's advocacy of restructuring springs from a concern about the inappropriateness of most school structures for the needs of modern society. With their single-classroom, single-lesson, single-teacher formats, such structures are more suited to late

nineteenth- and early twentieth-century preoccupations with mass education in basic skills and rigid educational selection of fixed, future work roles
than to the complex needs of the postindustrial order. For Schlechty, the
challenge of educational change is posed by the global information society. In this context, Schlechty proposes that children should be construed
as "knowledge-workers" and schools be defined as being in the business
of "knowledge-work."

> It is reasonable to expect that, as the American economy becomes more
> information based, and as the mode of labor shifts from manual work to
> knowledge work, concern with the continuous growth and learning of citi-
> zens and employees will increase. Moreover, the conditions of work will
> require one to learn to function well in groups, exercise considerable self-
> discipline, exhibit loyalty while maintaining critical faculties, respect the
> rights of others and in turn expect to be respected. . . . This list of character-
> istics could as well be a list of the virtues of a citizen in a democracy. (p. 39)

Both Schlechty and Sarason see a need for new skills and qualities in
postindustrial society and for new structures to generate them. Sarason describes these in broad social and political ways. For him, they are the skills
and problem-solving capacities needed to cope with and respond to a complex, changing, and threatened social world. They are cultural and political
skills as well as occupational ones. By contrast, for Schlechty, the purposes
of education in the twenty-first century are driven by more specifically
corporate concerns. While many of these points are similar to Sarason's,
the corporate context of Schlechty's agenda nonetheless narrows the range
of the qualities and characteristics thought appropriate as outcomes in the
schools of the future. There is talk of respect, but not of care—either for
other persons or for the environment. Justice and equity are also absent.
Productivity is paramount. This does not distort, but it does restrict what
is seen as appropriate for schools to do.

The corporate context of Schlechty's advocacy has especially striking
implications for his views of power and leadership in restructured schools.
Participatory leadership is advocated but not on the grounds of truth,
beauty, or justice. The grounds of organizational effectiveness are the ones
that are invoked. While Schlechty appears superficially to support changes
in power relationships, essentially only the "symbols of power" are to be
rearranged. Much of the mechanics of leadership may change, but ultimately control of the organization is vested in "strong leaders"—leaders
who are the architects of their respective organization's vision.

This view of power and leadership is quite different from Sarason's
more democratic view, for it is deeply rooted in the corporate perspective.
Schlechty advises administrators to read more widely outside education,

but all the references he lists are in the corporate and economic domain. Moral philosophy, organizational politics, and human development are excluded. Moreover, he posits that "those who are leading the restructuring schools and those who are leading the restructuring of America's enterprises are in the same business" (Schlechty, 1990, pp. 14–15). Schlechty's version of restructuring is therefore essentially a corporate one—corporate in its proposed structures for schooling and corporate in its desired outcomes for learning. This corporate perspective gives Schlechty a limited purchase on power relationships and teacher empowerment—one where bold rhetoric masks balder realities, where professional growth is subsumed under a framework of administrative control.

Together these two scenarios remind us that there is nothing inevitably good or inherently bad about restructuring. Much depends on who controls it, who participates in it, and the purposes to which it is put. The agenda of restructuring poses many important dilemmas that involve profound ethical and political choices about values and purposes.

At the heart of these dilemmas is a fundamental choice between *restructuring as bureaucratic control* (where teachers are controlled and regulated to implement the mandates of others) and *restructuring as professional empowerment* (where teachers are supported, encouraged, and provided with newly structured opportunities to make improvements of their own, in partnership with parents, principals, and students). Our wish for consensus and our desire to maintain the momentum of change often deflect us from addressing the fundamental and difficult dilemmas posed by restructuring. Yet if we do not grapple with them and resolve them to our own satisfaction, others will only resolve them for us later in ways that, perhaps, jar with and undermine our deeply held values and commitments. In the remainder of this chapter, I want to plumb beneath the current consensus of restructuring to expose the dilemmas of value, of purpose, and of control that we must confront and resolve as we address the educational challenges of the next century.

DILEMMAS OF RESTRUCTURING

Restructuring involves many choices and dilemmas. Some of these, like the choice between centralization and decentralization, are familiar ones and have already been widely discussed (see Caldwell & Spinks, 1988; Wise, 1988). Here I want to review four equally important but less widely discussed dilemmas of restructuring—ones that have powerful implications for the purposes of restructuring and the directions it will take and for the processes of teacher development contained within it. All four dilemmas (vision or voice, mandates or menus, trust in people or trust in processes, and structure or culture) are characterized by fundamental tensions between bureaucracy and professionalism.

Vision or Voice?

One of the key tensions in restructuring is between vision and voice. This tension is not peculiar to restructuring in education; it has its roots in the restructuring of contemporary society as a whole. The transitions currently being experienced within and across many societies from industrial to postindustrial, modern to postmodern, or liberal to postliberal forms are well documented in a burgeoning literature. The outcome of these transitions is, for most analysts, uncertain. As the use of the prefix *post* suggests, there is apparently greater clarity about what we are moving beyond than what we are moving toward (Fleming, 1991). Most writers agree, however, that the globalization of information, communication, and technology is at the heart of the transitions.[5] Globalization has led to a compression of time and space and an increase in the pace of productivity and decision making. Computerization along with satellite communication and fiber-optic telecommunications have made international trading in information and currency markets ceaseless. Turnover of goods and services has increased and economic corporations have spread their interests and expertise across national boundaries, utilizing local markets, labor resources, and land opportunities, while maintaining instantaneous connection and coordination across the whole network of operations through modern communications technology.

The globalization of trade and economic activity is weakening the significance of national boundaries as the world reorganizes into a smaller number of larger, more robust economic units. All customs and trade barriers have now been removed in the European Economic Community. The once unthinkable goal of a common European currency has been agreed to in principle. And the eventual opening of the Channel tunnel between England and France will consummate a physical and technological union that has already been achieved economically. Free-trade agreements already secured between the United States and Canada, and Mexico, have similarly elevated economic unity and flexibility above national identity on the North American continent.

In many respects, the globalization of economic life is coming to mean that the nation state as a separate economic, political, and cultural entity is under threat and in decline. In response to these threats, attempts have emerged to protect and reconstruct national identities, not least through the development of national curricula, in which elements of national culture and heritage figure strongly. Goodson (1990) sees such an attempt to revive and reconstruct a floundering national identity within the reassertion of traditional academic subjects proposed by the National Curriculum of England and Wales:

> The globalization of economic life, and more particularly of communication, information and technology, all pose enormous challenges to the existing modes of control and operation of nation-states. In this sense, the pursuance of new centralized national curriculum might be seen as the response of the more economically endangered species among nations. (p. 220)

Dealing with the specific case of history, he continues:

> The balance of subjects in the national curriculum suggest [*sic*] that questions of national identity and control have been pre-eminent, rather than industrial or commercial requirements. For example, information technology has been largely omitted, whilst history has been embraced as a "foundation subject," even though it is quite clearly a subject in decline within the schools. (p. 221)

This is particularly so, he argues, given the high emphasis accorded to British history within the history curriculum.

British history, Canadian content—these are the stuff of national cultural reconstruction, where the burden of reinvented traditions is placed, like most other social burdens, on the shoulders of education. More important still, as globalization intensifies, as a McDonald's restaurant opens in Moscow and sushi bars prosper in New York, as international urban landscapes become ever more alike in the global commodification of community living, we are witnessing the resurgence of ethnic, religious, and linguistic identities of a more localized nature. The quest to reconstruct meaningful identities and attachments in the face of globalization can be seen in the recent struggles of Latvians, Lithuanians, and Estonians to secede from the former Soviet Union and in the conflicts within the former Yugoslavia. It can also be seen on Canadian soil, in the attempts of francophones to secure recognition for themselves as a distinct society and for the province of Quebec as a politically autonomous unit, in the struggles of first nation peoples for self-determination as "nations-within-a-nation," and ultimately in the collapse of the Meech Lake Accord of 1990 and the most recent national referendum (1992) on changes to the Constitution.

What we are witnessing here is the emergence in the context of post-modernity of the voices of those who have previously been unheard, neglected, rejected, ignored—the voices of those who have formerly been marginalized and dispossessed. Gilligan's (1982) influential book, *In a Dif-*

ferent Voice, drawing attention to the undervalued women's perspective on moral development, is an instance of this phenomenon. As Harvey (1989) puts it, "The idea that all groups have a right to speak for themselves, in their own voice accepted as authentic and legitimate is essential to the pluralistic stance of postmodernism" (p. 48).

In educational change and educational research, the formerly unheard and undervalued teacher's voice has been accorded increasing respect and authority in recent years. Here also, especially in elementary schools, the teacher's voice usually belongs to a woman. Elbaz (1991) notes how much of the emergent work on teachers' knowledge, thinking, and empowerment is centrally concerned with the notion of voice. When the notion of voice is used, she says, "the term is always used against the background of a previous silence, and it is a political usage as well as an epistemological one" (p. 10). Goodson (1991) argues that teachers' voices are rooted in their lives, their lifestyles, and their point in the life cycle. The teacher's voice, says Goodson, articulates the teacher's life and its purposes. To understand teaching, therefore, either as a researcher, an administrator, or a colleague, it is not sufficient to observe the behavior, skills, and actions of teaching. One must also listen to the voice of the teacher, to the person it expresses, and to the purposes it articulates. Failure to understand the teacher's voice is failure to understand the teacher's teaching. Indeed, our priority should be not merely to listen to the teacher's voice, but also to sponsor it as a priority within our teacher development work.

The rise of dissident voices, however, threatens traditional centers of power and control. Struggles for regional autonomy and linguistic or ethnic separatism, for instance, challenge longstanding patterns of central domination. Similarly, in education, the bureaucratic impetus to guide the process of change and improvement from the center may silence or dismiss as "mere" resistance the voice of the teacher who doubts or disagrees with the change. Consequently, as the forces of bureaucratic control and teacher development wrestle with one another, one of the greatest challenges to the emergence of the teacher's voice is the orchestration of educational vision.

The development of a common vision, commitment to shared goals, or the development of clarity in understanding the goals being implemented by others are commonly advocated components of the change and improvement process. They are seen as essential to developing confidence and consistency among a community of teachers. Educational leaders are viewed as vital to the development of motivating visions. According to Achilles (1987), for instance, leaders "must know what is needed to improve schools. They must know how to administer the schools to achieve the desired results. As a starting point, principals must envision better schools, articulate this vision to others, and orchestrate consensus on the vision" (p. 18). There is a strong sense here that the vision is primarily the principal's vision, a vision to be articulated to (not developed with) others, a vision around which the orchestration of consensus will subsequently follow.

These criticisms are not intended to dispute the importance of vision, shared purpose, and direction among a school's staff. Rather, they are meant to raise the crucial question: Whose vision is this? For some writers, the principal's role in promoting school improvement and helping develop the culture of the school becomes one of manipulating the culture and its teachers to conform to the principal's own vision. Deal and Peterson (1987), for example, urge that once principals have come to understand their school's culture, they should then ask: "If it matches my conception of a 'good school', what can I do to reinforce or strengthen existing patterns?" "If my vision is at odds with the existing mindset, values or ways of acting, what can be done to change or shape the culture?" (p. 14). For Deal and Peterson, who, like Schlechty, write very much from a corporate perspective, this is part of the solution to the challenge of school leadership. I would argue that it can be seen as part of the problem.

The corporate folly of vision building being spearheaded by strong and single-minded leaders is revealed in an account of how Air Canada's president, Claude Taylor, tried to turn the company around. "To show the new way, Taylor wrote a mission statement for the airline, framed it on his private meeting room wall and sent a copy to every employee's home" ("Hello Cruel World," 1991, p. 36). Part of the solution? Or part of the problem?

"My company," "my vision," "my teachers," "my school"—these proprietary claims and attitudes suggest an ownership of the school and of change that is individual rather than collective, imposed rather than earned, and hierarchical rather than democratic. This ownership is typically male ownership in which power is exercised over women. With visions as unitary and prescriptive as this, teachers soon learn to suppress their *voice*. Management becomes manipulation. Collaboration become co-optation. Worst of all, having teachers conform to the principal's vision minimizes the opportunities for principals to learn that parts of their own vision may be flawed, that some teachers' visions may be as valid, if not more so, than theirs.

This does not mean that principals' visions are unimportant. The quality and clarity of their visions may have helped mark them out for leadership. But principals have no monopoly on wisdom. Nor should they be immune from the questioning, inquiry, and deep reflection in which teachers are asked to engage. Principals' visions should therefore be provisional ones that are open to change. They should be part of the collaborative mix.

The authority of principals' views should not be accepted uncritically because of whose views they are; rather, they should be appreciated for their quality and richness.

Ultimately, the responsibility for vision building should be a collective, not individual, one. Collaboration should mean creating the vision together, not complying with the principal's version. All stakeholders should be involved in illuminating the mission and purposes of the school. Leithwood and Jantzi (1990) describe a practical example of developing shared school goals for school improvement, in which the responsibility for the task was delegated to school improvement teams. This, they note, "prevented the principal's goals from dominating the process," although the authors add ominously in parentheses—"or from being seen to dominate the process" (p. 13).

Exclusive emphasis on vision or voice is constructive neither for school restructuring nor for teacher development. A world of voice without vision is a world reduced to chaotic babble where there are no means for arbitrating between voices, reconciling them, or drawing them together. This is the dark side of the postmodern world, a world from which community and authority have disappeared. It is a world where the authority of voice has supplanted the voice of authority to an excessive degree. Research studies that go beyond understanding teachers' stories to endorsing and celebrating them, and research traditions that give arbitrary credence to teacher accounts over (neglected) accounts of parents or students, for instance, illustrate some of the difficulties of this postmodern perspective.[6] Voices need to be not only heard but also engaged, reconciled, and argued with. It is important to attend not only to the aesthetics of articulating teacher voices, but also to the ethics of what those voices articulate.

We have seen that a world of vision without voice is equally problematic. In this world where purposes are imposed and consensus is contrived, there is no place for the practical judgment and wisdom of teachers, no place for their voices to get a proper hearing. A major challenge for educational restructuring is to work through and reconcile this tension between vision and voice, to create a choir from a cacophony.

Mandates or Menus?

The paradox of postmodernity is that with the globalization of information, communication, and economic life come tendencies and capacities to adapt, respond to, and emphasize local and immediate production needs and consumer wants. This move from massification to diversity in economic activity, together with the localized and regionalized revitalizations of cultural, ethnic, and linguistic identity described in the previous section, have profound implications for knowledge and belief systems and the expertise that rests on them. What we are witnessing here at the societal level is a shift from a small number of stable singularities of knowledge and belief to a fluctuating, ever-changing plurality of belief systems.

Confidence in universalizing, all-encompassing belief systems is in decline. Our growing understanding of the imminence of environmental catastrophe on a global scale has seriously undermined our faith in technology as a way of accurately and reliably predicting and controlling our world in the rational pursuit of progress. The spread of information, along with the globalization of economies, has also undermined beliefs in the scientifically predicted inevitability of socialist transformation, a change both symbolized and stimulated by the collapse of the Berlin Wall. Such grand theories and metanarratives of human understanding are in disrepute.[7] Even narrative knowing itself, as something that seeks to understand the allegedly inherent "narrative unities" that make up people's lives, has been subjected to vigorous criticism on the grounds that people's lives and biographies are characterized as much by inconsistency, contradiction, and fragmentation as they are by any purported unity (Willinsky, 1989).

The movement from vision to voice is therefore accompanied by a movement from single and relatively stable belief systems to multiple and rapidly shifting ones. It is occurring because the globalization of information also compresses space and time, leading to an increasing pace of change in the world we seek to know and in our ways of knowing it—a flux that continually threatens the stability and endurance of our knowledge bases, making them irretrievably provisional. In addition, the diversification of knowledge and belief is due to the expansion of travel and of multicultural migration, bringing different belief systems into increasing contact with one another. Lastly, the shift is also due to an ever-tightening and recursive relationship between social research and development, where the social world changes even as we study it, not least as a response to the very inquiries we make of it (see Giddens, 1990).

This transformation in our ways of knowing in many respects marks a movement from cultures of certainty to cultures of doubt and fallibility. This diminishing credibility of traditional knowledge bases, along with declining certainty attached to research expertise, has immense implications for education and its restructuring. These implications are expressed in an emerging tension between *mandates and menus* as preferred ways of delivering and developing educational improvement. These tensions make themselves felt in a number of areas, two of which I will illustrate here: the implementation of new teaching strategies and the development of different kinds of collegiality.

The implementation of new teaching strategies. In teaching strategies, as in other areas, a key issue is whether to recognize and sponsor single or multiple versions of excellence, whether to acknowledge only one route to salvation or to concede that many such routes are possible. Many, perhaps most, of our reform efforts over recent years have been predicated on single models of excellence. These have been grounded in and legitimated by the allegedly incontrovertible findings of educational research. Hunter's (1984) renowned model of elements of instruction is one example. This model organizes training in effective teaching around closely prescribed principles of "direct instruction." For a time, the model was widely adopted and mandated in many American and Canadian school districts as a required focus for staff training in methods of supposedly "proven" effectiveness. In many districts, adherence to the model has been used as a basis for teacher evaluation. In at least one district, effective compliance with the model has also been used to evaluate teachers' suitability to be mentors of new entrants to the profession (see Popkewitz & Lind, 1989).

Direct instruction has subsequently been criticized on the following grounds: that it is not universally applicable but effective only in particular settings—especially those emphasizing basic skills (see Hallinger & Murphy, 1987); that its widespread adoption in a school prejudices the growth of more risk-taking, open-ended teaching strategies;[8] and that it fosters dependency and inflexibility among those who use it (Smyth & Garman, 1989). It would seem, then, that efforts to improve teaching and to implement policies of evaluating and promoting teachers on the basis of their presumed effectiveness have actually been based not on broad criteria of effectiveness but on particular and limited versions thereof— indeed, on versions that may actually inhibit the growth of different kinds of effective characteristics and behaviors in teachers.

Similar criticisms have been directed at the models of teaching reviewed by Joyce and Weil (1986) that have been used as a basis for programs of in-service teacher training through peer coaching. In *Student Achievement Through Staff Development,* Joyce and Showers (1988) promote strategies of peer coaching to secure the adoption of preferred teaching strategies such as cooperative learning and mastery teaching, whose usefulness and effectiveness are said to be solidly grounded in the findings of educational research. Joyce and Showers's work has been criticized on the grounds that it undervalues the practical insight and wisdom of teachers and requires teachers to comply with the knowledge, expertise, and prescriptions that are the property and prerogative of a small cadre of scientific "experts" (Hargreaves & Dawe, 1990). Robertson (1991) sees in their technologically optimistic claims to scientific certainty not only an unjustified warrant for bureaucratic intervention in teachers' work but also an overconfidence in the authority of "hard research" having strong gender connotations. As she puts it:

> One can hear a stereotypically masculine overconfidence when the authors quote Ron Edmonds in their introduction: "We can, whenever and wherever we want, successfully teach all children whose schooling is of interest to us. We already know more than we need to do that." Such certainty and predictability are familiar aspects of a masculine view of reality, as is the dependence on external rather than internal inquiry. The "we" to whom Edmonds is referring is assuredly not classroom teachers; this claim for the power of knowledge and instrumentalism refers only to those whose expertise is validated within hierarchical systems. The authors give no indication that they believe teachers might already know enough to teach more children better, but rather that experts can train teachers in observable and tested behaviours which will produce predicted results. (p. 46)

Reliance on the imposition of unitary models of teaching expertise can create inflexibility among teachers and make it hard for them to exercise proper discretionary judgments in their classrooms. It can lead to teacher resistance because of implicit rejections of the worth and value of the rest of a teacher's repertoire, and of the life and the person that has been invested in building it up. It can also lead to an overly narrow focus on particular techniques just when we are beginning to understand that effective instruction in real classroom settings involves teachers' possessing a wide repertoire of teaching strategies, which they apply flexibly according to the needs of the child and the moment.

The pathways of educational reform are strewn with discarded certainties of the past. Reading schemes, language laboratories, programmed learning, even open classrooms—reforms such as these would be appropriate exhibits for any museum of innovation. Today's solutions often become tomorrow's problems. Future exhibits in the museum of innovation could easily include whole language, cooperative learning, or manipulative math. We do not know yet. The point is, our knowledge and understanding of the effectiveness of these methods are often provisional and always contingent on their being used in particular circumstances. Unitary models of expertise that rest on an allegedly dependable research base are, in this sense, built on epistemological sand.

Multiple models of excellence are grounded in and arise from collective wisdom in the community of teachers and other educators (including but not confined to research). They acknowledge the provisional and context-dependent character of the knowledge base of teaching. They respect and leave space for teachers' discretionary judgments in their own classrooms. And by endorsing the possession and application of broad teaching repertoires, they permit gradual and selective adaptation to and integration of new approaches without this necessarily implying wholesale rejection of the old.

Development of different kinds of collegiality. In addition to all this, multiple models of instructional excellence also foster greater collegiality among teachers by acknowledging that teachers have complementary instructional expertise as a basis for partnership. In a study of elementary teachers' use of preparation time, Hargreaves and Wignall (1989) found that teachers generously acknowledged their colleagues' complementary expertise when it was rooted in subject matter. They readily acknowledged they might need help and could get support in, say, art, physical education, or music. They were less likely to acknowledge complementary expertise in classroom management or styles of instruction. This may be because teachers find it easier to accept diversity of content and content mastery than they do a legitimate range of alternative teaching styles. For many teachers, to acknowledge expertise in another's teaching style is not to appreciate the value of another version of teaching, but to defer to someone else's superior skills as a teacher and therefore to cast doubts on the adequacy of one's own. This state of affairs exists because teachers have typically been exposed to unitary models of classroom practice. For all these reasons, multiple models of classroom excellence are to be preferred over singular ones. Menus from which to choose are to be preferred to mandates which have to be implemented.

A second area in which menus should prevail over mandates is that of teacher collaboration and collegiality. Collaborative work among teachers can take many different forms. Teachers can collaborate, for instance, on developing school goals or mission statements. They can collaborate in curriculum and other kinds of planning. They can collaborate through structured systems of help and support in the forms of peer coaching or mentor programs. They can collaborate in systematic inquiry or action research. And they can collaborate in classroom practice through team teaching. Yet administrative systems sometimes act as if collaboration takes only one form and pressure teachers to adopt it. Mandatory peer coaching, compulsory team teaching, required collaborative planning, stilted systems of school development planning—measures as inflexible and insensitive as these rest on singular models of collaborative excellence. They fail to recognize the diverse forms that collaborative work can take. They prescribe narrow techniques that may not suit some people or contexts, and they lose sight of the broader collaborative principle that gave rise to them and could command wider support. They therefore offend the discretionary judgment of teachers that is at the core of teacher professionalism.

Despite administrative rhetoric, mandating specific kinds of collaboration is not empowering but disempowering.

Where such unitary models of collaboration are adopted, what transpires is what I have elsewhere called *contrived collegiality* (Hargreaves, 1991): a form of collaboration that is forced rather than facilitated, that meets the implementation needs of bureaucratic systems rather than the development needs of teachers and schools, that is designed to be administratively predictable rather than instructionally flexible in its outcomes, and that, as a result, might be viewed as stereotypically male rather than female in its style of operation. *Collaborative* teacher *cultures,* on the other hand, comprise many different and interconnected forms of collaborative work, some quite informal; they offer teachers much discretion in choosing the kinds of collaborative work in which they want to be involved; they evolve more slowly around the trust and patience that is needed to build supportive relationships; and because of the levels of teacher involvement and control, they are more unpredictable in terms of their specific outcomes. This can cause particular difficulty for bureaucratic and hierarchical systems of administration seeking to incorporate collaborative work into existing systems of administrative control.

Putting menus before mandates means not forcing through one particular approach. It means developing awareness of, commitment to, and experience in the general collaborative principle of working together for continuous improvement. Administratively, it is important to commit to this collaborative principle; it is, however, equally important to empower teachers to select from a wide range of practices the ones that suit them best. However, while commitment to collaboration is important, overcommitment or compulsion can be damaging. Increasing the commitment to collaborative work and having most teachers try some aspect of it is probably vital. But working for a 100% adoption rate is unrealistic and undesirable. Most teachers will plan or teach some things better alone than together. And there are some who teach better entirely alone. The solitary mode has its place.[9]

Not all teachers who choose to work on their own are weak teachers. Some are strong, even excellent, classroom practitioners. They may be eccentric prima donnas, difficult to work with as colleagues, but nonetheless skilled in their own classrooms. The idiosyncratic excellence of such teachers should not be punished in pursuit of a collegial norm.

While commitment to collaboration is important, then, it should not be pursued with administrative and ideological inflexibility. Above all else, even above collaboration, respect for teacher discretion is paramount, provided this does no harm to students. This is why menus should prevail over mandates. Such a choice is ultimately a struggle for professional, dis-

cretionary control among a community of teachers at the school level
against the retention and reconfiguration of bureaucratic control by administrators and their systems.

Trust in People or Trust in Processes?

In the struggle between bureaucratic control and personal empowerment
that marks the transition to postmodernity, collaborative relationships and
the particular forms they take are central. Such relationships, I have argued,
can help give people voice or they can contribute to the reconstitution of
central control. They are at the core of the restructuring agenda and all its
contradictory possibilities.

   A pervasive theme that runs throughout the literature on shared leadership and collaborative cultures is the truism of trust. The establishment
of trust, it is argued, is essential to the buildup of effective and meaningful
collaborative work relationships. For Lieberman, Saxl, and Miles (1989),
"trust and rapport . . . are the foundation for building collegiality in a
school" (p. 154). Louden (1991), for instance, describes the importance of
trust in the establishment of a collaborative relationship between himself
as a researcher and the teacher with whom he worked:

> The trust we developed was quite personal in character. We found that we
> liked each other, we became friends and the project became more than a
> piece of work for both of us. I enjoyed working with Johanna and partici-
> pating in the life of the school, she liked having me around and hoped my
> study would go well. (p. 195)

   The value of such trust in collaborative working relationships is so
widely acknowledged and understood that we rarely probe more than
superficially into its meaning and nature. One exception is Nias, Southworth, and Yeomans (1989), who note that "to talk of trust as if it explained
everything is . . . to make it into a 'black box', an abstract word packed with
individual meanings" (p. 78). They maintain that trust has two dimensions—predictability and common goals. "For trust to exist," they argue,
"people must find one another highly predictable and share substantially
the same aims" (Nias et al., 1989, p. 72). To paraphrase Nias and colleagues,
we might say that trust is a process of personal and predictable mutuality.

   This understanding of trust and the social–psychological heritage from
which it springs certainly helps illuminate our understanding of the dynamics of interpersonal relationships in the context of small-group collaboration. But it does not illuminate all forms of trust, only trust in particular
circumstances. These are ones of interpersonal relationships that remain
relatively stable and persistent over time. As Giddens observes, however,

there are other variants of trust. These can be found in contexts where interpersonal relationships are much less stable and persistent over time. Giddens (1990) alludes to these contrasts in his core definition of trust: "Trust may be defined as confidence in the reliability of a person or system, regarding a given set of outcomes or events, where that confidence expresses a faith in the probity or love of another, or in the correctness of abstract principles" (p. 34). Trust, in other words, can be invested in persons or in processes—in the qualities and conduct of individuals, or in the expertise and performance of abstract systems. It can be an outcome of meaningful face-to-face relationships, or a condition of their existence.

The movement from small and simple to massified and modernistic societies brought with it transformations in the forms of trust that were dominant in people's lives. These transformations can be seen particularly clearly in the changing relationships evident in these two forms of society. There is a reciprocal relationship between trust and risk.[10] In simple societies, risk was associated with permanent danger, with threats of wild beasts, marauding raiders, famines, and floods. Personal trust in family, friends, and community helped people cope with these persistent risks. Risk in simple societies was something to be minimized or avoided. In modern, mass organizations and societies, risk and trust took on different qualities. In secondary schools, for instance, there are often too many adults to know everyone well. Personnel, including leaders, could change frequently. Trust in individuals was no longer sufficient. When key players left or leaders moved on, exclusive reliance on personal trust could cause massive instability. In part, these sorts of problems in societies of growing industrial complexity gave rise to, and constituted a persuasive case for, bureaucratic forms of organization. Advancing change and complexity led to a decline in traditional forms of authority. Even innovative schools spearheaded by charismatic leaders often reverted to mediocrity when the leaders left. In modern, mass societies and organizations, another kind of trust was called for: trust in processes and abstract systems.

Tragically and ironically, however, as Weber's (1968) work reveals so clearly, the iron grip of modern bureaucracy simply perverted the course of system trust. Predictability turned into inflexibility. Relationships and responsiveness became strangulated by rules and regulations. Once they had grown and become established, modern bureaucratic organizations became too inflexible and self-serving to respond to local circumstances and changing needs. The interests of persons were blocked by the inertia of procedure. Trust in impersonal authority and technical expertise therefore declined. Confidence in abstract principles was undermined.

Modern secondary schools, for instance, were and still are criticized for being vast bureaucratic organizations unable to build a sense of community, to secure loyalty and attachment among their students, and to be responsive to the changing social world around them. In other words, they are an integral part of the malaise of modernity. Similarly, prevailing patterns of educational change and reform have been criticized for their top-down, standardized, bureaucratic application across entire systems in ways that neglect the purposes and personalities of individual teachers and the context in which they work.

The transition from modernity to postmodernity marks the emergence of new kinds of process trust, along with the reconstruction of more traditional kinds of personal trust. In postmodern societies, the form and articulation of corporate activity changes from the large mass factory to smaller, dispersed centers of enterprise, connected by rapid communications and efficient means for processing information. These developments give rise to two important trends in the reconstruction of trust.

First, there is the reconstruction of personal trust. There is extensive and increasing advocacy in the corporate and educational worlds for making the local unit of enterprise more meaningful to those working within it and more empowered to respond to the needs of its local environment. Emphasis is placed on the reconstruction of intimacy, warmth, and personal trust in the building of rewarding and productive collaborative work relationships. With these ends in view, many school districts have initiated programs of school-based management. Large and impersonal secondary schools are also looking increasingly generously at the possibilities for creating smaller, self-contained minischools or subschools within them that are more meaningful and self-determining for students and teachers alike.[11]

This reinvention of personal trust is double-edged, however. Personal trust can build loyalty, commitment, and effectiveness in the enhanced capacity that comes from shared decision making. But it can also reintroduce problems of paternalism and dependency that characterized traditional forms of authority and organization. Indeed, a number of writers (e.g., Nias et al., 1989) have noted that what appear to be collaborative school cultures seem to prosper most in smaller organizations under conditions of exceptionally strong leadership of a personalized nature. As Acker (1989) suggests, this state of affairs can transform internal collective confidence into collective complacency, carrying with it reduced capacity and willingness to network and learn from other kinds of expertise from outside that are not grounded in immediate and trusted personal relationships. Too much reliance can be placed on the principal to be responsible for external linkages.

Exclusive reliance on personal trust and the forms of collaboration that are built on it can lead, then, to paternalism and parochialism. Additional trust in expertise and processes helps postmodern organizations develop and solve problems on a continuing basis in an environment where problems and challenges are continuous and changing. Processes to be trusted here are ones that maximize the organization's collective expertise and improve its problem-solving capacities. These include improved communication, shared decision making, creation of opportunities for collegial learning, networking with outside environments, commitment to continuous inquiry, and so forth. Trust in people remains important, but trust in expertise and processes supersedes it. Trust in processes is open-ended and risky. But it is probably essential to learning and improvement.

This means that in postmodern school systems, risk is something to be embraced rather than avoided. Risk taking fosters learning, adaptability, and improvement. The trust it presumes may need to extend beyond the close interpersonal understandings that make up the collaborative cultures described earlier. These understandings and cultures are important, especially in smaller schools and teams. But larger and more rapidly changing schools require teachers who can also invest trust in processes, who can trust their colleagues provisionally, even before they know them well. This is not to advocate contrived collegiality, which can substitute managerial tricks for organizational trust. But it is to advocate a kind of trust that extends beyond the deep knowledge of interpersonal relationships.

The establishment of trust is central to the restructuring of education. The challenge of trust is to reconstruct collaborative working relationships among close colleagues that enhance personal meaning without reinforcing paternalism and parochialism. It is also the challenge of building confidence and connectedness among teachers, who may not know one another that well, by investing mutual trust in complementary expertise—but without this leading to burgeoning bureaucracy. The challenge of trust is one of restructuring and ultimately choosing between enhancing genuine empowerment or reconstructing administrative control.

Structure or Culture?

A fourth tension in educational restructuring is that between *structure* and *culture* as a proper focus for change. This tension is highlighted by Werner (1991) in an incisive analysis of recent restructuring efforts within the province of British Columbia in Canada. Werner refers to the provincial minister's call in 1989 for "a fundamental restructuring of the provincial curriculum with a focus on the development of problem solving and creative thinking" (see Brummet, 1989, p. 3). This proposed restructuring included an ungraded primary curriculum; an integrated, common curriculum; and a strengthening of assessment and accountability procedures.

Werner (1991) dismisses the proposed restructuring for British Columbia as "a classic curriculum fix," reflecting a pervasive and deep-rooted belief in the power of curriculum reform to secure effective change (especially if supported by some in-service training and supervision). Against this structural orientation to change, Werner draws on a submission by the British Columbia Principals' and Vice-Principals' Association to suggest an alternative strategy: "to encourage teacher development, strengthen school culture, and build upon those good practices already in place in schools" (p. 228). In effect, Werner supports the strategy of improving schools from within rather than reforming them from without. More significant than centralized control of curriculum development and implementation, he argues, "will be groups of teachers who search out and discuss ways to better understand and organize their programs, and who take action in and within the structure of their own schools" (p. 228). Werner's concern is that, despite the rhetoric of empowerment and the appearance of devolving power to teachers by giving them more responsibility for planning and organizing curriculum integration, the British Columbia ministry "retained control of curriculum by strengthening student testing and program evaluation. In essence, this meant that power relations around the curriculum would change little" (p. 234).

Werner is here counterposing politically popular *structural* solutions to educational change against less fashionable but more enduring and effective *cultural* ones. The contrast is striking and persuasive. Structural changes of the sort initially proposed for British Columbia underestimate the traditions, assumptions, and working relationships that profoundly shape existing practice. Consequently, they also overestimate the power of structural changes to alter such practice, even with the support of in-service training for teachers. The image is of a powerful, determining structure acting on a relatively malleable body of practice. The important thing about change in this view is to get the structures right so that they support your educational goals, then have practice conform to them.

The cultural view, by contrast, sees existing practice as heavily determined by deeply rooted beliefs, practices, and working relationships among teachers and students that make up the culture of the school and the traditions of the system. In this pattern of deep cultural determination, structural reforms are perceived as small, transient, and ineffective—little match for the power of the existing culture. Change, in this view, is brought about by acting on and supporting the culture itself so that teachers are enabled to make change as a community in the interests of the students they know best. Promotion of change in this cultural view is achieved by what Werner (1982) has elsewhere called policy support strategies—ones that create release time for teachers to work together; assist them in collaborative planning; encourage them to try new experiences (such as a new practice or grade level); involve them in goal setting; create a culture of collaboration, risk, and improvement; and so forth.

While there are growing indications that deep cultural changes of this sort are much more likely to be effective in improving classroom practice than quick structural fixes, there are nevertheless limits to the effectiveness and applicability of Werner's cultural model. Werner's writing, like a good deal of other writing on teacher development and the culture of the school, treads a fine line between respecting the beliefs and perspectives of teachers and romanticizing them. In the quest for collaborative professional development and improvement, the inherent generosity and altruism of all teachers cannot always be presumed. Teachers' beliefs and practices are grounded not only in expertise and altruism but also in structures and routines to which they have become attached and in which considerable self-interest may be invested. Such structures have often evolved historically to meet political and moral purposes that are very different from those which many of us would now consider important. Effective teacher development in the building of collective improvement therefore depends on more than the release of moral virtue. It also depends on controlling vested interests. For example, stronger forms of collegiality in the teacher work culture may require modifications to the subject-specialist, departmentalized secondary school curriculum that currently isolates teachers from many of their colleagues and ties them to the Balkanized domain of departmental politics and self-interest (Fullan & Hargreaves, 1991; Hargreaves, 1993b; Hargreaves & MacMillan, in press).

In some cases, therefore, especially in larger secondary schools, it is not possible to establish productive school cultures without first effecting structural changes that increase opportunities for meaningful working relationships and collegial support among teachers. The importance of the structural option of restructuring, therefore, may be less in terms of its direct impact on curriculum, assessment, ability grouping, and the like, than in terms of how it creates improved opportunities for teachers to work together on a continuing basis. The challenge of restructuring along the lines of changed power relationships proposed by Sarason, therefore, is not one of choosing between structure and culture as targets of reform. Nor is it one of "managing" school cultures so that teachers cheerfully comply with structural goals and purposes already fixed by the bureaucratic center. Rather, it is a challenge of redesigning school structures away from nineteenth and early twentieth century models so as to help teachers work together more effectively as a community in collaborative cultures of positive risk and continuous improvement. As an essential precondition for productive interaction, this much at any rate may need to be mandated! Structures are not neutral. New structures will threaten some existing interests. Teachers cannot therefore be relied on to create them entirely of their own volition. Collaborative cultures require collaborative structures. The reality of restructuring is that these structural prerequisites of teacher collaboration may need to be imposed so that teachers can create continuous cultural change and generate future structural change themselves.

CONCLUSION

Restructuring, I have argued, has no single, agreed-upon definition. Its meaning, rather, is to be found in the context and purpose of its use. In the centralization of curriculum change and assessment demands, wherein restructuring is a camouflage for reform, it can support intensification of bureaucratic control. Strong, singular visions and imposed, inflexible mandates—these are the stuff of such control. Equally, however, restructuring can also propel us into a world of postmodern indeterminacy and ephemerality—into a cacophony of voices of undistinguished moral validity, without any common vision or purpose, a world in which the decision-making power invested in school cultures is arbitrarily shaped by the inertia of historical tradition and ingrained interest rather than the virtue of collective moral choice.

The challenge of restructuring in education and elsewhere is a challenge of abandoning bureaucratic controls, inflexible mandates, paternalistic forms of trust, and quick system fixes in order to hear, articulate, and bring together the disparate voices of teachers and other educational partners. It is a challenge of opening up broad avenues of choice that respect teachers' professional discretion and enhance their decision-making capacity. It is a challenge of building trust in the processes of collaboration, risk, and continuous improvement as well as the more traditional kinds of trust in people. And it is a challenge of supporting and empowering school cultures and those involved in them to develop changes themselves on a continuing basis. But in relaxing and relinquishing administrative control, the challenge of restructuring in postmodern times is also one of not losing a sense of common purpose and commitment. In trading bureaucratic control for professional empowerment, it is important that we do not trade community for chaos.

This chapter is not a litany of solutions to these complex dilemmas; rather it has sought to sketch out ways of approaching them. Its purpose has been to show that the resolutions are not ideologically simple but profoundly complex, that they involve more than straight choices between restructuring and reform. Restructuring is not an end to our problems but a beginning. In this chapter, I have tried to point to ways in which the concept and practice of restructuring may itself need to be restructured, if the purposes of professionalism and empowerment are to be pursued with seriousness and integrity.

NOTES

1. This chapter has benefited from valuable comments and feedback from my colleagues Sandra Acker, Michael Fullan, and Ken Leithwood. It is an adapted version of a paper of the same title, reprinted with permission from *The Journal of Education Policy* (1994).

2. For a more extended discussion of the impact of National Curriculum reform on teacher development, see Hargreaves (1989).

3. For evidence and examples, see Hargreaves and Dawe (1990), Smyth and Garman (1989), and Popkewitz and Lind (1989).

4. See the collection of papers in *Educational Evaluation and Policy Analysis*, Vol. 12, No. 3, Fall 1990.

5. See, for instance, Harvey (1989), Menzies (1989), Naisbett and Aberdene (1990), and Giddens (1990). The ensuing account of the developments in postmodernity at the societal level draws on these sources.

6. In Chapter 4 of my book *Changing Teachers, Changing Times* (Hargreaves, 1993a), I critique approaches to teacher development that present it exclusively as a process of self-development as being narcissistic and self-indulgent:

> Teacher development can be misleadingly and narcissistically grandiose . . . when the . . . self of the teacher is invested with the unlimited power for personal change, and unrealistic moral obligations for professional improvement that are untempered by any practical and political awareness of the contexts and conditions which currently limit what any one teacher can reasonably achieve; and which teachers and others must confront if more than trivial gains are to be made. (p. 91)

The kind of work that is vulnerable to this kind of critique is work that not only validates but also celebrates teachers' personal and practical knowledge (see, for example, Clandinin, 1986; Connelly & Clandinin, 1988).

7. See Harvey (1989) for a development of this.

8. See the articles in the issue of *Educational Evaluation and Policy Analysis*, Vol. 12, No. 3, Fall 1990.

9. I develop this argument elsewhere (Hargreaves, 1991).

10. See Giddens (1990, pp. 34ff), from whom much of the following account of trust and risk is drawn.

11. For account of these developments, see Hargreaves and Earl (1990).

REFERENCES

Achilles, C. M. (1987). A vision of better schools. In W. Greenfield (Ed.), *Instructional leadership: Concepts, issues and controversies* (pp. 17–37). Boston: Allyn & Bacon.

Acker, S. (September, 1989). *It's what we do already but . . . Primary teachers and the 1988 Education Act.* Paper presented at a conference on Ethnography, Education and Policy, St. Hilda's College, Oxford, UK.

Brummet, A. (1989). *Policy directions: A response to the Sullivan Royal Commission on Education by the Government of British Columbia.* Victoria, BC: Queen's Printer.

Caldwell, B. J., & Spinks, J. M. (1988). *The self managing school.* Lewes, UK: Falmer.

Carnegie Forum on Education and the Economy. (1986). *A nation prepared: Teachers for the 21st Century: Report of the Carnegie Task Force on Teaching as a Profession.* Washington, DC: Carnegie Forum.

Clandinin, D. J. (1986). *Classroom practice: Teacher images in action.* Lewes, UK: Falmer.

Connelly, F. M., & Clandinin, D. J. (1988). *Teachers as curriculum planners: Narratives of experience.* New York: Teachers College Press.

Deal, T., & Peterson, K. (1987). *Symbolic leadership and the school principal: Shaping school cultures in different contexts.* Unpublished manuscript, Vanderbilt University, Nashville, TN.

Elbaz, F. (1991). Research on teachers' knowledge: The evolution of a discourse. *Journal of Curriculum Studies, 23*(1), 1–19.

Fleming, T. (1991). Canadian school policy in liberal and post-liberal eras: Historical perspectives on the changing social context of schooling 1846–1990. *Journal of Education Policy, 6*(2), 183–200.

Fullan, M., & Hargreaves, A. (1991). *What's worth fighting for?: Working together for your school.* Toronto: Ontario Public School Teachers' Federation.

Giddens, A. (1990). *The consequences of modernity.* Oxford, UK: Polity Press.

Gilligan, C. (1982). *In a different voice: Psychological theory and women's development.* Cambridge, MA: Harvard University Press.

Goodson, I. (1990). Nations at risk and national curriculum: Ideology and identity. In *Politics of Education Association Yearbook* (pp. 219–252). Philadelphia: Taylor & Francis.

Goodson, I. (1991). Sponsoring the teacher's voice. In A. Hargreaves & M. Fullan (Eds.), *Understanding teacher development* (pp. 110–121). New York: Teachers' College Press.

Hallinger, P., & Murphy, J. (1987). Instructional leadership in the school context. In W. Greenfield (Ed.), *Instructional leadership: Concepts, issues and controversies* (pp. 179–203). Boston, MA: Allyn & Bacon.

Hargreaves, A. (1989). *Curriculum and assessment reform.* Milton Keynes, UK: Open University Press.

Hargreaves, A. (1991). Contrived collegiality: A micropolitical analysis. In J. Blase (Ed.), *The politics of life in schools* (pp. 46–72). New York: Sage.

Hargreaves, A. (1993a). *Changing teachers, changing times: Teachers' work and culture in the postmodern age.* New York: Teachers College Press.

Hargreaves, A. (1993b). Individualism and individuality: Reinterpreting the culture of teaching. *International Journal of Educational Research, 19*(3), 227–246.

Hargreaves, A., & Dawe, R. (1990). Paths of professional development: Contrived collegiality, collaborative culture, and the case of peer coaching. *Teacher and Teacher Education, 6*(3), 227–241.

Hargreaves, A., & Earl, L. (1990). *Rights of passage.* Toronto: Queen's Printer.

Hargreaves, A., & MacMillan, R. (in press). Balkanized secondary schools and the malaise of modernity. In J. W. Little & L. S. Siskin (Eds.), *Perspectives on departments.* New York: Teachers College Press.

Hargreaves, A., & Wignall, R. (1989). *Time for the teacher: A study of collegial relations and preparation time among elementary school teachers* (Final research report). Toronto: Ontario Institute for Studies in Education.

Harvey, D. (1989). *The condition of postmodernity.* Oxford, UK: Polity Press.

Hello cruel world: Claude Taylor fought for a decade for privatization. Now he confesses, Air Canada wasn't ready. (1991). *The Globe and Mail Report on Business, 7*(8), 36.

Hunter, M. (1984). Knowing, teaching and supervising. In P. Hosford (Ed.), *Using what we know about teaching* (pp. 169–192). Alexandria, VA: Association for Supervision and Curriculum Development.

Joyce, B., & Showers, B. (1988). *Student achievement through staff development.* New York: Longman.

Joyce, B., & Weil, M. (1986). *Models of teaching* (3rd ed.). Englewood Cliffs, NJ: Prentice-Hall.

Leithwood, K., & Jantzi, D. (April, 1990). *Transformational leadership: How principals can help reform school culture.* Paper presented at the annual meeting of the American Educational Research Association, Boston.

Lieberman, A., Saxl, E. R., & Miles, M. B. (1989). Teachers' leadership: Ideology and practice. In A. Lieberman (Ed.), *Building a professional culture in schools* (pp. 148–166). New York: Teachers College Press.

Louden, W. (1991). *Understanding teaching.* New York: Teachers College Press.

Menzies, H. (1989). *Fast forward and out of control: How technology is changing our lives.* Toronto: Macmillan.

Murphy, J., & Everston, C. (Eds.). (1991). *Restructuring schools: Capturing the phenomena.* New York: Teachers College Press.

Naisbett, J., & Aberdene, P. (1990). *Megatrends 2000.* New York: Morrow.

National Governors' Association. (1989). *Results in education.* N.G.A., Washington, DC.

Nias, J., Southworth, G., & Yeomans, A. (1989). *Staff relationships in the primary schools.* London: Cassell.

O'Neil, J. (1990). Piecing together the restructuring puzzle. *Educational Leadership*, 47, 4–10.

Popkewitz, T., & Lind, K. (1989). Teacher incentives as reforms: Teachers' work and the changing control mechanism in education. *Teachers College Record*, 90(4), 575–594.

Robertson, H. (1991). Teacher development and gender equity. In A. Hargreaves & M. Fullan (Eds.), *Understanding teacher development* (pp. 43–61). New York: Teachers College Press.

Rudduck, J. (1989). Accrediting teacher education courses: The new criteria. In A. Hargreaves & D. Reynolds (Eds.), *Education policies: Controversies and critiques* (pp. 178–190). Philadelphia: Falmer.

Sarason, S. (1990). *The predictable failure of educational reform*. San Francisco: Jossey-Bass.

Schlechty, P. (1990). *Schools for the twenty-first century*. San Francisco: Jossey-Bass.

Smyth, J., & Garman, N. (1989). Supervision as school reform: A critical perspective. *Journal of Education Policy*, 4(4), 343–361.

Tyack, D. (1990). Restructuring in historical perspective: Tinkering toward utopia. *Teachers College Record*, 92(2), 170–191.

Weber, M. (1968). *Economy and society: An outline of interpretive sociology* (G. Roth & C. Wittoch, Eds.). New York: Bedminster.

Werner, W. (1982). *Evaluating program implementation (school based)* (Final project report). Vancouver: Centre for the Study of Curriculum Instruction, University of British Columbia.

Werner, W. (1991). Defining curriculum policy through slogans. *Journal of Education Policy*, 62, 225–230.

Willinsky, J. (1989). Getting personal and practical with personal and practical knowledge. *Curriculum Inquiry*, 9(3), 247–264.

Wise, A. (1988). The two conflicting trends in school reform: Legislative learning revisited. *Phi Delta Kappan*, 69(5), 328–333.

A PERVASIVE CONTEXT
OF INAUTHENTICITY

Part II contextualizes the ideas put forward by Lieberman, McLaughlin, and Hargreaves. Woods examines the relationship between manifest conditions for teacher development and the larger social context in which the enterprise takes place. His thesis is that teacher development has to be considered within a framework of economic and political trends and events that, in large part, determine what is possible in teacher development, what is considered desirable by interest groups, and how it will occur. He begins by describing three models of teaching that have come about in England and Wales as a result of the macro-political context. The first two models, "personal qualities" and "opportunities to learn," have seriously constrained teacher development to the extent that the optimistic tones of the first section about restructured roles and responsibilities in professional discourse communities of positive risk and continuous improvement are largely rendered impracticable. The third model, "opportunities to teach," is less pessimistic but also less widespread than the other two. Woods uses these three models to characterize three scenarios about conditions for teacher development. When the constraints from the macropolitical context are few and teachers are given many opportunities to teach, the conditions for creative teaching and the chances of development are enhanced. When constraints force teachers to modify their teaching according to externally derived instructional practices, development consists largely of strategically refining coping skills. When the constraints on teachers are overwhelming and restrict opportunities to teach to a minimum, teachers experience regression. The economic and political trends and events over the last few years in Britain have rendered the latter two scenarios more prevalent than the first.

Chard picks up the context described by Woods to explore the responses of teachers to the implementation of the National Curriculum

in England and Wales. This educational reform, essentially brought
about by political fiat, was part of the government's larger political aim
of reducing the power and influence of the professions in British life.
Despite this and the intimidating educational climate that it produced,
Chard documents how teachers articulate their role as holding onto the
social democratic, egalitarian, and child-centered ideas that had characterized British education (particularly at the elementary level) over the
previous two decades and subverting the implementation of the
National Curriculum through devious means of pretense and contriv-
ance. Caught in the cross-fire (because of their position at the nexus of
information flow) between the teachers and the government are the
elementary school principals. They have always regarded themselves
primarily as teachers, and the government's expectation that they now
manage the implementation of the National Curriculum puts them in a
particularly difficult spot. This difficulty is shared by teachers when it
comes to the government's assessment procedures. Here, the positive
subversion turns into a siege mentality. This, together with the additional
professional demands that the new curriculum is making on teachers,
has created considerable professional and personal stress. Consequently, despite great determination on the part of teachers to hang
onto a view of learning that the National Curriculum has set out to
change, this politically motivated educational reform has made tremen-
dous inroads into the everyday work world of teachers. Forces in the
macropolitical context have thus changed dramatically what is understood by and enacted as teacher development.

Siskin focuses on a similar kind of invasion, but in this case the outside elements affecting practice are found in the micropolitical context.
She documents how an experiment to change a school's organizational
and instructional structures, which began back in 1976 under favorable
conditions, became derailed by pressures exerted by external and internal contexts. Her chapter is important to teacher development because
the case of Rancho High School provides insightful commentary on the
current press for restructuring. It calls into question the implicit assumptions about the school as a professional community on which much
school restructuring is based—namely, that schools could and should be
given increased site-level autonomy and that shared goals, norms, and
objectives can and will be established when such favorable conditions
pertain. The case of Rancho High School demonstrates how, even under
favorable conditions, any attempt at changing the structures of schools
is subject to the forces at work in the external communities of which the
local schools are a part and in the internal subcommunities that partition
those same schools. External to the school, an unanticipated tax bill cur-

tailed the favorable conditions and luxuriant resources the school enjoyed. Internally, the departmental divisions, deliberately targeted for extinction in the planned change, proved to be remarkably resilient as the change was implemented. The department, more so than the school, became the professional community that ultimately held sway, leading Siskin to question the axiomatic assumption of many reform efforts that the school is the unit of change. Siskin's case study provides an example of planned change, of a series of unplanned changes that result from the school's embeddedness in the larger, turbulent community of policy makers, and of the power and resilience of departmental boundaries in defining vital subcommunities within the high school.

Ceroni and Garman write about the power and resilience of bureaucratic hierarchies in educational systems to prevent genuine teacher empowerment from occurring. Their chapter examines the metaphor of "empowerment" and shows how a shallow understanding of what teacher leadership involves can, in fact, produce the opposite effects to what is typically expected. They describe how an initiative designed to restructure leadership roles and responsibilities essentially lost its way because of political co-optation and administrative intransigence. When principals provided a moral, financial, and organizational framework of support within which teachers could construct the role of lead teacher, the initiative produced highly positive outcomes. In the main, however, this kind of support was lacking and teachers felt frustrated, unsupported, confused, and ultimately disempowered in the lead teacher role. Ceroni and Garman argue that the Lead Teacher Program did little to address the unequal power relations that existed between and among teachers, policy makers, and administrators. By attending only to the status of one subgroup of teachers and ignoring other features of the organizational mosaic, the attempt to institute lead teachers was analogous to tinkering at the margins of a longstanding educational structure whose history, tradition, overlearned attitudes, and unrealistic time perspectives ensure turmoil. As a consequence, teachers rarely emerged with the necessary credibility that authentic leadership requires. Rather, the initiative succeeded in establishing another layer in the hierarchy that ultimately prevented genuine collegiality from occurring.

What, then, has happened to the emerging theoretical patterns of restructured roles and responsibilities, professional discourse communities, and teachers' voice proposed by Lieberman, McLaughlin, and Hargreaves? Are these theoretical ideas simply impracticable? Or is there something else at work in the mix?

Part II alerts the reader to the possible ways in which useful ideas can be co-opted and/or vitiated during implementation. Factors in the various contexts of education that are alien to both the purposes and broadened concept of teacher development essentially disrupt any attempt to redefine learning from the perspective of teachers and students. New ideas require hospitable cultures in which to take root and grow. Teachers' struggle for authentic development essentially occurs at the micropolitical level of the education system. Real power still resides at the macropolitical level that frames the changing educational context in which teacher development takes place.

CHAPTER 4

The Conditions for Teacher Development

PETER WOODS

Teacher development does not take place in a social vacuum. It has to be considered within a framework of social, economic, and political trends and events. These have a strong influence on what is possible in teacher development. Also, different interest groups have different views on what kind of teacher development is desirable.

This chapter begins by contrasting three models of teaching and their respectively different implications for teacher development. An integrated model is then proposed, followed by three possible scenarios of teaching. These scenarios of creative teaching, strategic teaching, and stressful teaching are explored within the context of educational reform as it has been experienced in England since 1988. While the conditions for teacher development have deteriorated considerably for many teachers during this period, the chapter concludes with more optimistic signs for developing teacher professionalism.

MODELS OF TEACHING

I want to begin by outlining three models of teaching that stand in some contrast to one another and that, taken separately, have vastly different implications for teacher development. The first two, "personal qualities" and "opportunities to learn," have been very influential in England in recent years; the third, "opportunities to teach," less so.

"Personal Qualities" Model

The "personal qualities" model is heavily implicit in a series of major government reports of the 1980s (Department of Education and Science, 1983,

1985a, 1985b). Teachers' personal qualities are considered to be the deci-
sive factor in effective teaching. However, it is never quite clear what these
qualities are. They tend to be interpreted in terms of their product. For
example, they include good relationships between teachers and students,
good classroom management, use of a range of teaching techniques, and
varied dialogue between teachers and students. The reports were very
critical of some teachers, finding nearly a quarter of new recruits "poorly
equipped" for teaching. Such a model presents an ideal state of teaching,
the assumptions of which are not made explicit, and asks how teachers
measure up to it. It emphasizes the selection and training of teachers and
the weeding-out of those considered unsuitable. This model has to be seen
within the context of growing central control of the education system, in
which the criteria of successful teaching are centrally determined and rating systems set up against which to measure teachers. Meeting the prescribed requirements has to take place within the prevailing system and
with existing, or possibly fewer, resources. This political context has a
strong bearing on how personal qualities are defined and the kind of development implied.

"Opportunities to Learn" Model

Another very influential model has been one that holds that successful
teaching depends on the opportunities a teacher gives students to learn.
This has been called the "opportunities to learn" model. The opportunities include the time allocated to tasks; devising, choosing, and presenting
tasks in an appropriate manner; and assessing and diagnosing the results.
The concern here is with "matching" tasks to students and making them
appropriate in every particular, for example, in degree of difficulty. One
research study (Bennett, Desforges, Cockburn, & Wilkinson, 1984) found
a high level of mismatching among the primary teachers in their research
(as much as 60% in language and mathematics, the two subjects studied);
that is, teachers set tasks that were either too easy or too hard for the students involved. Even though the teachers in this research were experienced
and able, the researchers concluded that the problems lay with teachers
and various kinds of misjudgment that they had made. It is not so much a
lack of "personal qualities" as a matter of misjudgment. The policy indicated is one of in-service teacher development designed to aid teacher skills
of diagnosis. Research and teaching combine to pinpoint problem areas,
which can then be rectified.

    Such models as these above tend to take for granted how teaching is
defined and what it means to teachers. They also take no account of the

social context of teaching and how that affects decisions that are made or actions that are taken, what possibilities it allows, and what it prevents. What we need, therefore, is an "opportunities to teach" model.

"Opportunities to Teach" Model

This model revolves around factors internal to the teacher having to do with commitment and interests, and external factors having to do with constraints. These factors interact on one another. Thus the constraints on teaching may affect teachers' commitment to the job and how and where they perceive the realization of their interests. "Personal qualities" will play a part in the perception of constraints and how they are tackled, but they cannot operate independently of them. They are part of the overall holistic activity of teaching. They can be made, or broken, by other factors. The main components of this model are the following.

• *Teacher commitment*. This has to do with teachers' motivation. A great deal is heard of student motivation, which is often presented as the major factor in successful teaching. Teacher motivation tends to be taken for granted. However, not all teachers are as committed to teaching as others, or in the same way. Sikes, Measor, and Woods (1985) identified different forms of teacher commitment: vocational commitment (love of teaching and/or children), professional commitment (reflecting teaching as a skilled, professional accomplishment that can be improved through teacher development), and instrumental commitment (reflecting purely material interests in terms of salary, holidays, a comfortable job, and so forth). Any given teacher can have one form of commitment or a mixture of them. A teacher's commitment can vary over time, between different places, and among different groups of teachers and students. It might vary in strength as well as in kind. Thus there are core, mixed, or peripheral types of commitment. A teacher can have a core professional commitment but also have peripheral instrumental interests. In critical periods for the teaching profession as a whole (involving loss of status, depressed salaries, and weakening professional control of the curriculum), one might expect a shift from vocational and/or professional to instrumental and from core to peripheral kinds of commitment.
    • *Teacher interests*. Pollard (1985) has identified elements of primary and secondary self-interest by which the personal survival of the teacher is defined. Keeping order and instructing children in this respect are secondary interests. Primary interests are maximizing enjoyment, controlling the workload, maintaining one's health and avoiding stress, retaining auton-

omy, and maintaining one's self-image. The importance of order and instruction lies in the extent to which they can advance the primary interests.

• *Societal constraints.* Society has contradictory goals for the education system. For example, the goal of teaching individuals to their maximum potential runs counter to the goal of selecting and socializing students. Moreover, teaching policy and practice are affected by levels of funding (Hargreaves, 1988). There are also ideological constraints that affect practice, such as traditionalism, progressivism, vocationalism, or multiculturalism, which might exert pressure on teachers to teach in certain ways. Finally, there is the degree to which teachers have autonomy to exercise their personal qualities as they see fit. In recent years, teachers in England have lost a degree of control over what they teach and under what conditions. They have also lost status, a vital ingredient in teacher motivation.

• *Institutional constraints.* Societal demands are mediated through the school. Schools differ in the way they adapt. Prominent in studies here is the notion of school ethos, which some have claimed to be the main factor in school achievement (see, for example, Mortimore, Sammons, Lewis, & Ecob, 1988; Rutter, Maugham, Mortimore, & Ouston, 1979). Measor and Woods (1984) have noted that schools speak of "our way" of teaching. Denscombe (1985) has identified schools with a "low-achievement orientation," while Reynolds (1985) and others argue that "schools do make a difference" against what is taken to be the alternative argument that "education cannot compensate for society" (Bernstein, 1970).

AN INTEGRATED MODEL: THREE POSSIBLE SCENARIOS

These three models focusing on personal qualities, cognitive matching, and social factors are not necessarily competing explanations. All figure in teaching in some way. But they have to be seen in interrelationship. "Opportunities to learn" are contingent on "opportunities to teach." The useful idea of cognitive matching needs to be seen within the context of a range of social factors. Teachers will differ to some extent in how they manage these factors according to personal abilities and interests, but the analysis cannot be reduced to those aspects alone.

Taking this integrated model as a guide, I shall look at three contrasting characterizations of teachers' experience and development (see Woods, 1990, for a fuller account):

   1. The constraints on teachers are few, and there are many opportunities to teach and use "personal qualities." This permits "creative teaching" and provides maximum chances for development.

2. The constraints force teachers to modify their teaching in restrictive ways. Development here consists largely of refining strategical coping skills.

3. The constraints on teachers are overwhelming and restrict opportunities to teach to a minimum, thereby inducing stress. Teachers thus experience regression rather than development.

The consequences for individual teacher development from these scenarios are not inevitable. They are general tendencies, not hard-and-fast distinctions.

Creative Teaching

Creative teaching involves innovation (something new), ownership (it belongs to the teacher concerned), control (the teacher has control of the processes involved), and relevance (it is productive in terms of student learning). Many kinds of creative teaching have been observed, particularly in elementary schools, which are less constrained than secondary ones. They include creative teaching around a structured base, teaching as discovery, creative projects, managing the teacher role, generating a productive school climate or ethos, and exceptional educational events.

Creative teaching around a structured base. One example of this occurs when teachers go beyond the specified ways of using graded reading schemes to maximize student learning in different ways. These schemes are self-contained and might be regarded as being almost "teacher-proof." Creative teachers, however, regard them as only another resource, making plays out of them, extending vocabulary, tackling any sexism or racism in them, and adapting them to students' interests.

Teaching as discovery. This is finding out "what works" or "ways in," for example, identifying clues in the student's culture that will aid his or her understanding. This involves experimenting, probing, asking questions, "trying anything," as one teacher said, and constant vigilance for the slightest sign of understanding that indicates learning has begun. Sometimes a student will experience a sudden enlightenment, a breakthrough, freeing a blockage and achieving an enormous advance. A teacher might have employed a wide range of imaginative techniques to achieve this.

Creative projects. These are planned exercises in the first instance, involving whole classes of students and potentially more than one teacher, that develop in unpredictably productive ways. One interesting example is a school exchange project, which reached inspirational levels when conceived and controlled by the teachers involved, in contrast to a previous exchange (Grugeon & Woods, 1990). In the successful project, the children of our class in a multiethnic urban elementary school exchanged places for a day with children in an all-white rural school. The exchange itself was a catalyst for the impressive developmental work that took place beforehand and the consolidation afterwards. The children were excited and highly motivated by their new "friends" in the other school, and they made great strides across the curriculum, especially in language and in social and personal development. All recognized it as a high point in the school year. This project had been conceived, planned, and carried out by the two teachers of the two classes, with the support of their principals. When asked why the prior event concerning the multiethnic school and a different school had not fared as well, one of the teachers replied that it had been "thrust upon them." It had been someone else's idea (that is, the principal's), and the guidelines had been laid down for them without consultation. This is not to say that it was an outright failure but that the "spark" between two teachers and two different schools evident in the highly successful project was missing. The ownership and control elements were clearly crucial in this case.

Managing the teacher role. There is an art in how the skilled teacher handles conflictual elements in the role, cultivating warm personal relationships with children and a caring ethos in the school, on the one hand, while managing some problems of control with more discipline-oriented techniques, on the other—all the time exhibiting a seamless web of activity that flows productively regardless of all problems and hazards. The main techniques identified for doing this are establishing and maintaining friendship and a family spirit, orchestration (the ability to put conflicting elements of the teacher role together in a harmonious whole), and omniscience (appearing to know everything that is happening in a classroom, even things occurring behind one's back!). I recall saying to a young student that I thought he had a good teacher, and he said, "Yeah, Mrs. Brown knows everything." And so she did. She was able to see around corners, could hear silence in a room full of noise, and seemed to know how all her various students felt and what they needed to do.

Generating a productive school climate or ethos. Measor and Woods (1984) described one example of this. They characterize it as a "middle-ground culture," the result of an attempt by teachers to interlock key communicative elements in students' background culture into their curricular–instructional concerns. Teachers tried to meet the students half-way, largely through symbolic forms of language, humor, and appearance. While there was a school uniform, and certain basic requirements had to be met, there were many areas of flexibility as a result of student–teacher negotiations in the past—types of shoes, knots in ties, and hair styles, for example. The teachers had developed a classroom language shared among themselves, the local community, and the world of mass advertising, not one derived from their own professional culture. This established a bond with students on common linguistic ground. The bridging qualities of humor were also well deployed, with liberal use of jokes, taking part in "ribbing" and banter, and acting as comedians. The middle ground was distinguished by openness and flexibility, by equality of treatment, by sincerity, and by friendliness. But the ethos only worked if students responded in the expected way. If unwritten rules were transgressed, it collapsed and more authoritarian structures came into play. A middle-ground ethos does not just happen—it has to be worked at, constructed, and maintained. It is another example of teacher creativity, in this case a collective accomplishment. It shows that, if the teachers of a school can agree, they can exercise considerable influence on institutional constraints and opportunities by acting together and contributing to the environment in which their individual teaching takes place.

Exceptional educational events.   I recently studied some outstanding examples of inspired and inspiring teaching and learning (Woods, 1993b). These are creative projects on a grander scale than those mentioned above, bringing radical change in both students and teachers. Several of the schools involved had won prestigious awards. These events included the publication of a well-known children's book, on-site history when the foundations of a school's extensions revealed an Iron Age settlement, the design of a new heritage center in Winchester, the production of a community video in a Suffolk school, "fun" science in a school in Reading, and a smash-hit drama in a Northamptonshire comprehensive school.

   In all of these creative enterprises stretching across the curriculum there is communal growth. Students and teachers learn together. For example, the teacher responsible for the community video, Melanie, commented:

> I wanted the pupils to feel involved. I wanted it to be their thing, and obviously I had to have a steering influence, and I had more knowledge, at least in the first place, of the techniques we were going to be using than they did but then again it was only a bit elementary. I'd never done it before. So we were all learning as we went along. I mean I would make great cock-ups like not press a certain button when we were first filming, using the camera for the first time, and each time the children were using the camera, it was for

the first time . . . but they improved tremendously, very quickly. (Woods, 1993b, p. 55)

Melanie's skills as camera-person, editor, director, producer, and teacher of this activity were not learned in any courses. "I got some books out of Norwich [a city in England] library, which I took a few notes from, and I asked a couple of friends, and that was it" (p. 56).

This was on-the-job learning for all, deriving from the inspiring qualities behind the project, which, in turn, led to the discovery of new skills and knowledge both within herself and among her students. She spoke at length of the things that she would do "slightly differently" another time—cutting short the logging time, making sure the children were happy with their parts (necessary for full motivation), encouraging them to be shorter on their use of film, and so on. Melanie only likes that sort of teaching

> when you're working on something which is creative, that there's going to be something good at the end, and it goes on longer than the children might otherwise go on, but hopefully they see the point of that involvement and effort, so that it's all worth it. You know, that it can be worth sustaining something past a certain point. (p. 57)

The teacher/producer of the smash-hit musical *Godspell* at Roade Comprehensive School in Northamptonshire was a new person as a consequence of this critical event. I present this quote in full here, as recorded on tape, since it is instructive to see the manner of the teacher's reflection as well as its content. There is affective, cognitive, career, personal, and social development, and also a certain quality of development. At times this is difficult to express. Teachers may sense this development tacitly. They experience it without always feeling the need to articulate it:

> Well, I suppose it's changed my life in that it's taken over a year of my life, . . . fully, and almost excessively. . . . You can't be the same person after that —if anything takes over your life for a year, you're going to change, depending what it is. On this occasion, . . . it's difficult to say exactly how—I feel much more vulnerable in some ways as a person because it opened up . . . whole ranges of emotion that I hadn't experienced to such depth before and it gave me tremendous faith . . . in young people. It's given me some very wonderful friendships with some of them, two or three particularly, which I value even though I know young people change, particularly from sort of 18 to 21/22. . . . But it's given me those people to care for, and it's made me much happier as a person, just from being through it because it's such a wonderful memory to have. . . . I mean it was so wonderful to see that on stage and it just made me very happy to have thought I'd created that and of course very proud, and it's given me much more confidence in myself.

There's knock-on effects—I mean Clive Walker the guy who runs the National Students' Drama Festival—has now asked me to direct a production in Edinburgh next year for him and so there's knock-on effects from that, so inevitably it changes—practically-speaking it's changed my life because it's led to other things and probably will continue to do so—it's given me an insight into what we see at more professional theatres, the Derngate and places like that. It's just made me feel more relaxed and much happier about life in general because it gives you so much hope when you see people working like that, and you see what they get out of it, and it suddenly makes everything worthwhile. . . . But on the whole what we're aiming for is this relationship within a group where you can work positively, constructively, and creatively together and learn to negotiate compromise and build. But it's very difficult—I mean it happens obviously within timetable time, within the curriculum, it happens within the Expressive Arts—but it doesn't happen to such an extent because there isn't the long term project that there was with this and the length of time that it continued, and you're just building, building, building all the time, building relationships, and again I tried to say it to them in the letter that I wrote to them—I hope that you'll be able to retain that feeling of great unity, or to find it again at another point in life, remember what it felt like, and be able to pick that up more easily because of that. I'm much more positive now and I'll go into lessons and expect the best and I suppose in that sense the work actually has improved . . . that's one of the reasons why I'm so pleased with my teaching over the last few months—it's probably exactly that reason, because I am much more positive about what can be achieved . . . I mean, I never consider that this is a grotty group or anything—I always think in terms of the positive, which is interesting, very interesting. (Woods, 1993b, pp. 126–127)

This seems to be a kind of ultimate in teachers' experience. It is perfect in its own terms. It reaches heights unthought of in the initial conception, brings out hidden or dormant qualities in the self, and opens up new educational possibilities. What are the conditions pertaining to this kind of work? All the projects studied had the following features (in addition to those of ownership, originality, and control mentioned earlier):

- Strong vocational and professional commitment on the part of the organizer(s); *and* of the *schools* concerned
- Resourceful and entrepreneurial staff and head-teachers (in some cases this secured extra finance for the project)
- A holistic view of learning, which saw the whole neighborhood (and sometimes beyond) as school, and the whole day as learning time. These projects also had a high degree of cross-curricula relevance.
- A democratic and cooperative view of teaching and learning. Each project had a strong measure of teamwork, in contrast to the individualism of the typical teacher culture.

- The use of other professionals, such as novelists, architects, drama-lecturers, computer experts, who considered these experiences as contributing to their own professional development.
  I have argued elsewhere that these critical others enhance the role of the teacher by supplying a charismatic element (Woods, 1993a, pp. 546–549).

This seems to indicate a mixture of personal qualities (highly motivated and able staff) and making the most of opportunities presented. But it is not as simple as that, for the opportunities available have something to do with the motivation; and the abilities of staff were not always fully evident at the beginning of these events, but rather were revealed or developed by them. In short, the opportunities to teach must be there for the seeds of such creative enterprises to take root and grow.

Strategic Teaching

When teaching is more circumscribed, teachers resort to employing coping strategies. There may be a great deal of creativity, but it is directed toward the managing of constraints rather than the promotion of teaching. Such constraints include poor buildings and equipment, low levels of resources, difficult students, a "low-achievement" ethos, little recognition and few rewards, but high expectations from parents, superordinates, and employers altogether at variance with the problems faced. At its most extreme, teachers employ "survival strategies" in which survival ("getting through the day" and maintaining one's position and sanity) becomes almost the sole aim. Various survival strategies have been noted, including negotiation, fraternization, and absence or withdrawal (Woods, 1979). Some schools had a (hidden) rotation for teacher absence. They claimed they would not have lasted without it, nor indeed without a considerable rate of truancy among the students.

Clearly constraints can vary from system to system and from school to school, and they can be experienced and interpreted differently from person to person. For example, teachers differ in terms of interests and commitment as well as the choices they make. Some lines of inquiry here have used the method of life histories as a way of characterizing the teacher's career in a whole-life perspective (Ball & Goodson 1985; Sikes et al., 1985). In one study (reported in Woods, 1990) I examined two teachers with similar educational interests, aims, and dedication in the same school. I was concerned to discover why one succeeded to some extent while the other chose to leave teaching. I argued that an explanation lay, to some extent, in the self and identity that each had constructed and sought to promote. What helped one maintain an admittedly precarious teaching existence, but nonetheless an ideologically intact one, was a range of commitments, both within the school and in the community at large, among which he could juggle or negotiate his general interests depending on circumstances at any given time. In addition to being a teacher, he was a member of the local artists' confederation, a member of the village community group, and director of the adult education service. He was thus able to take advantage of what opportunities presented themselves and, on occasion, to create them. He also had a number of bridging devices (such as "fair procedures"—scrupulous and manifest observation of agreed-upon rules in decision making concerning student work and career progress) that enabled him to cross the divide between ideals and practice. A factor playing a large part in the other's resignation from teaching was the need to preserve his own chosen radical identity. This teacher operated on the margins of the education system. He had moved to three different schools in as many years. He wanted to be a reformer, and *each* of his brief excursions into these three schools gave him a glimpse of that characterization before threatening to undermine it. He introduced reforms, notably into the social studies curriculum. But he also tried to subvert the governance structure of the school by establishing a school council for the students, forming a "ginger group" (a forum for stimulating ideas for change) among the staff, and submitting the legitimacy of the principal's position to general appraisal. All institutions have a certain elasticity, where norms and rules may be ill-defined and their guardians take time to marshal their defenses. This teacher exploited the area of "give" before the guardians (especially principals!) rallied their forces and catapulted back. Resignation was, therefore, an act of self-preservation.

This study illustrates how teachers differ in their chosen identity, with different implications for development. It also illustrates how coping strategies entail analysis both of how society and institutions bear on the individual and of how the individual's own biography and identity contribute to the manner of coping. Biography and identity are further illustrated in the life history of an art teacher (also in Woods, 1990) showing that a teacher's self both finds expression in, and gives expression to, a curriculum area. From childhood, this teacher had developed values, beliefs, and dispositions to do with such things as creativity, expressivity, romanticism, love of beauty, freedom, individuality, sociability, independence, questioning, a critical attitude, and holism. Art clearly allows room for creativity and beauty. Its relatively low status within the curriculum and need for creative space means there are fewer constraints than in some subjects and hence more room for individual expression. It is integrative and holistic in its approach to people, yet separatist within the overall curriculum of the school. It has distinct social and community aspects, which emphasize relationships; and it permits scope for creating the kind of environment and atmosphere the teacher wishes. In the life history of this art teacher, there are institutional influences such as head teachers and school ethos; macro-considerations having to do with socioeconomic and political events; structural factors such as social class; and "private life" considerations, deriving from family and leisure interests and commitments. The analysis shows how this teacher steered a personal course through various configurations of these factors, trying to preserve the predominance of the self; it also traces the strategies employed in this task of survival to roots deep in his past. It suggests how teachers both make and are made by their chosen subject areas.

An illustration of how he accomplished this comes from a period in a school when he was fundamentally opposed to the educational philosophy of the head but, for domestic reasons, unable to leave. Among the strategies he cultivated were: (1) compromising—but only "to seem to give way in smaller battles in order to win larger wars"; (2) bargaining—offering his services for what others saw as unwelcome tasks (such as teaching a difficult class) in exchange for more freedom; (3) marginalizing—"I just lived in a little island within the school"; (4) compartmentalizing the self, reserving his real, substantial self, on occasions, for outside school; and (5) indulging in creative strategies in his day-to-day interaction with students. For example, when staff were required to carry out a uniform inspection (to which he objected), he accomplished this task in such a way as to convince the hierarchy that he was doing it properly and his students that he was not. His subject, art, offered good opportunities for this strategic activity, preserving and protecting as well as promoting his desired image of self.

Stressful Teaching

Stress occurs when the constraints exceed the coping capacity of a teacher. Stress is not just a product of pressure or problems, for it is all part of a teacher's job to withstand pressure and resolve problems as they arise. To understand what job stress is for teachers requires a broader perspective. For example, one might envisage a school norm exhibiting a dominant climate of harmony among a number of key factors, such as teacher and student interests; government, local district, and school policy; the demands made on teachers, the resources to meet them, and the rewards to be gained thereby. A potentially stressful situation comes about when a teacher's personal interests, commitments, or resources not only get out of line with the other factors but actually pull against them. A classic example is having too much work to do, together with a strong moral imperative to do it but not enough time or energy. Add to this the provision of inadequate resources, as well as the receipt of little reward or recognition, and the situation is compounded. Here, elements grate against one another, as in losing an idyllic and restorative free period and being asked to stand in for an absent colleague with a difficult class. If such situations continue over a long time, a teacher becomes gradually worn down, and a single incident or event, such as a particularly frustrating and troublesome lesson, can induce breakdown.

Principals and vice-principals are especially prone to stress since they occupy positions of extreme role conflict. In recent years in England, however, stress has also become more of a feature among rank-and-file teachers. Some have said they have been unable to cope with student behavior, and there have been some lurid descriptions of this (see, for example, Woods, 1990). Some women teachers, for example, have been subjected to sexual harassment from male students. In some areas male teachers have been observed being harassed by female students (Dubberley, 1988). Dubberley's analysis is framed in terms of "working-class resistance" on the part of students, but the experience is no less stressful for the teachers concerned. Other teachers have found themselves doing things and becoming people they do not like. Some have felt their individual identity submerged beneath bureaucracy and lost in the overwhelming expectations associated with the teacher role. Some have felt eaten up by "the greedy institution" (Coser, 1974)—the more it consumes, the more it wants.

These points are well illustrated by Andrew Bethell, an ex-head of English at a London secondary school. He had wanted to take a year off from teaching for his own personal development, but his employers would not grant him leave, even unpaid. So he left. Why is this such an unusual thing to do? It may be because people view careers as the best vehicles for realizing their personal and professional goals, be they vocational or instrumental. There are also the more mundane reasons of security and other forms of cushioning. As Bethell (1980) wistfully remarks, "you can fail in education and never be confronted with the blunt implications of your failure" (p. 23). But Bethell points to other reasons within teaching—the general ethic "which keeps the rest of them at it," the "constant pressure of immediate demands," which he had "internalized" so that attendance day after day was "not just a routine, it was a deep-seated imperative" (p. 23). These routines were so ingrained that he had to force himself to construct similar ones after he had left teaching. At school he had a strong sense of moral obligation—his "every action" as a teacher "was tainted by guilt" (p. 23). However much he did, there was more to do and a strong feeling that he should do it. But these were the very pressures that, in the long run, caused him to take the year off. His job was stunting his growth rather than promoting it. The educational possibilities lay in finding out what he did best, the personal control of his time and activities and the flexibility it afforded, and ultimately in the discovery of "whole areas of my life, which my job, while giving me much else, had denied me" (p. 23). The crucial point for Bethell is that this was a quest for "personal enrichment" and not simply "professional improvement" (p. 23). This is not to say that these activities are inevitably separate and distinct for all teachers (Nias, 1989).

Loss of status for the profession as a whole, depressed salaries, loss of negotiating rights, weakened control of the curriculum, new demands for accountability and appraisal remove potential cushions for blows and create new sources of stress. In addition, the Education Reform Act of 1988 has required teachers in England and Wales to implement with few additional resources a new National Curriculum. This has brought serious problems of overload among teachers (Campbell, Evans, Neill, & Packwood, 1991) and support for theories of intensification (Apple, 1986) and deskilling (Ozga, 1988) of teachers' work. These arguments contend that the labor process for educated workers in advanced capitalistic economies is being radically changed in the quest for more productivity. Overload, increased bureaucracy, new forms of accountability, externally devised and imposed objectives and curricula, and decreased opportunities for creativity are typical features.

One way of dealing with these new pressures is for teachers to redefine their commitment from vocational or professional and total to instrumental and partial, devoting their creative energies to other activities *outside* teaching. However, teachers with high vocational commitment (arguably the best teachers) find this impossible to do, as they also do with regard to engaging in "survival strategies." They are among those, therefore, who are most prone to stress. Others include:

- Teachers in positions of high role conflict (such as principals and vice-principals)
- New recruits who have not yet adapted to the rigours of teaching
- Midcareer teachers who became teachers during the educational boom years of the 1960s and early 1970s

Many midcareer teachers have experienced arrested or impeded development, career blockage, and even "spoiled" and "terminated" careers because of the changes that have taken place since the mid-1970s. For example, many have been redeployed, and there have been a number of early retirements. Escape committees have been formed to help resolve the unbearable conflict between commitment and constraint and to facilitate exit from the profession. This is a long way from the teaching ultimates mentioned earlier in the section on creative teaching. Clearly, this is not a matter of personal qualities, for those arguably with the best qualities, those closest to the ultimates, are among those most at risk. This reveals the poverty of "personal qualities" models.

THE FUTURE FOR TEACHERS

Teachers in England have gone through a period that has depressed their salaries, status, and morale. They have also witnessed a deterioration of the conditions in which they do their work. But there are signs that the pendulum has already begun to swing back again. Among the factors indicating this are the following.

• Research is beginning to appear that shows that, while the government might make policy, there is scope for teachers to implement it in line with their own beliefs and values (see, for example, Acker, 1990; Ball & Bowe, 1992; Vulliamy & Webb, 1993). My own research (Woods, 1993c) is indicating that self-determination is finding expression through a range of adaptations, including appropriation (the National Curriculum is made to work largely for teachers' own aims), resistance (some aspects are vigorously opposed, in the process aiding development through closer collaboration and sharper articulation of views), and retreatism (the self is salvaged, for example, through retirement).

• Some of the more extreme aspects of the Education Reform Act of 1988 are being modified—the National Curriculum is being slimmed down, the number of compulsory subjects has been reduced, testing is being reduced, attainment targets at the elementary level have been reduced, the program working groups devising the content of the curriculum have become sites of struggle, and some of what many teachers regard as the best educational features of past practice are being retained.

• Gains made in teacher research and teacher development remain. In addition, there is more collaborative work between practitioners and academics (Woods, 1989; Woods & Pollard, 1988).

• Reforms widely regarded as beneficial to education—such as the new 16+ examination, the General Certificate of Secondary Education (GCSE), profiling, records of achievement, and new understandings of learning, notably constructivism (Bruner, 1986; Donaldson, 1978; Edwards & Mercer, 1987)—continue.

Above all, many teachers continue to derive great satisfaction from their work and face the future with confidence. One primary school for 5- to 7-year-olds has recently won two major awards for its innovative approach to the teaching of science (Woods, 1993c). These teachers' basic philosophy is that "learning is fun." They regard "attainment targets"—specified objectives for all children across the curriculum in the new requirements— as "entertainment targets." The Education Reform Act holds no fears for them. In some cases, then, creativity can win over constraint, even transforming it into opportunity. There must be some flexibility in the arrangements for this to occur. There is still this while teachers retain control of the educational process and have latitude in the choice of books and materials they use to support their teaching. Teachers also enjoy increased collaboration among themselves (for example, peer tutoring) and with academics, and there has been an increase of school- and classroom-oriented in-service work and research. In all these features of teacher discretionary decision making lie the seeds, perhaps, of a new professionalism.

Thus a combination of modification of structures by the government and an indomitable spirit on the part of teachers is yielding a negotiated settlement in some areas. As Golby (1989) has noted, "We may for the present have to take to the hills as guerrillas, but there is a hope that we may return to power with renewed vision" (p. 163). For the present, a sense of struggle pervades the system, struggle for the kind of education that teachers believe in, for the kind of system that they perceive offers the best chances for all children, and for the kind of teacher development that will lead to personal growth and advanced professionalism rather than deskilled proletarianization. In the long term, teaching might not be much different from that experienced by the following teacher, who retired 13 years ago:

> I had a good time. I'm not saying it was all sweetness and light . . . there were some difficult times—all the changes, the reorganization, the comprehensivization, schools getting big, difficult colleagues and some kids who were nasty pieces of work. But you come through it all, and if you like it and if you're right for it, it's a damn good life all round. (Sikes et al., 1985, p. 244).

REFERENCES

Acker, S. (1990). Teachers' culture in an English primary school: Continuity and change. *British Journal of Sociology of Education, 11*(3), 257–273.

Apple, M. W. (1986). *Teachers and text: A political economy of class and gender relations in education.* New York: Routledge & Kegan Paul.

Ball, S. J., & Bowe, R. (1992). Subject departments and the "implementation" of National Curriculum policy: An overview of the issues. *Journal of Curriculum Studies, 24*(2), 97–115.

Ball, S. J., & Goodson, I. F. (Eds.). (1985). *Teachers' lives and careers.* Lewes, UK: Falmer.

Bennett, N., Desforges, C., Cockburn, A., & Wilkinson, B. (1984). *The quality of pupil learning experiences.* London, UK: Erlbaum.

Bernstein, B. (1970). Education cannot compensate for society. *New Society, 387,* 344–347.

Bethell, A. (1980, March 21). Getting away from it all. *Times Educational Supplement,* pp. 22–23.

Bruner, J. (1986). *Actual minds, possible worlds.* Cambridge, MA: Harvard University Press.

Campbell, R. J., Evans, L., St. J. Neill, S. R., & Packwood, A. (1991). *Workloads, achievements and stress: Two follow-up studies of teacher time in key stage 1.* Policy Analysis Unit, Department of Education, University of Warwick, UK.

Coser, L. (1974). *The greedy institution.* New York: Free Press.

Denscombe, M. (1985). *Classroom control: A sociological perspective.* London: Allen & Unwin.

Department of Education and Science. (1983). *Teaching quality.* London: Her Majesty's Stationery Office.

Department of Education and Science. (1985a). *Better schools.* London: Her Majesty's Stationery Office.

Department of Education and Science. (1985b). *Education observed 3 good teachers.* London: Her Majesty's Stationery Office.

Donaldson, M. (1978). *Children's minds.* London: Croom Helm.

Dubberley, W. (1988). Humour as resistance. *International Journal of Qualitative Studies in Education, 1*(2), 109–123.

Edwards, D., & Mercer, N. (1987). *Common knowledge: The development of understanding in the classroom.* London: Methuen.

Golby, M. (1989). Teachers and their research. In W. Carr (Ed.), *Quality in teaching* (pp. 163–172). Lewes, UK: Falmer.

Grugeon, E., & Woods, P. (1990). *Educating all: Multicultural perspectives in the primary school.* London: Routledge.

Hargreaves, A. (1988). Teaching quality: A sociological analysis. *Journal of Curriculum Studies, 20*(3), 211–231.

Measor, L., & Woods, P. (1984). *Changing schools: Pupil perspectives on transfer to a comprehensive.* Milton Keynes, UK: Open University Press.

Mortimore, P., Sammons, P., Lewis, L, & Ecob, R. (1988). *School matters: The junior years.* London: Open Books.

Nias, J. (1989). *Primary teachers talking: A study of teaching as work.* London: Routledge.

Ozga, J. (1988). Teachers' work and careers, unit W1. In course EP228 *Frameworks for Teaching.* Milton Keynes, UK: Open University Press.

Pollard, A. (1985). *The social world of the primary school.* London: Holt, Rinehart & Winston.

Reynolds, D. (Ed.) (1985). *Studying school effectiveness*. Lewes, UK: Falmer.

Rutter, M., Maugham, B. P., Mortimore, P., & Ouston, J. (1979). *Fifteen thousand hours*. London: Open Books.

Sikes, P., Measor, L., & Woods, P. (1985). *Teacher careers: Crises and continuities*. Lewes, UK: Falmer.

Vulliamy, G., & Webb, R. (1993). Progressive education and the National Curriculum: Findings from a global education research project. *Educational Review, 45*(1), 21–41.

Woods, P. (1979). *The divided school*. London: Routledge & Kegan Paul.

Woods, P. (Ed.). (1989). *Working for teacher development*. Dereham, UK: Peter Francis.

Woods, P. (1990). *Teacher skills and strategies*. Lewes, UK: Falmer.

Woods, P. (1993a, August). The charisma of the critical other: Enhancing the role of the teacher. *Teaching and Teacher Education, 9*(4), 545–557.

Woods, P. (1993b). *Critical events in teaching and learning*. Lewes, UK: Falmer.

Woods, P. (1993c, September). *Self-determination in the National Curriculum*. Paper presented at the British Educational Research Association conference, Liverpool, UK.

Woods, P., & Pollard, A. (Ed.). (1988). *Sociology and teaching: A new challenge for the sociology of education*. London: Routledge.

CHAPTER 5

The National Curriculum of England and Wales

Its Implementation and Evaluation in Early Childhood Classrooms

SYLVIA C. CHARD

The Educational Reform Act (ERA) of 1988 in England and Wales reflects the most comprehensive restructuring of education in Britain in this century; "almost all the taken-for-granteds in the system are being shaken up at once," as Pollard (1990, p. 74) puts it. The ERA gives the British Secretary of State for Education "hundreds of new powers" (Lawton, 1989b, p. 1). The National Curriculum is part of the ERA. It is a common curriculum designed to raise standards in education by specifying the range of subjects that students should be taught, offering clear programs of study with levels of attainment that students should be expected to reach in four "key stages" of schooling. Students are tested at the end of each key stage, at ages 7, 11, 14, and 16. Implementation of the National Curriculum was mandated in all state-maintained schools on and after September 1989.

This chapter discusses the implementation of the National Curriculum, the innovation at the heart of the ERA. First, it presents the views of several recent educational commentators on the changes taking place, reflecting the depth of professional concern felt in response to the reforms. Second, it provides a discussion of issues explored in interviews with teachers in different parts of England on the effect of the new policies on the schools in which they work and on their own professional lives.

THE PROFESSIONAL CHALLENGE OF THE NATIONAL CURRICULUM

The ERA has served two main political goals for the Conservative party, which has governed Britain during the past decade. First, it is one part of the more general political intention to reduce the power of local government in favor of increased central control. From the Conservative point of view, local government has worked through expensive bureaucratic planning and encouraged cooperation rather than competition among schools in improving services to the public (Lawton, 1989b, p. 118). The ERA is an "attack on local government and its control, through democratic procedures of local school systems" (Simon, 1990, p. 32). Local authorities in areas other than education are also being effectively curtailed.

Second, the ERA serves the political intention to reduce the power and influence of the professions in British life. Privatization is an important Conservative principle, and competitive commercialism is seen as an appropriate means of improving standards in professional activity. However, as Kelly (1990) suggests, the appropriateness of commercial competition to the professions is questionable. "For it must introduce extraneous, strictly irrelevant, and in some contexts even dangerous, considerations into the minds of those who plan and practise in these areas" (p. 49). Again, education is only one of the professions suffering in this way; medicine and law are also affected. Kelly (1990) has provided an excellent critical review of the government's means of achieving this second goal in the field of education. The National Curriculum has been designed mostly by political planners who have taken little account of professional expertise. As a result, nationwide school-based curriculum planning is being seriously encumbered because professional knowledge and understanding have not been incorporated into the documents setting out the central government's requirements of teachers (Jeavons, 1990).

It is important to recognize the wider political purposes of the educational reforms in Britain because the vulnerability of institutions in the state can threaten the practices and values of the individuals who work within them (Kemmis, 1987). At the same time, there should be concern for individuals because "the best structures in the world will not work when human beings do not want them to work and quite poor structures work very well if the human beings concerned have common purposes, shared values and efficient working partnerships" (Sallis, 1990, p. 26). The schools as institutions cannot easily defend the practices and values of those who teach in them when these positions conflict with the government view. If they did so they might put their own existence at risk. This is especially problematic in times of radical reform when the changes in demand on individual classroom teachers involve significant shifts in the values currently inherent in their ways of working with children. And there are many teachers and head teachers who are opposed to what the government is requiring them to do. "The dilemma of accountability for teachers is that they have to accept responsibility for implementing policy for which they are not in fact accountable" (Silcock, 1990, p. 7). Head teachers in the front line, who are under considerable pressures themselves, have responded carefully.

In Britain the life of a school owes a great deal to the personal and professional qualities of the head teacher (the British equivalent of the North American principal). "The Educational Reform Act has radically altered the statutory and professional context within which heads operate and changed their relationships with LEA's [local education authorities], governors, parents, staff and children" (Boydell,1990, p. 20). Traditional reasons for aspiring to headship were "a desire based on proven ability as an expert teacher, to establish their own philosophy in their 'own' school" (Boydell, 1990, p. 23). Now they are required to take more of a managerial role and attend to the financing of a wide range of the school's functioning, for which they had not previously been responsible. The main complaint from the head teachers has been the time they have not been able to spend in classrooms with teachers and feelings of powerlessness under increasing pressure from a variety of sources outside the school itself.

Individual teachers, who are faced with reforms with which they do not agree, have to reflect critically on their professional options: *either* (1) leave the field of education for retirement or other employment, *or* (2) submit uncritically to new directives in order to keep their current teaching post, *or* (3) endeavor to mediate between institutional direction and personal professional values. This mediation can be achieved if teachers distance themselves from the inconsistencies created by the changes. This distancing can be seen in schools where teachers continue to maintain current practices in the classroom while at the same time colluding with the head teachers, whose role it is to mediate between the institution and the outside authorities. The collusion involves the teachers' agreeing in principle to make changes without actually altering their practice in any significant way and the head teachers' accepting the teachers' assurance. Such collusion appears necessary in order for the heads to defend their institutions by stating that the teachers are carrying out the required reforms. They are, after all, responsible for the continued reputation of the institution in a competitive world in which each school is to be publicly compared with others on the basis of mandated standard assessment.

In this threatening climate head teachers have played down their role in implementing change in favor of their role in sustaining it. Many claim to be more concerned with the quality of relationships among staff, with teamwork, and with job fulfillment than with mandated educational change. Monitoring or evaluating were not high on their agenda among current pressures (Boydell, 1990). Kemmis (1987) writes, "Schools can no more change without the informed commitment of teachers than teachers can change without the informed commitment of the institutions in which they work; that schools and systems (local clusters of schools, or LEA's) are similarly interdependent and interactive in the process of reform" (p. 74). Yet the power does lie in the hearts, heads, and hands of teachers to take active steps to resume authority when the new policies are shown to be unworkable. Such a response by teachers would help them should they once again be exposed (as they have been in recent years) to public blame for the failure of education to meet the needs of children and parents as well as those of the prevailing society. Openly questioning or challenging government directives in the current climate in Britain might be considered a subversive activity (Kemmis, 1987; Postman & Weingartner, 1969), but it could also be professional suicide for individual teachers.

Kelly (1990) writes of the professional responsibility teachers could undertake to limit the damage inevitable in the wake of the implementation of the new education policies. He has attempted to outline the inadequacies of the National Curriculum, which was constructed with "little reference to professional educators or teachers and thus without the 'knowledge, skills and understanding' of those whose professional concern it has been to plan educational provision and to implement the plans so made" (p. 129). Brighouse (1990) suggests that the current policies present an opportunity to examine a range of educational practice in terms of what will and will not work so as to be ready for the inevitable "collapse" of the education system as currently conceived. Some writers take comfort in those ERA reforms other than the National Curriculum. These can be seen to offer opportunities for increased communication between parents, teachers, and other members of the public about education, its aims, and its professional practices (Sallis, 1990). In Sallis's view "the greatest danger of all is that because of negative attitudes on the part of teachers, and particularly head teachers, to some of the new structures, we shall miss the chance to find allies for the good fight" (p. 26).

Implementation of the National Curriculum began in September 1989. British primary education has for decades been internationally renowned for the "social democratic, egalitarian and child-centred ideas to which most teachers have subscribed" (Pollard, 1990, p. 74). From the mid-1960s, the curriculum had evolved through the influences of a "network of interactions and communications with other institutions, and with individuals outside the school, which connect the school to society" (Taylor, Reid, Holly, & Exon, 1974, p. ix). The resulting pluralism in education allowed teachers to work with considerable autonomy in their classrooms (Pollard, 1990, p. 66). The principles supporting the new legislation are very different.

Today, by contrast, teachers are dependent on a centrally dictated curriculum. This state of affairs has produced many critics. O'Connor (1987) sees it as "the gravely flawed product of amateurs, a hasty shallow, simplistic sketch of a curriculum, reductionist in one direction, marginalizing in another, paying only dismissive lip-service to the professional enterprise and initiative on which all progress depends" (p. 34). Pollard (1990) states that "the legislation imposes a National Curriculum and a framework for its delivery both of which represent a serious curtailment of teacher autonomy" (p. 63) with the attendant dangers of teachers becoming "mere deskilled functionaries" (p. 63). He concludes: "to a great extent, the content of the curriculum which they [teachers] teach will be prescribed and they will be required to monitor pupil achievement much more closely, precisely and publicly than in the past" (p. 73).

An interesting perspective for North American readers is given by Hatch (1990) in an article, aptly entitled "Exchanging Places?", pointing out the opposite directions in which reform movements are going in the United States and the United Kingdom. It appears that the emphasis in the United Kingdom is on removing power from the teachers and putting it in the hands of politicians, parents, or future employers so as to require the schools to respond to the social functions of education. By contrast, in the United States there is talk of "empowering teachers," of giving back some authority for educational decision making to the teachers, to those who understand most about what children are like. This comparative perspective helps to explain the nature of the resistance to some of the requirements of the National Curriculum by many teachers. The second part of this chapter, then, presents discussion of selected responses to this reform by teachers from four dissimilar schools in different parts of England. In spite of the variation in the circumstances and location of these teachers, all have similar views on the issues raised with them in interviews. The teachers' views represent their accommodation to the far-reaching implications of the new curriculum requirements. The voices of these teachers must be heard in the context of increasing central government control, commercialism, and competition, which characterizes the wider tide of cultural change in Britain, change that has seriously affected educational provision.

THE TEACHERS' VOICES

The teachers were interviewed in the summer of 1990, at the end of the first year of the implementation of the National Curriculum.[1] The interviews took place in the seventh year of a longitudinal study of teachers' professional development (currently in progress). The teachers were all in their mid-20s and in their third year of full-time employment. Two of the four had already worked in two schools in different parts of the country. They are all regarded as effective teachers of young children, all having shown considerable commitment to their chosen career over the past seven years.

Three main themes emerge from the teachers' discussion of the National Curriculum requirements and the effects of these on the teachers in their schools. The first theme concerns the response to the implementation of the National Curriculum at the school level. There seem to be substantial differences between the response of small and large schools, particularly in regard to their different approaches to the issue of subject specialization. The second theme concerns the changes teachers have had to make in their classroom teaching to respond to the demands of the National Curriculum. Curriculum integration in project work and the cross-curricular study of topics were less feasible. There are also implications for class size, scheduling, planning, assessment, and record keeping, and one of the major problems was the pressure of having to achieve more under difficult conditions than was possible in the time available. The third theme concerns the other professional demands being made on teachers in terms of in-service training, professional development, and communication with other teachers both within each school and among schools in a local area. The effect of the National Curriculum policies on the teachers' perception of their career development and opportunities for advancement within the profession was also explored. There was concern with status and promotion prospects, with professional commitment, and with responsibilities to be assumed. Each of these three themes will be discussed in turn.

The School Response to the National Curriculum

The four selected schools represent a range of responses to the new legislation at the local level. Jill taught at a very small rural elementary school with fewer than 70 children enrolled. Diane and Stella taught at large urban schools. One of these was a primary (K–3) school with about 270 students and the other an elementary school with about 400 students. The elementary school was in a catchment area with a very high proportion of children of Asian origin. The fourth teacher, Sally, taught at an elementary school for some 180 children in a low-cost housing subdivision in a small rural town.

Some advantages of the National Curriculum were perceived in terms of communication and solidarity among staff in the school. As Diane put it: "One emphasis of the school is that we are all going to learn together. No one is actually seen as the absolute expert, and if you do not have a subject specialization then you are seen as a good generalist all-round teacher; therefore you're going to teach anything well."

Sally had felt very isolated during her first year of teaching two years earlier. For her the National Curriculum had opened new opportunities for her to talk with her colleagues, to learn from them as well as share some of her expertise in a way that she had found impossible before. "I think the best thing is that the infant [primary] staff are getting together to plan and talk about what they're doing. We started to get together because we were studying the same theme of water and there's a lot of 'well, I tried this . . .' and 'have a go at this!' There's a lot of cooperation that wasn't there before."

In the small rural school, Jill commented on the communication among teachers required by the new curriculum. This involved meeting with groups of teachers from other schools. "We've all been trying to work in our little groups on how to keep these assessments, the best way to keep records." One of the main problems for the small schools, however, was access to subject-specialist expertise. Some teachers were being asked to become experts in several areas and to share the knowledge they were acquiring through in-service courses. Jill, a young teacher, was supposed to take responsibility for language, drama, and art, early childhood education (5- to 7-year-olds), and integrating the preschool (children and parents) one afternoon a week, in addition to deputizing for the head teacher when he was increasingly required to be out of the school building. So much responsibility, even though the school was a small one, was proving quite stressful for this teacher.

At the school level the teachers welcomed the collegiality brought about by the requirement to have a common understanding of planning and assessment. Some head teachers were managing to delegate more responsibility than they had previously and in so doing had expressed faith in the ability of their staff. However, there were signs that the collaboration was being done under too much pressure and with inadequate direction, leading to a feeling among school staffs that some very difficult times lay ahead.

There was agreement that the National Curriculum had far-reaching consequences at the school level. Some of the communication had more defensive undertones. Stella commented:

I think it's had a big effect on our school. Last year when I came here the school was writing policies, pre–National Curriculum things, what we believe in, what we feel is good for governors and parents. I think we weren't sure what the National Curriculum was going to contain. We wanted a statement so we were not forced into doing things that we haven't agreed on. Compared with my last school, they're very keyed up, they knew what was going on, and they were getting prepared for it.

This teacher felt pleased to have made the move from the other school, which she felt was not in touch with imminent changes: "I know if I'd stayed at that school I would still be thinking 'Oh no! What's the National Curriculum?' I'm sure I would; I can't imagine them having the sort of motivation to get on and do anything about it."

Changes in Classroom Teaching

The second theme emerging from discussion with the teachers concerned the changes that seemed to be required of them in their day-to-day classroom teaching. Generally, the most immediate response was that the National Curriculum was going to make little difference to the way they taught. Jill spoke about her belief that she had been well trained in preparation for teaching and that she was well able to implement her daily plans:

> It's not changed how I work with the children in any way. I mean, I do my records and my little tick sheets at the end of the term, then I don't look at them again till the end of the next term when I fill in a few more boxes. It doesn't influence me at all. No, I can't see any point. Whereas when I'm teaching I'm always noticing; I store my knowledge about the fact that, say, Jonathan's nearly there, I mean he just needs a little extra help right now to understand something.

However, she did say that her planning had been affected in that she would check the National Curriculum for content: "I did electricity, batteries and magnets and things, last term because it fitted in with my topic anyway. Perhaps I wouldn't have done that if it hadn't been for the National Curriculum."

All the teachers either asserted or hoped that they were going to try not to relate any differently to the children as they were teaching them. However, they expected to be required to plan, assess children, and record progress in new ways. Planning was clearly to be much more publicly shared among teachers within the school. However, there was some concern that the children's learning might suffer because it would be more difficult to follow the children's interests or take advantage of the "teachable moments" arising for individual children. There was a fear that there would be more pressure on classroom time to accomplish prespecified planning objectives leading to more whole-class teaching and less curriculum integration in the form of project work. As Sally put it: "It's going to make more demands on you when you're planning your activities. You are going to have to keep thinking, 'I haven't done this or that, so I'll have to get it in,' instead of letting a project run and following the children's lead a bit, then bringing them back to some main concepts through their interests."

She went on to describe a science lesson based on the National Curriculum program of studies in which she was teaching the concept of "water-proof" through trying out different materials to find which one might most effectively cover an umbrella. During the course of the lesson she discovered that several of the children (age 5 and 6) became intrigued with absorption, which materials absorbed the most water from the bowl, how different fabrics felt and reacted when squeezed. They appeared to have little practical experience of that concept. This involved her in a change of plan so that she could provide the children with a variety of activities leading to a more tactile appreciation of absorption. Sally was afraid that having to cover a set range of required topics would make such changes of plan more difficult to justify. However, teachers have appreciated the science curriculum content that offers suggestions of specific concepts to explore that otherwise might not be approached by some teachers.

Concern was expressed over the need for subject specialists to come into the classroom to teach. In Jill's case, the head teacher came into her multiage class to teach history while Jill taught art to another class. She was afraid that, in the interests of giving some history to her class, there would be less time for the integration of history with geography and local studies. Blyth and Bish (1990) suggest that "each school should have a co-ordinator for history with a special allowance to attend in-service courses, plan the work in her school, and help her colleagues to teach history well" (p. 17). These authors do, however, go on to say that "this has serious implications for small schools, and would probably require the grouping of such schools to share expertise and resources" (p. 17).

Another concern was that class size would rise. I recently spent three days observing in a classroom with one teacher and 39 5- and 6-year-olds. This teacher was very concerned that she could not teach as well as she had previously, with so many children and no ancillary help. There are predictions of an increasing shortage of teachers and large numbers of teachers leaving the profession. Yet the teachers interviewed were as concerned as ever to get to know the children well as individuals so as to teach effectively. Where there were still fewer than 25 children in the class, there were still many examples of the individualization frequently observed in good British early childhood classrooms.

One teacher (Jill) with a small class described her teaching in this way:

> You need to be moving about the classroom noticing what's going on
> with each child because you know the children and you know their pro-
> gression. Jonathan has just gone through this stage when he's doing his
> own emergent writing. He just did lots of lovely rows of little letters and
> then one day he just grouped them and that was a step forward because
> each group was a word. Next day he went back to doing lines of letters so
> I stopped with him and we looked at a book and off he went! He was just
> half-way there. Like Jenny working today. What is exceptional for one
> child is not for another. If Susie did a piece of writing or a story, that
> might just be a beautiful picture and some scribble. Genna does lots of
> lovely circles and writes IG's everywhere and I praise her for that, but
> Hayley I expect much more from, and I get it. So you're making judg-
> ments all the time for each individual child.

However, it is likely that there will be increasing pressure on teachers to
adopt a more collectivist rather than individualist approach to their teaching. "The National Curriculum imposes a standardized structure on all
classrooms which invites standard, not differentiated methodologies" (Silcock, 1990, p. 8).

Assessment. One of the reforms arousing the most suspicion and apprehension in the minds of teachers is that of standard assessment. What precisely
is the National Curriculum requiring in the way of assessment? For each
of the nine subjects to be taught in the elementary school, there are a number of "attainment targets" (ATs) specified. For each of these ATs there
are 10 levels of attainment through which children should progress. Four
"key stages" have been identified at which most children should be expected
to have attained particular levels of attainment. In the elementary school
age range there are two key stages. At key stage 1, the children (age 7) are
expected to be performing at levels of attainment 1–3 and at key stage 2
(age 11), at levels 2–5. There are "programmes of study" built on a series
of statements of attainment for each of the levels in the attainment targets.
For example, in the case of science there are 16 attainment targets consist-
ing of 157 statements of attainment. Assessment will be undertaken at the
end of each key stage through standard assessment tasks. Ways of assessing children at age 7 were piloted in the summer of 1990 in a small number of schools to examine the feasibility of proposed assessment procedures.
At the time the interview data reported here were collected, there were
already reports that the pilot schools were experiencing much teacher and

child stress. As Stella expressed it: "The assessment, that's the other thing really. Teachers are worried about it. I know we do it anyway but it's the standard tests looming in the background somewhere and I'm not looking forward to doing that at all. Some of the pilot schools have said they're a work of art." By "work of art" Stella was referring to the type of assessment required by the tests. These tests were not simple paper-and-pencil activities but rather something like the "authentic assessment" procedures currently being devised in the United States (see Darling-Hammond & Snyder, 1992). They were to be undertaken while the children were engaged in an authentic learning activity. Such assessment is found to be perfectly possible as part of the regular teaching process, but almost impossible to do in order to produce and record a rating for an official report.

All the schools were discussing how best to assess progress in each of the subjects and devising ways to record assessments efficiently and in detail. There is still considerable confusion about how this can be done. One of the problems concerns the optimum generality or specificity of records of progress. As Jill put it:

> We've got these sheets that are quite general, and we've got others that
> we are trying out that are too detailed. You think, for instance, whether
> they know the difference between on top and underneath—I think they
> do but I haven't actually tested them. But it's the sort of thing you'd
> notice when you asked a child to pick up something, 'Oh look, there's a
> pencil under there' and they pick it up because they look under the table.
> So am I supposed to sit there then with my little notebook to ask each
> child if he understands *underneath* then *next to* and so on?

Campbell (1990) discusses the confusion teachers are experiencing, as exemplified in these comments by Jill. In an editorial on the report by the Department of Education and Science (1989) on the implementation of the National Curriculum, he refers to "a lack of clarity and helpfulness in the information from local and central government or in the case of assessment and recording, lack of information" (p. 2). As the information flow increased in the area of assessment, it proved in some cases to be quite unworkable. As Silcock writes (1990) about schools in one LEA, "There is considerable in-school discussion about National Curriculum monitoring producing a diversity of models—each it seems, flawed fatally by the time they take to use" (p. 6).

The confusion over the relative importance of effecting and recognizing real progress in skill and understanding, on the one hand, and the need for curriculum delivery in the form of "coverage," on the other, is problematic. Two examples are of particular interest here. Silcock (1990) reports one teacher's pedagogical dilemma as follows: "Although she could cover the ground adequately she could not guarantee that children would actually learn anything" (p. 6). Referring to an action research project she had carried out, this teacher described how she and a colleague had begun each day by trying to discover what the children (age 5 and 6) remembered from the day before. They found that very little was remembered. She reflected: "How many times do we have to teach anything before we can be sure children know or can do it? How much time do we have?" (p. 6). She was afraid that teachers would be checking children on lists as having learned something whether or not it was true. Then teachers would be recording according to what they knew about the children, as they always have previously, rather than according to their direct observation of the children. A claim could be made, then, that teachers' knowledge of student understanding is built on the cumulation of evidence about the child's understanding gained through daily teaching conversations over a long period of time. Silcock (1990) makes the point that "coming to understand something" is not like "becoming ill with recognizable symptoms" but is more like "a transforming experience which affects many behaviors often manifested over a long rather than a short term" (p. 6).

An example of such long-term learning in young children is given in Bruce and colleagues' (1989) *Early Childhood Education*. There is a description of how children's understanding of plant growth might develop during the course of one academic year through the common kinds of experience children have of growing things in the classroom. The description also offers some indication of how different levels of understanding in various children might be developed in diverse ways through similar classroom experiences:

> It is typical of young children that experience is built up over weeks and months, interest is generated and sustained through interaction with the teacher, and knowledge is acquired, sometimes in small increments, and at other times through considerable leaps of understanding as it is relevant to their experience. (p. 17)

The second example is given by Smith (1990), who describes the teaching of subtraction. The match between past experience, current understanding, and new information is important for learning. Yet this match is different for different children. Therefore the teacher instructing a whole class or even a group may need to attend to misunderstanding on an individual basis. Smith describes a young child who does not understand the meaning of the words *how much more* in the context of a question about difference. He describes the process of trying to learn how close the child is to understanding the concept and trying to seek out exactly that point at which connections are not being made. He makes the point that learning is not a simple "either you know it or you don't" kind of matter.

Smith (1990) describes the "territory teachers are working in constantly, mediating between what the children can bring and trying to get them to extend themselves into the half-known" (p. 12). He refers to the mind as "'what she knows' bordered very hazily by a grey area of what she's working on, her work-in-progress, what she can do with a bit of help" (p. 12). He then makes the point that "summative assessment is nothing more than bureaucratic and reductive convenience" (p. 12). The formative part of the assessment process is that which the teacher makes as part of teaching each child every day "on a moment-by-moment scale"; it is based on evidence that is fluid, uncertain, repetitious, now here, now gone again. "Learning is a messy rather than a neat process and the consequence of this can often be the realization that too much of what we do amounts to the mere laying down of a superficial veneer of 'ability' which is all too rarely transferable" (Smith, 1990, p. 12). This is reminiscent of the analogous situation of news media reporters in a war zone attempting to search out the truth as accurately and quickly as possible. They find themselves asking soldiers or airmen just back from a mission to report on numbers of enemy planes seen or numbers of prisoners of war captured. Yet this most often proves to be an unsatisfactory strategy because the individual in the thick of the action can rarely supply the kind of reliable information required for meaningful reporting.

In trying to make sense of the assessment procedures of the National Curriculum, school staffs were going to considerable lengths to understand what was likely to be required of individual teachers. Some ingenious possibilities were being explored to enable one staff to understand what was meant by the levels of attainment described in the official documents. Sally describes what was happening:

> All the schools in this area are looking at samples of children's work in English and we're seeing if we can agree on what might be early level one, middle level one, and late level one work. We got some work from the reception class that we agreed was early level one. I thought James's work was early level one, but then when I saw what Sophie had in her class you could see that there was a stage before that. So James fit into middle level one. And there was so much that was late level one that was definitely not level two. So we thought we had better divide each level into three to make it easier.

The problem besetting these teachers in this noble enterprise of clarification was that of agreeing on a nine-level progression instead of a three-level one. It would be easy to imagine what would happen if such a procedure were adopted to clarify teachers' understanding of each of the levels of attainment in the other eight subjects across all the attainment targets at the first three levels. The teachers' world was further complicated by the additional expectation that they aggregate results of assessment across the different subjects to give a single score for each student. As Sally put it: "Some of the children are so varied, though. In some things they might be level two, yet they're level one in others, and there's quite an imbalance."

Lack of time. One of the main problems following from the need teachers had to gain some common understanding of the different levels of attainment was that the process of coming to agreement was extremely time-consuming. Jill tells of the way the demands on her time are increasing, thereby eroding her ability to manage the classroom learning environment as she would like to:

> I think I'm not in my classroom enough after school, I'm dashing away to do something else and my displays have been up for about a month and I haven't time to change them when I should, so they start to peel or get dirty and I'm uneasy with the classroom because I want to change things and don't have time. There's always some extra demand.

Stella tells a similar story:

> Time! That's what we're finding the worst thing, trying to plan what we're doing. The time to sort out what we're *supposed* to be doing. The time to evaluate what we *are* doing and then to plan the *next* lot as well as all your normal preparation time. That the worst thing, there just isn't enough time.

The teachers expressed concern that this lack of time posed a threat to the quality of life in the classrooms for which they were responsible.

The problems created by time pressure may also give rise to a kind of siege mentality among teachers. Sallis (1990) warns against this and its impact on the public at a time when teachers most need to maintain good and open relations with those outside the field:

> Schools must work to share their thinking with governors and parents, not feel they have to be a step ahead because they are professionals. In a situation where change comes so fast and all the service has indigestion, a huge obstacle to progress is the professionals' feeling that they must possess understanding themselves before they can share, keep a step ahead, have the answer book. (p. 30)

Her worst fears are that the teachers may "retreat into even more territorial habits, as power to the parents and governors gets all mixed up in peoples' minds with the fear of the market place philosophy and all the destructive things it could do to schools" (p. 31).

There was evidence in the schools visited that the teachers were accommodating successfully in many ways to the new demands on their time and energy. However, the quality of life for both teachers and children seemed to be threatened, leading to stress and to feelings of apprehension. Throughout his book, Armstrong (1980) describes the importance of close observation of teaching. The teachers I interviewed shared a similar view of teaching, claiming that time to observe and understand the children personally contributed to their professional self-confidence. The teaching role entails providing a range of experiences for children and building on their interests and on the sense that they are able to make for themselves of those experiences. Close observation of and responsiveness to children's own meaning-making are important aspects of the teacher's role. Scheirer's (1990) description of the teacher's role also underscores the need for the teacher to be sensitive to individual children: "The teacher acts as a bridge between the children and knowledge; the teacher both interprets knowledge for the child in order to facilitate learning and helps the child make personal meaning of the knowledge confronted" (p. 109). Ayers (1986) further emphasizes recent views on the nature of learning, which the collectivist National Curriculum approach may be threatening: "Knowledge acquisition is active and involves children in construction and reconstruction, with the teacher as an 'interactor' who activates others in their engagement with 'object matter'" (p. 50). The National Curriculum has therefore begun to threaten a view of learning that is framed around active engagement, knowledge construction, and spontaneous individual and social processes.

The Professional Demands on Teachers

The third theme explored in discussion with teachers was that of the nature of the professional demands being made on them outside the classroom teaching environment. Some of the kinds of activity in which the teachers have been engaged have already been described. There have been many meetings with other teachers to plan, implement, and evaluate curriculum innovations. There have been in-service courses attended by teachers to increase their understanding of the implications of the National Curriculum for their teaching. Many have been involved in teaching their peers in such courses. There is a massive attempt to share the subject expertise that already resides in one school or one geographic area. Where procedural guidelines are unclear or nonexistent, teachers have spent enormous amounts of time discussing the feasibility of many alternatives. Jill describes the demand:

> There just seem to be more and more meetings for various reasons and more you've got to plan for too! For instance, I'm going to a meeting on Saturday on art because I want to go. So fine, if that's the only one I had that week, but I've got something on Thursday to go to and I've got to find out some things for it. Then by the time you get back from a meeting after school then you have a meal then you've got to start your preparation for teaching next day, soon the whole evening's gone!

Another demand is for each teacher to take on special responsibility for different subjects of the curriculum or resources for learning. Sally was responsible for the school's policy on children with special educational needs, using the computer in the classroom, history, physical education, and swimming. Jill was responsible for drama, art, music, liaison with parents and the local preschool, and deputizing for the head teacher when she was out of the school. "I get so worried with having to assume all the authority. I guess it's just the thought—if things go wrong, it's all going to be my fault." Yet in each case these teachers were not considering doing anything else but teaching. Diane had been offered a job by her brother (company car, high salary, other additional perks) but she seemed more determined than ever to stay in teaching. "If I left it might be fine for me but what about these children? I feel I understand these children. I can't just turn away and say 'Oh, let someone else teach them!'" Sally said, "but I can't imagine myself doing anything else but teaching the children. When I'm in the class, I enjoy my job and it's lovely to see the children making progress. It's just when you get to weekends and then you sort of think 'oh dear!'" When asked if she had considered leaving the profession, Stella put it this way: "No, not at the moment really. I'll wait and see when all this is settled. If we are called upon to publish the results and do all sorts of ridiculous things like that, I'd think about it. But I like being with the children because it's so interesting, it's so different every day." Some of the teachers remaining in teaching seem to be resolute and determined to do the very best they can for the children, their schools, and the profession. As Pollard (1990) has commented: "Teachers may find it hard to achieve the idealized aims to which they aspire, but they show considerable determination and creativity in attempting to reconcile such ideals with the practical realities within which they must work" (p. 71).

CONCLUSION

Times are changing in Britain, and the educational scene reflects the political reforms that have been initiated and successfully pursued by the Conservative government under the strong leadership of Margaret Thatcher. It appears both from reading the work of educational commentators and from talking with teachers and head teachers that the reforms are having considerable impact on school life. However, it is interesting to make the links between the critical writing of educators and the views of professionals who work in schools with children on a day-to-day basis.

Those who are in a position to publish critical accounts of the implications of government reforms are doing so with considerable fluency and assertiveness. Excellent critical writing is being made available to readers at great speed following events designed to impose change in a very short time frame. Such critical commentary is most valuable at times of rapid professional adaptation, since teachers are accountable for the results of their work irrespective of the circumstances in which they are required to teach. The teaching profession is working under duress at the present time not only because of the rate of change but also because the change is seen by many teachers as threatening professional standards. Yet the teachers are not in a position to assert their professional perspective against the current government position.

The processes of teaching and learning that have been developed in British elementary schools over the past 20 years or so are threatened by the introduction of the National Curriculum and its assessment procedures. Simons (1988) has described the effect of the National Curriculum as "a demoralizing demotion of teachers and the virtual extinction of creativity in curriculuar action" (p. 89). Lawton (1989a) refers to this problem in an account of the opposing forces of teacher professionalism and bureaucratic accountability. On the one hand, professionals are concerned with the process of teaching and emphasize the importance of understanding children's learning needs. On the other hand, bureaucrats, primarily concerned with accountability, seek the efficiency of results that can be reported in statistical form. The increasing professionalism teachers have enjoyed in the recent past has been supported within a system that has encouraged school-based initiatives and permitted innovations to be developed by teachers themselves. The National Curriculum documents, however, emphasize external direction and centralized control, giving the Secretary of State for Education many new powers over teachers. Lawton (1989a) writes of school-based reforms introduced by government: "Evaluation can easily become, for example, part of very mechanistic accountability exercises on a regional or national scale which have the effect of tying teachers down to rigid requirements or guidelines rather than being able to develop the potential for creative innovation" (p. 89).

When the emphasis shifts from teaching to assessment, there are implications for the relationship between the child and teacher in the classroom. Gipps (1988) suggests that this relationship will be "not so much that of a guide and mentor, but more one based on instruction and assessment" (p. 73). There is concern that teachers, in implementing the National Curriculum, will be constrained to follow educational practices that they do not believe are in the children's best interests. Yet in carrying out the statutory requirements, they might also lose some of the skills of interdisciplinary teaching and learning for which British elementary education has become renowned.

Among the teachers interviewed, however, there is a strong determination to continue to teach by means of strategies that best support children's learning even when such strategies are seen to be undermined by central government directives. Meanwhile, internationally there seems to be greater recognition than ever that the practical knowledge that teachers use in their work is highly complex and constructed on the basis of personal experience with children in classrooms (Calderhead, 1988; Clandinin, 1986; Elbaz,1983; Grimmett & MacKinnon, 1992; Smyth, 1987). Such a view of professional expertise indicates the value of empowering teachers to develop the curriculum in their own classrooms rather than designing standard curriculum materials to circumvent the potentially negative effects of individual differences among teachers.

In conclusion, however, there appear generally to be grounds for some optimism about reform in primary education in Britain, since rapid change can bring opportunities for teachers to rethink their priorities. As Pollard (1990) puts it, "Ways in which the legislation will be interpreted and enacted will depend on professional judgement, on aims and values at the point of delivery" (p. 76). However, he goes on to say that "this can only be influential if teachers have the self-confidence and sense of perspective to use their remaining autonomy and responsibility. Power can be created and enacted by individuals. There are many responsibilities which remain, squarely, with the teaching profession" (p. 76).

POSTSCRIPT

The last year or two has seen a growing resistance among teachers to implementing statutory procedures when they judge them not to be in the children's best interests. During 1993 many schools have opted to boycott the standard assessment tests. Two major teachers' unions won a legal victory in the High Court in London, and the test boycott was legally cleared. In the *Sunday Observer* O'Connor (1993) reports: "It seems that most parents support the teachers and believe this Summer's tests should be abandoned." The story continues . . .

NOTE

1. The real names of the teachers are known only to the researcher. To protect their anonymity and confidentiality, pseudonyms have been used.

REFERENCES

Armstrong, M. (1980). *Closely observed children: The diary of a primary classroom.* London: Writers and Readers.

Ayers, W. (1986). About teaching and teachers: Thinking about teachers and the curriculum. *Harvard Educational Review, 56*(1), 49–51.

Blyth, J., & Bish, P. (1990). History 5-11: Issues raised by the National Curriculum. *Education 3–13, 18*(2), 15–19.

Boydell, D. (1990). '. . . The gerbil on the wheel': Conversations with primary headteachers about the implications of ERA. *Education 3–13, 18*(2), 20–24.

Brighouse, T. (1990). The present state of education and its future prospects. In T. Everton, P. Mayne, & S. White (Eds.), *Effective learning: Into a new ERA* (pp. 41–48). London: Jessica Kingsley.

Bruce, T., Chard, S., Hurst, V., Lally, M., Pascal, C., & Scott, W. (Eds.). (1989). *Early childhood education: The early years curriculum and the National Curriculum.* Stoke-on-Trent, UK: Trentham Books.

Calderhead, J. (Ed.). (1988). *Teachers' professional learning.* Lewes, UK: Falmer.

Campbell, R. J. (1990). Editorial. *Education 3–13, 18*(1), 2–3.

Clandinin, D. J. (1986). *Classroom practice: Teachers' images in action.* Lewes, UK: Falmer.

Darling-Hammond, L., & Snyder, J. (1992). Framing accountability: Creating learner-centered schools. In A. Lieberman (Ed.), *The changing context of teaching* (Ninety-first yearbook of the National Society for the Study of Education, part I) (pp. 11–36). Chicago: University of Chicago Press.

Department of Education and Science. (1989). *The implementation of the National Curriculum in primary schools.* London: Her Majesty's Stationery Office.

Elbaz, F. (1983). *Teacher thinking: A study of practical knowledge.* London: Croom Helm.

Gipps, C. (1988). What exams would mean for primary education. In D. Lawton & C. Chitty (Eds.), *The National Curriculum* (pp. 71–79). London, UK: Kogan Page.

Grimmett, P. P., & MacKinnon, A. M. (1992). Craft knowledge and the education of teachers. In G. Grant (Ed.), *Review of Research in Education* (Vol. 18) (pp. 385–456). Washington, DC: American Educational Research Association.

Hatch, J. A. (1990). Exchanging places? Primary education in the US and UK. *Education 3–13, 18* (1), 4–7.

Jeavons, I. (1990). Learning to do as they are told. *Forum, 32*(2), 1–4.

Kelly, A. V. (1990). *The National Curriculum: A critical review*. London: Paul Chapman.

Kemmis, S. (1987). Critical reflection. In M. F. Wideen & I. Andrews (Eds.), *Staff development for school improvement: A focus on the teacher*. Philadelphia: Falmer.

Lawton, D. (1989a). *Education, culture and the national curriculum*. London: Hodder & Stoughton.

Lawton, D. (1989b). *The Education Reform Act: Choice and control*. London: Hodder & Stoughton.

O'Connor, M. (1987). *Curriculum at the crossroads: An account of the School Curriculum Development Committee national conference "Aspects of curriculum change."* London: School Curriculum Development Committee.

O'Connor, M. (1993, May 16). National Curriculum update. *Sunday Observer*, p. 10.

Pollard, A. (1990). The aims of primary school teachers. In N. Proctor (Ed.), *The aims of primary education and the National Curriculum* (pp. 63–77). Lewes, UK: Falmer.

Postman, N., & Weingartner, C. (1969). *Teaching as a subversive activity*. New York: Delta.

Sallis, J. (1990). Schools and their governors: Building effective partnerships. In T. Everton, P. Mayne, & S. White (Eds.), *Effective learning: Into a new* ERA (pp. 25–31). London: Jessica Kingsley.

Scheirer, E. A. (1990). The triangular relationship of the teacher, knowledge, and the child: Accountability in action. In T. Everton, P. Mayne, & S. White (Eds.), *Effective learning: Into a new* ERA (pp. 108–115). London: Jessica Kingsley.

Silcock, P. (1990). Implementing the National Curriculum: Some teachers' dilemmas. *Education 3–13, 18*(3), 3–10.

Simon, B. (1990). How to achieve effective learning in spite of the Educational Reform Act. In T. Everton, P. Mayne, & S. White (Eds.), *Effective learning: Into a new* ERA (pp. 32–40). London: Jessica Kingsley.

Simons, H. (1988). Teacher professionalism and the National Curriculum. In D. Lawton & C. Chitty (Eds.), *The National Curriculum* (pp. 78–90). London: Kogan Page.

Smith, R. (1990). What doesn't Anita know? *Education, 3–13, 18*(3), 11–12.

Smyth, J. (1987). *Educating teachers*. Lewes, UK: Falmer.

Taylor, P. H., Reid, W. A., Holly, B. J., & Exon, G. (1974). *Purpose, power and constraint in the primary school curriculum*. London: Macmillan.

CHAPTER 6

Is the School the Unit of Change?

Internal and External Contexts
of Restructuring

LESLIE SANTEE SISKIN

This chapter reports a study of a single high school in California, here called Rancho, which back in 1976 began an experiment: a planned change in its organizational and instructional structures. A case study of a single school always raises questions about the possibility, and the advisability, of attempting to generalize; and this story may be particularly suspect, since in one sense, it is a story of a school that might have been—a case of planned change that did not quite turn out the way anyone planned. Moreover, since the experiment began almost 15 years ago, this might be considered ancient history in educational research. But that time span allows for a rare glimpse into longitudinal data, as teachers[1] remember what was and connect it to the long-term effects (and noneffects) of a planned change effort. Moreover, this effort, and its effects, are particularly salient now, since Rancho's planned change looked very much like what we presently call "restructuring"—a kind of change that educational researchers, policy makers, and practitioners are almost unavoidably entangled with today, when "the political climate has made [it] hard to resist" (Boyd, 1987, p. 94).

Restructuring attempts depend on implicit assumptions about the school as a professional community—one to which increased site-level autonomy could and should be granted and in which shared goals, norms, and objectives can and will be established. These are assumptions that the Rancho case calls into question and that the established literatures on professional and occupational communities take as problematic, for the focus there has been to highlight interdependence and interconnectedness rather than autonomy, and internal divisions and groupings rather than unitary goals. Huberman (1990), for example, directly challenges the restructuring advocates, declaiming that "I would submit that the logic of using the school building as the unit of analysis and intervention, when we are talking about at least 25–30 teachers and support staff and 500 pupils, is a goofy logic" (p. 32). When we are talking about high schools with even larger staffs and student bodies, his point is particularly apt. An alternative logic, drawing on more complex models of extended and fragmented professional communities, suggests that in examining the case of Rancho, or any attempt to restructure, we need to look not only at the school as unit of change, but also at the external communities of which the local schools are a part and the internal subcommunities that partition local high schools (see, for example, Ball & Bowe, 1991; Little, 1990a, 1990b; McLaughlin, Talbert, & Bascia, 1990; Rosenholtz, 1989; Siskin, 1991, 1994; Van Maanen & Barley, 1984). The strong suggestion emerging from this work is that context matters (McLaughlin et al., 1990) and that relevant contexts may include only portions of a school, with departments being a prime example, or may extend well beyond its boundaries. As Ball and Bowe (1991) found in their study of the recent British reform efforts, the "power" to change what goes on in schools "is strongly circumscribed by the contextual features of institutions over which the State may find that control is both problematic and contradictory" (p. 28). The purpose of this chapter, then, is to look at the case of Rancho's attempt at school-level restructuring within a context of problematic and often contradictory features of institutions within and surrounding the school.

THE CONTEXT OF RESTRUCTURING

The early 1980s were a difficult time for schools and educators, as claims of crisis and charges of failure were levied from all sides. From the media came headlines such as "Why Public Schools Fail" (1981) and "Help! Teacher Can't Teach" (1980); from business leaders came demands for "quality control" over products from our schools that left them unable to compete in the international marketplace; from a spate of national reports came titles such as *A Nation at Risk* and the rhetoric of impending doom: "We have been committing an act of unthinking, unilateral educational disarmament" (National Commission on Excellence in Education, 1983, p. 5); and, finally, from the legislators came a virtual explosion of activity (Kirst, 1983) culminating in over 1,000 pieces of state legislation largely aimed at tightening controls over teachers and teaching (Darling-Hammond & Berry, 1988). By 1983, the year the National Commission on Excellence in Education released *A Nation at Risk,* 38 states had mandated student testing requirements, 35 had launched new curriculum development efforts, and 30 had imposed district- or school-level planning requirements (Education Commission of the States, 1983).

Within a few years, however, a so-called second wave brought to center stage an apparently miraculous intervention, as educational rhetoric moved from *A Nation at Risk* to *A Nation Prepared* (Carnegie Forum on Education and the Economy, 1986). The language of doom escalated to apocalyptic promise as advocates sought to bring us to the dawn of a new era: The state of New York, for example, released its "Compact for Learning" with the opening phrase "As the millenium approaches." On the same rhetorical level, the Canadian Association for Teacher Education pronounced its 1991 convention "On the threshold of a new age: Restructuring teacher education." The Nabisco corporation offered $100,000 to $250,000 annual grants to what it calls "Next Century Schools"—schools that develop "restructured" structures to include shared commitment by school and community. Such plans for "sustained, wide-ranging change" must "extend beyond traditional concepts or the status quo" because "the next century is just around the corner" (*Fortune*, 1990).

Emerging from the fallout is the growing sense that what education and the nation need is a complete restructuring of schools and, even more surprising, that teachers need to be involved in the decision-making process for the effort to work. This is something on which a wide range of reformers, observers, practitioners, and policy makers agree, although—or perhaps because—there is so little agreement on what, specifically, "restructuring" means. Taking its lessons from research on "effective schools" (Purkey & Smith, 1983) and from a generation of change studies that suggest policy makers "cannot mandate what matters" (McLaughlin, 1987, p. 172) and cannot make effective policy without considering the level of the school, this reform attempt seems to have moved beyond those findings to assume that change must occur at the level of the individual school and that the school is therefore the appropriate unit of change. Advocates argue not only for a new structure but also for local schools to have the ability and responsibility to develop, modify, and design the appropriate structure themselves (Schlechty, 1991).

It is this assumption, that the school is the most appropriate unit of change, as well as the apparently underlying assumption, that the school is a discrete and unitary body, that the Rancho case leads us to question. There has been a tendency in the restructuring movement to think we can, and should, consider the school as a unit that is both discrete (as if somehow we could isolate it from the larger communities within which it is inextricably embedded and interconnected) and unitary (as if a common, and commonly shared, goal would override patterns of complex, and sometimes competing, internal divisions).

Rancho, then, serves as a case history of an early attempt at what is now being promoted as restructuring and illustrates the interaction of a restucturing attempt with external and internal community forces. For, according to a former principal, "Rancho seems to be ahead of its time. It embodied what all the new commission reports recommend." And, since it was "ahead of its time," it allows us to see what time has done to the early visions of what this school could, and should, become.

THE RANCHO PLAN

In 1976 a team of administrators and teachers, selected before the school was even built, were authorized by a supportive district to "be something different" and to develop what resembled a site-based management program. This was a growing community, with a fairly stable middle-class population, and the team spent the first planning year analyzing local student needs, visiting innovative programs, and devising structural alternatives. Although the district relied primarily on local taxes for funding, they obtained extra funds available through a state program for what was then called "school improvement" but that sounds much like the grants currently available for "restructuring"—grants for school sites that would put forward innovative proposals and would include, in some form, community involvement (with community involvement defined to include faculty, staff, student, and parent input in decision making).

After a year of planning, of assessing students and community needs, the team put forward their "Rancho Plan." As one of the original teachers remembers it:

> At that time there was a strong message from the district to decentralize. Rancho was supposed to be different. The school improvement council was supposed to be a viable, powerful body. As a teacher I would have input over what happened in the school. We had leadership training, training in conflict resolution, shared decision making. We were on the cutting edge. We could generate our own curriculum to match student needs; we had resources, time, money.

Through the Rancho Plan, they were given free rein to define what they saw as necessary to develop a good school for their particular student body—to design new staffing patterns, curricula, even to be involved in the design of the building itself; through district support and state funding they were given the resources to put their design in place. Both alterations in "rules, roles, and relationships" and attention to desired "results" —the characteristics Corbett (1990) uses to identify restructuring—came into play as the Rancho team created what one participant called "a special vision in terms of educational design."

By all accounts it was an exhilarating period. An administrator recalls it as the "Camelot period where things were possible and funding was possible. A different time." And a former social studies teacher remembers how "I said all these years I've been putting my fingers in curricular dikes. Wouldn't it be grand to build one? Build a program the way it should be?" He likens the feeling of creativity and potential in those first years to "kind of walking with the gods." With this apparently almost euphoric sense of mission, the team began to implement the Rancho Plan.

The vision this team developed called for deliberate restructuring of traditional organizational design, replacing departmental divisions and hierarchical levels with three advisory units. All staff, including administrators, 85 teachers, counselors, and clerical staff, were divided into these units, called "learning houses." Each unit would operate to some degree independently, but all shared the same central function: advising students. Each unit member had a core group of about 20 students to meet with during a once-a-week advisory period and to act as advocate for during the students' entire time in the school. Advisers would be "monitors for success as well as for failure" and would be able to develop the close relationships with their students that traditional high school design makes so difficult. The Rancho design centered around the needs of the students, since, as an English teacher explains, "student needs would drive what the units would produce," but it was also attentive to the needs of staff for collegial relationships, in that the units would provide "a sense of community" that the school as a whole was too large to permit. Other teachers confirm the value of these units to their own needs: "The unit provided a structure for community, a means of support" observes one teacher; "It makes the school smaller and mitigates alienation" notes another.

The staff who were chosen for this school, and who chose to come to Rancho, were by all accounts a special group of people—on a number of dimensions. They were strong academically. They were also, as one teacher remembers, "leaders, opinion setters." Another describes them as "the risk takers. It was a very innovative school; it was going to try to set a brand new trend in education." Yet another describes them as "boat rockers" and "rebels" among other, more graphic terms ("shit disturbers"), adding that their former schools were at least as happy to be rid of them as Rancho was to welcome them. They either came in as, or were quickly converted to, advocates for the special mission of caring for students. Their commitment to the students, and to a caring relationship with them, appears at times extraordinary. One teacher recalls how she had a problem with one student:

> It was about five years ago. She was being abused, and I said "Why don't you come home, you know, feel that you can stay at my house if it gets

really bad . . ." That night there was the daughter, there was the mother, and there was the son. They moved in. Of course, I allowed it to happen, but they moved in. They stayed with me so long [about 6 weeks] that I was afraid that I was going to have to buy a six-foot Christmas tree.

Yet even with the extraordinary staff selected by and committed to the Rancho vision, even with the extra resources and the support to "be different," there was an awareness of the difficulties inherent in what they were trying to do—for the Rancho Plan was a deliberate challenge to what Sarason (1971) has called the "regularities" of schooling. Of particular concern was the potency of the traditional departmentalized boundaries, which the new structure set out deliberately to break down. Like Sizer (1984), these planners cast the departmentalized structure of the high school as a villain, fragmenting the school for teachers and learning for the students. Their Rancho Plan would "get away from" that divisive structure:

> It was designed in order to allow people to meet people outside of their department. It was to get away from The English Department, The Math Department. So people were in units where they were mixed . . . that was the whole idea to have the units: to get away from each department for themselves.

The administrators who were coming into the school all saw strong departments as a threat to what they wanted to accomplish. One explains that "the three administrators who came here when the school opened were all strong department chairmen in their own schools. And I think we all saw the dangers of a school that has a department, for whatever reason, that becomes sort of the tail that wags the dog." For these administrators, the units were a way of avoiding the fragmentation, and the competition, that they had seen in their own experience:

> The units were really a way of having teachers structured in a nondepartmental fashion. And the thing they had in common was being advisers, and the focus was the role of the adviser. And the idea was that you would force teachers, because of the set that you would put them in, you would force them to really look at the total student. And to look at the educational experience from an organizational point of view. And so when you talk about organizational changes, or thrust, or looking at a new magnet focus, or trying to decide how to realign advisory, you do it through that arena. Now there are still some things that you can discuss in your department. The department focus is fairly narrow, isn't it? It has

been. They tend to look at English as the only thing that is of concern. And you know, perhaps that's the way it should be. You need to have some of that kind of an ethnocentric way of looking at it. But we wanted for each teacher to play both of those roles. To also look at the school as a whole, just as an administrator does, or a counselor. Most teachers don't have that experience in high school.

Yet the Rancho staff recognized that factors both external (in the expectations of the wider community) and internal (in the orientation of subject-specialist teachers) would push and pull on the unit structure. For these teachers refer repeatedly to their sense of belonging to the wider, subject-based community and the pull that community exerts: to science teachers' need "to go to science conferences and things like that"; to their friendships with teachers from within their fields but outside the school; to the demands of subject-based exams such as the College Boards and Advanced Placement tests; and to the feedback of returning students who reported on their performance in the subject in college. One of the original English teachers remembers the pull "from outside—colleges, district mandates," observing almost wistfully that Rancho was "intended to be interdisciplinary" but "the secondary school was simply too entrenched in their [traditional] structure, particularly in terms of curriculum," so that "everyone was willing, there was extra money to make it work, but the plan just didn't materialize." They tried a variety of experiments but they "couldn't resist the weight"; it was just "too much to take on."

Nor was the pressure coming exclusively from external sources, for the teachers themselves, by their training, interests, and experience, were well entrenched in the traditional departmental divisions. The vice-principal commented on the push from inside—from the strength of the individual teacher's orientation to subject:

> We had representatives from the units, that were elected by their constituents; they were to kind of represent the student and the school as a whole. And of course, none of that is that clean . . . no teacher is ever going to think about his role as an adviser and forget that he's a social studies teacher. But it's interesting, when people are given roles, they tend to somewhat fulfill those roles. I think that kind of happened.

From inside and outside, then, from the very beginning, the Rancho staff recognized the potency of curricular categories and subject-matter orientation that would challenge their efforts; for even in a brand new high school, with a new vision, "none of it is that clean."

STRIFE, STRESS, CHAOS

In the beginning, despite the push and pull of subject-specific pressures, the teachers, and the units, did "tend to somewhat fulfill these roles." The organizational chart of the school listed the names of all staff members in three columns, one for each unit. Within each column were groupings of "learning areas"—such as Communication or Cultural Skills—with departmental affiliation reduced to a parenthetical abbreviation. The unit offices, where teachers had their desks, began to fill with the trappings to make them more attractive and more of a home base—coffee makers, a microwave, a comfortable couch, posters and pictures. Although they were not designed to be thematically distinct, each unit began to take on a distinct identity, a personality of its own: "Unit 3 is argumentative; unit 1 has strong personalities; unit 2 is the good guys . . . [we] find it easy to make decisions, we get along" reported a perhaps somewhat biased member of unit 2.

Following quickly on the heels of the Camelot era, however, came a series of unforeseen and unforeseeable events, which created a period teachers characterize as one of "strife, stress, chaos." Even a site-based management school is embedded within the context of the larger educational community, and actions taken by the district, state, and even the courts played a critical role in shaping events at Rancho. A vice-principal recalls her experience vividly, characterizing the "contingency universe" within which a school operates:

> We had a year to plan this school. Then we had what we call the "We Agree" with the staff, commitments, and then moved from there. And the structure was that every four years you recommit . . . kind of a fine-tuning thing . . . that was nice, because we were a SIP [School Improvement Program] school, and we could use SIP days [for staff development], and then the board took those away, and said no, we do not want to have students that are not going to school, we want them in school for longer hours. And that was devastating. So, but that was only one thing. It was sort of like a contingency universe. You touch this one little thing there [that] didn't seem in and of itself all that significant, but it really had a rippling effect to all kinds of things.
>
> I can tell you, in the time that I was an administrator here we went through such horrendous . . . we went through a strike, we went through Proposition 13, we went through a reconfiguration of the total secondary program from a three-year high school to a four-year high school. In the meantime, after Proposition 13, we went from a six-period school day to a five-period day. Then we phased in, and this was all because of the bank-

ruptcy, we went back to a six-period day for ninth and tenth graders only. This all during the time that I was a curriculum VP here. Learning how to do this was really traumatic. But it just shows you, boy, I'll tell you, you survive and kids still learn, and things still go on.

In this swirl of activity, three sets of events stand out as critical to the functioning of the Rancho design—events that altered the financial, the demographic, and the curricular makeup of the school.

Proposition 13 and Financial Change

First, and almost immediately, came financial challenges. Proposition 13, the California taxpayer revolt, sharply curtailed local authority's capacity to raise taxes and dramatically increased the dependence of school districts on state aid. In the next few years, the district would lay off more than 500 teachers, cut the high school day to five periods, and eliminate support positions, such as counselors and department chairs, the former of which had been crucial to the Rancho design. Without this support, the teachers found themselves on overload, as "they changed the names but the work remained."

When the state, itself facing fiscal shortfalls, decided that districts with declining enrollments would receive no increases in aid, the district situation worsened. As relations between the school and the district grew increasingly tense, and strikes became a regular occurrence, the board closed 17 schools and moved the ninth graders into what had been 10–12 high schools. This reconfiguration brought into Rancho a new group of teachers who were neither selected for nor committed to the advisory program, at a time when the school no longer had the resources of counseling staff or in-service time to prepare them. At the same time, in response to the board's decisions to defer agreed-upon pay raises and to continue to lay off large numbers of staff, the teachers began what would become a persistent tradition of "work-to-rule" practice, refusing to perform any but contractually specified tasks—a hardship in any school, but particularly in one that depended on a model of participatory decision making and extracurricular advising. Department meetings, unit meetings, curriculum development, work on developing a new peer observation program—all came to screeching halt, since all such activities are dependent on teachers taking on more than they are obligated or paid to do. As one Rancho teacher put it, "We aren't going to kill ourselves when we don't feel there is any payoff there." Another noted that the problem "shows up in class. Teachers say they are not working as hard; they pretend to be working. They're unhappy; their hearts are not in their work."

Desegregation and Demographic Change

The second major challenge to the Rancho Plan came from a court-ordered desegregation plan, which dramatically changed the student body, dispersing the neighborhood students whose needs the plan had been designed to serve and bringing in new students with new sets of problems. As one teacher said, "We've gone from being a school that was very, very middle-class and upper-middle class to a wide range of students and all the problems they bring." And students brought these problems from longer distances: The districtwide magnet program meant students came from diverse and distant neighborhoods. For a school structured around community input and involvement, this made getting parents into the building almost impossible; and the busing schedule made altogether impossible the extra contact, the before- and after-school conferences with teachers, which had been a cornerstone of the program. Teachers felt that the court-ordered solution ignored the realities of their lives and those of their students: "The court monitor should ride the bus for one solid month, every day, to see what it's really like for these kids, and to be subjected to the same gang aspects on the same bus, and to be subject to the insults and the inconvenience."

With the arrival of these new students, many of whom did not speak English, teachers found themselves having to develop new skills to teach new assignments, such as ESL classes and transition classes; although they wanted to maintain the school goals of personalization and caring, they were not always sure how to do so. In addition, district support was often absent, since the staff development days and support staff had been lost to the budget cuts, or in some instances devastatingly present, but dissonant with the school goals—as when the district brought in a consultant to work with teachers around an adopted transition program. A frustrated teacher recounted how one day a student (unsure of what a word in the story had meant) had asked a question, so the teacher turned to the class to see if anyone else could provide the answer. The consultant, who happened to be in the room, later "just got all over my case and said 'never have another student answer another student's question . . . don't take time with her, she's just sidetracking you; you've got to keep this pace up.' It was just awful." What was now being defined as "sidetracking" was what the teachers had seen as central to the personalized mission of the school: responsiveness to the individual needs of a student.

Standardized Access and Curricular Changes

In another move, which made the district's presence devastatingly felt, the central office responded to the desegregation order by moving to standardize curriculum to assure the monitors that all students had an equal opportunity to learn. From the superintendent's perspective, this was essential: There was "no choice. We need to be consistent. We have to standardize access and curriculum. It is not a matter of philosophy; it is a matter of necessity. Suddenly, people at the district level are working on aligning, standardizing, and so forth. Teachers resent this." The teachers at Rancho clearly did resent this, for it undermined the essence of what they thought their school was all about and removed the sense of control over decisions critical to their work:

> You had staff input, shared decision making; you felt like you had control
> of your fate. When they centralized they took away the control of the
> school; they made edicts outside the school. It just goes on and on and
> you felt totally helpless. . . . As the board became more and more conser-
> vative and started to become centralized, it started reviewing some of [the
> principal's] decisions. And once you did that he had to take the responsi-
> bility for our decisions and he started overriding decisions that the School
> Improvement Council made, or not using the sic as a vehicle.

Also undermining the teachers' sense of control were the effects of the first wave of educational reform, as the state omnibus education bill began to hit the classrooms in a series of "framework" guidelines covering texts, content, and teaching techniques, as well as tests to monitor their adoption. While this bill was adopted back in 1983, it had taken several years for the actual guidelines to reach the schools. Increasingly, then, curricular decisions were seen as centralized, standardized, and distanced from the classroom and the school decision-making structures.

This list may seem like an extraordinary litany of disasters and may call into question what this case can possibly have to do with other attempts at restructuring—for how could such a bizarre confluence of crises ever be repeated? But even a quick look at recent events suggests that the Rancho case may not be unique, as the educational system struggles, "despite trends toward increasing centralization," with "a fairly extensive movement toward site-based management" amidst the added stress of fiscal crises (Sergiovanni, Burlingame, Coombs, & Thurston, 1992, p. 26). The San Francisco schools, as they move to embrace "restructuring," face growing state and district budget deficits, while the centralized California frameworks are still coming down the system and the new tests coming up. In New York City, where there has been a strong push for restructuring and site-based management, the system is confronting fiscal crises strong enough to keep a presidential contender out of the race, while the Regents Board is redesigning and tightening curricular requirements at the state level. And, across the country, while teachers are concerned with the need to reconfigure programs to meet the challenges of changing neighborhoods and of changing needs of diverse groups of students, there is increasing talk and active research on the feasibility of a uniform national test. Such contextual features surely present current reformers with "problematic and contradictory" issues of control (Ball & Bowe, 1991).

REASSERTION OF DEPARTMENTAL COMMUNITIES

Whether or why restructuring attempts are likely to face formidable external challenges is not, however, central to this present inquiry. Rather, my thesis is that in *making the school the unit of change* these efforts risk neglecting both external and internal contextual features that may play critical roles in the outcome. The Rancho case demonstrates how—under conditions of stress from the external educational community—even a group of teachers dedicated to restructuring design, convinced of the need to overcome departmental fragmentation and divisiveness, committed in extraordinary ways to the needs of students, and willing to take extraordinary means to address those needs, ultimately retreated into the traditional departmental divisions that they had originally defined as part of the problem.

Over time, the departmental boundaries at Rancho have been reasserted. The members of each subject area have retreated into the familiar territory of the department, and within each have developed distinctive norms, values, and relationships to sustain themselves. The internal pull toward the department is strong; one of the chairs notes that even administrators tend to gravitate toward their former subject areas: "More attention is given to that department. I'm sure it's because it's their comfort zone; it's where they feel most comfortable" and with the other areas they "feel like they're out of their league. I don't mean that as a put-down; I just mean that's the way it is." Under the stressful conditions, Rancho teachers needed to find a "comfort zone."

Science was the first to go, breaking off even before the state guidelines hit. Despite the initial aim of breaking down departmental divisions and scattering teachers across the units, the science classes remained architecturally clustered around the water and gas lines of their labs. Built as spokes around a central common hub, without walls, this classroom structure meant that science teachers early and inevitably became closely connected. They could see and hear what was going on in one another's classes and found it necessary to coordinate planning, so that one class would not be taking a test while the group next door was listening to a clearly audible lecture.

Although all teachers were assigned originally to desks in the unit offices, the science teachers found themselves as connected to their lab stations as the gas lines were: "In science, and I would think in classes like home economics and shop, activity-oriented classes, it's impossible. You can't do your preparation away from your materials. You cannot do that from a unit office. It's impossible."

Several members told, with relish, the story of how they came into the unit offices early on and moved their desks (all are men): "You can't do your preparation away from your materials. And so we just, one at a time, carried our desks over here. And the principal at the time was real upset about it. He didn't say anything to us, but he was real upset about it, the fact that we had left our unit offices and come out here and isolated ourselves." They literally picked up and left the unit offices, and they now report that they have little reason to venture out from their stronghold.

When they do venture out of their stronghold, it is with collective strength and purpose. With their close contact and early frustration with the "they" that could not understand their needs and had provided them with inappropriate conditions and materials, the science teachers quickly coalesced into a distinct and distinctive subgroup; a social studies teacher explained that "they were nicknamed, at one time, the swarm." They found that as a group, as a "swarm" of science teachers, they were able to make demands on the system. The principal describes how "science is very independent and good, but they complain the most. I like them. They've filed a lot of grievances."

The particular architectural arrangements of the labs created another set of constraints for the science teachers, for not only were the gas lines fixed, so too were the numbers of stations at which students could work. This became an issue when district budget cutting took away the release time for department chairs, making it difficult to accomplish what had been their routine responsibilities: "They change the name, but the person still gets to do all the work." In most departments, however, teachers negotiated to increase the size of their own classes, thereby relieving the chair of one class assignment. But, because there are only a limited number of stations in each lab, the science teachers did not have this option. Their alternative was to share the work. They divided most of the administrative responsibilities among four teachers, but much of the decision making has involved the whole department and has continued the centripetal force pulling department members together into a collective group.

The collective strength of the department also served as a base for political action—several of the science teachers are or have been active as union representatives, and one described how the fears of administrative retaliation for union activism are lessened because of the privileged status of science teachers, since "to an extent the science teachers are an endangered species." An active union member, who is not in science, commented on the disproportionate representation of science teachers in union activities, saying that "there's something about mathematicians and scientists when they get this social conscience that seems to say 'I know how to do this.'" One new teacher described how he was rapidly socialized into the shared political, as well as professional, values of this department: "The science department is very strong in the union," and eating lunch together "they'd talk about problems . . . and the more I found out the angrier I got" until he also became a union representative, despite the countervailing forces of his low status as a new teacher and high demands as a new father.

While science may provide the most dramatic examples of a department as a distinct community within Rancho, these teachers are far from alone in their departmental solidarity. The math teachers, for example, work together closely around curricular and instructional matters. As one describes it, "We do, as a department, plan what needs to be covered in a year, and we have what's called readiness tests" to determine who can go on to the next level, and supplemental materials "the department put together before I came here, and we've all agreed to use that in addition to the textbook." A number of teachers report sitting in on one another's classes to learn how the material is taught before they take on that course themselves. One tells how he sat in on a calculus class "even though I had to give up my own prep[aration] time to do it" and of how another teacher, who was assigned pre-algebra, which "she had never taught before, she came into my class every day; she gave up her prep [time] everyday . . . and would be two days behind me and just follow what I did. That seemed to help her."

In this department, teachers are tightly tied by the strength of their common assumptions and also by the length of their shared experience— several of the leaders have been teaching together since the late 1960s, and they have "brought [the others] in" from other schools. But rather than acting as a "swarm" that directs activity outward to school and district politics, the math department seems to observers to have retreated inward —to where they can count on a common understanding largely absent in the wider community. "It is an unhappy feeling, is it not?" observes one teacher from his vantage point outside the department, later referring to the department attitude as "this sort of inward withdrawal . . . it's the same syndrome of always fighting the last war sort of thing." As a group, they have refused to participate in a number of school activities, ranging from the first-year interviews for this study to a recent meeting called when the principal found he had additional monies to distribute: "I [the chair] told him 'I don't want to come to your meeting; we'll just take what we agreed to' . . . you'd think he would welcome it; there's never enough money, and this was one less voice fighting for it." While the principal hardly welcomed their nonparticipation, he found few ways that year to address the math department's siege strategy.

The sense of embattlement is very strong here, for in the recent movements to district standardization and state guidelines, the math department both has the most to lose and is the most likely to lose. Within the department, teachers share a set of assumptions about testing, placement, and tracking that are seen as essential to their own success and that of their students. Outside the department, these assumptions not only are not shared but are actively opposed by school, district, and state officials. "We think there are three levels of kids in this school below algebra 1, and most people don't want to believe that" said one math teacher, and to the math department the difference in these levels is obvious. But, he continued, "The movers and shakers in the educational business, at least in this district, want to deny [that]. . . . Folks that are saying that don't know; they just don't know. They're just on a political kind of trip." The decision to eliminate tracking has significant consequences to the math teachers, who have to deal with what they see as wrongly placed students: "They're just going to have a miserable year and fail, and I'll have a miserable year, the kids that are O.K. will have a miserable year; everything's miserable because . . . folks won't admit that they should be more attentive to where they put kids." From this perspective, the decision clearly has important consequences, but from outside the shared understanding of the math department, the situation looks quite different and is seen in more humorous light. One teacher from another department described "this convoluted little policy they had where there were 9,000 ways one got into mathematics. There was pre-algebra, pre-pre-algebra, pre-pre-pre-algebra, and things like that." The math teachers have largely given up trying to convince such an unresponsive audience; they can only retreat into their own territory and hope to wait out the opposition.

In English, the anger over recent changes is least obvious, and the retreat into departmental boundaries seems least deliberate—it just seems to have happened. A science teacher characterized this department as having only two or three activists around any issue; for the rest, "whatever happens, happens." But while they have not actively rebelled like the science department or withdrawn like the math department, what they have done is to congregate quietly within the unit to which their chair is assigned. When the administrators realized that this unit had a disproportionate number of English teachers (teachers had been given some choice of membership), they changed the official assignments, but the teachers have crept back, unofficially and quietly.

For the English teachers, the importance of the departmental community is described not in technical or political terms, but in social terms of friendship, of individual rather than group-subject identification. Often it is not directly stated at all, but comes out almost parenthetically; when asked about who her colleagues would be, one began, "Peggy, who's one of the other English teachers, and Denise, who's next door who's another English teacher . . . ; Nira is also an English teacher . . . we were young, bright, and eager English teachers together more years ago than we want to admit." Another echoed this same theme, with the personal identifications first, and the professional or pedagogical connections almost as afterthoughts: "Most of the time I spend with two other English teachers . . . then outside of school I have a lot of friends, who are also English teachers . . . with the teachers here I would say it's mostly social . . . although we do talk some about teaching, but the two I'm best friends with don't teach anything remotely like what I'm teaching . . . although [we] did at one time collaborate." Many of these English teachers mourn the decline of the unit structure, like the chair who observed, "You lose the sense of the whole [now] . . . we work more in isolation from one another; I miss it." Yet to collaborate, to socialize, or simply to commiserate, they turn almost inevitably toward their subject-matter colleagues, unintentionally contributing to the demise of the unit structure and the reassertion of the departmental one.

DEPARTMENT AS COMMUNITY

These stories of demise and reassertion can lead us toward an alternative logic for restructuring. As one teacher put it, "It's really strange to see us turning around and heading back, given all that we've been through. And you see all these national publications coming out and everything, saying where we should be, and we were there." For the faculty at Rancho, as at many schools, are experienced not only in teaching but also in weathering reforms (Louis & Miles, 1990). As veterans in both areas, they have good reason to raise questions about the substance of these new efforts at restructuring and about the sustained commitment necessary to see them through. In particular, they raise two sets of concerns about viewing the school as the unit of change.

First, they remind us that, while restructuring advocates may have moved to agreement on taking the school as the "focus of change" (Goodlad, 1991), we need to keep a watchful eye on the rest of the system and become mindful of how that context matters (McLaughlin et al., 1990). Rancho's story provides an instructive example of how schools and their staffs operate within a "contingency universe" wherein events outside their borders, and beyond their control, have profound consequences. State budget changes, new tests or curriculum guidelines, the election of new officials—all can disrupt even the best-laid local plans. As Darling-Hammond (1992) has argued, for restructuring to "make these changes last," we need complementary policy development and political support to accompany the current emphasis on professional development (p. 17). When these three components do not move in concert, they often conflict—leaving schools such as Rancho and their staffs in untenable positions.

Second, as either restructuring efforts or the "rippling effects" of this contingency universe come into large comprehensive high schools, they meet the complex structural and cultural divisions of subject departments, where school visions are reinterpreted in sometimes diverging and conflicting ways, and where specialist teachers grapple with their own subject-specific contingencies (Siskin, 1994).

Departments are, as the Rancho English teachers suggest, a likely site for personal connections that support and sustain individuals, "comfort zones," which may unobtrusively encourage professional development or simply afford a sympathetic ear. They are a site for professional identity among faculty who have chosen and studied their particular subjects, belong to subject associations, and work within a single content area—and where, as the administrator above observed, a teacher is unlikely to "forget that he's a social studies teacher." Departments provide, as the math teachers' experience attests, a mechanism for getting specialized work accomplished—and an arena for having it valued. And, as the ripples of external events touch only one department (as with new curriculum guidelines), or have differential effects (increased class size), this sense of specialization is further reinforced. Departments can serve, as science teachers demonstrate, as a base for political action, for pulling in resources and for pushing agendas. Under increasing pressures for change but contracting resources, these micropolitical coalitions are likely to become particularly visible (Ball & Bowe, 1991). Supported by the external pulls of the larger educational community and the internal push of their own members, subject departments remain a likely site for clearly defined and potent subcommunities—even within a high school whose philosophical and organizational arrangements are designed to break them down.

This is not to suggest that departmental divisions are inevitable, but rather that they are remarkably resilient, even when deliberately targeted for extinction, and that they pose a particular challenge to restructuring efforts. Nor is it to suggest that departments are the only sites around which distinctive communities can form, but rather that the conditions within schools and the pressures from without make them highly likely sites. Understanding that there are likely, resilient, and consequential professional communities within high schools can further educators' attempts to analyze or to reform them.

We need to recognize the problematic nature of viewing the school— or at least the high school—as the unit of change. What Rancho provides is an example of planned change, of the contingency universes that result from the school's embeddedness in the larger, turbulent community of educational policymakers, and of the power and resilience of departmental boundaries in defining subunits within the high school. The Rancho Plan is not an example of failed change—for many of its original features are retained, are purposeful, and remain important to the staff—but of the changing nature of change efforts as they are implemented and interpreted in the internal and external contexts of multiple communities over time.

NOTE

1. Teachers and administrators at Rancho were interviewed, observed, and surveyed over a three-year period (1988–1991) during which they participated in a study conducted by the Center for Research on the Context of Secondary School Teaching, Stanford University. Research for that project, from which this chapter is drawn, was supported by funds from the U.S. Department of Education Office of Educational Research and Improvement.

REFERENCES

Ball, S. J., & Bowe, R. (1991). *Subject to change? Subject departments and the 'implementation' of national curriculum policy: An overview of the issues.* Centre for Educational Studies, King's College, London.

Boyd, W. L. (1987). Public education's last hurrah? Schizophrenia, amnesia, and ignorance in school politics. *Educational Evaluation and Policy Analysis, 9*(2), 85–100.

Carnegie Forum on Education and the Economy. (1986). *A nation prepared: Teachers for the 21st century.* Hyattsville, MD: Author.

Corbett, H. D. (1990). *On the meaning of restructuring.* Philadelphia: Research for Better Schools.

Darling-Hammond, L. (1992). Building learner centered schools: Developing professional capacity, policy, and political consensus. In J. A. Banks, L. Darling-Hammond, and M. Greene. *Building learner-centered schools: Three perspectives.* New York: National Center for Restructuring Schools, Education, and Teaching.

Darling-Hammond, L., & Berry, B. (1988). *The evolution of teacher policy* (No. JRE-01). Santa Monica, CA: Rand Corporation.

Education Commission of the States. (1983). *A survey of state school improvement efforts.* Denver, CO: Author.

Fortune. (1990, June). Advertisement. New York: Time Inc. Magazine Co, p. 31.

Goodlad, J. I. (1991). Why we need a complete redesign of teacher education. *Educational Leadership, 49*(3), 4–10.

Help! Teacher can't teach. (1980, June 16). *Time,* pp. 54–60.

Huberman, M. (1990, April). *The social context of instruction in schools.* Paper presented at the annual meeting of the American Educational Research Association. Boston.

Kirst, M. W. (1983). *State education policy in an era of transition* (Policy Paper 83-c7). Stanford, CA: Institute for Research on Educational Finance and Governance.

Little, J. W. (1990a). Conditions of professional development in secondary schools. In M. W. McLaughlin, J. E. Talbert, & N. Bascia (Eds.), *The contexts of teaching in secondary schools: Teachers realities* (pp. 187–223). New York: Teachers College Press.

Little, J. W. (1990b). The persistence of privacy: Autonomy and initiative in teachers' professional relations. *Teachers College Record, 91*(4), 509–536.

Louis, K. S., & Miles, M. B. (1990). *Improving the urban high school: What works and why.* New York: Teachers College Press.

McLaughlin, M. W. (1987). Learning from experience: Lessons from policy implementation. *Educational Evaluation and Policy Analysis, 9*(2), 171–178.

McLaughlin, M. W., Talbert, J. E., & Bascia, N. (1990). *The contexts of teaching in secondary schools.* New York: Teachers College Press.

National Commission on Excellence in Education. (1983). *A nation at risk: The imperative for educational reform.* Washington, DC: Author.

Purkey, S. C., & Smith, M. S. (1983). Effective schools: A review. *Elementary School Journal, 83*(4), 427–452.

Rosenholtz, S. J. (1989). *Teachers' workplace: The social organization of schools.* New York: Longman.

Sarason, S. (1971). *The culture of the school and the problem of change.* Boston: Allyn & Bacon.

Schlechty, P. C. (1991). Schools for the 21st century: The conditions for invention. In A. Lieberman (Ed.), *Schools as collaborative cultures: Creating the future now* (pp. 233–255). Lewes, UK: Falmer.

Sergiovanni, T. J., Burlingame, M., Coombs, F. S., & Thurston, P. W. (1992). *Educational governance and administration* (3rd ed.). Boston: Allyn & Bacon.

Siskin, L. S. (1991). Departments as different worlds: Subject subcultures in secondary schools. *Educational Administration Quarterly, 27*(2), 134–160.

Siskin, L. S. (1994). *Realms of knowledge: Academic departments in secondary schools.*
    Lewes, UK: Falmer.
Sizer, T. R. (1984). *Horace's compromise: The dilemma of the American high school.*
    Boston: Houghton Mifflin.
Van Maanen, J., & Barley, S. (1984). Occupational communities: Culture and
    control in organizations. *Research in Organizational Behaviour, 6,* 287–365.
Why public schools fail. (1981, April 20). *Newsweek,* pp. 62–65.

CHAPTER 7

The Empowerment Movement

Genuine Collegiality or Yet Another Hierarchy?

KATHLEEN M. CERONI
NOREEN B. GARMAN

As with any initiative in education, this decade already has its share of school reform analysts who speculate about the flurry of rhetoric and activity related to current reform efforts (Cuban, 1990; Gibbonney, 1991; Sarason, 1990). They share the hope that we can better understand why reforms return at various times in our history, yet seldom substantially alter the regularities of schooling. Cuban (1990) tells us that "the existing tools of understanding are no more than inadequate metaphors that pinch-hit for hard thinking. We can do better by gathering data on particular reforms and tracing their life history in particular classrooms, schools, districts, and regions" (pp. 11–12). "Empowerment" is one such metaphor. It has spawned a substantial movement in educational policy and practice, yet the term itself becomes problematic as it is used in the various school reform scenarios and texts. Within the "empowerment movement" a kind of illusion is created. There is a tacit understanding of what the term *empowerment* means and how it can be played out in the realities of school life. In the name of empowerment, imperatives are offered, programs are put into place, and people's lives are affected by the multiple understandings of what the word means. In the following pages[1] we attempt to characterize the empowerment movement, briefly mentioning various "empowerment" initiatives such as career ladders, site-based management, differentiated staffing, mentor programs, and lead teachers. The focus of our study is on the Lead Teacher Program in Pennsylvania. We describe the consequences of the program through the voices of participants themselves. We conclude with a discussion of observations and obstacles as lessons learned from these participants as well as our attempt to recover a deeper understanding of empowerment as a primary condition of educational life.

THE EMPOWERMENT MOVEMENT

The term *empowerment* originated in written form in 1645. This earliest citation in the Oxford English Dictionary reports that *empower* meant "to authorize or to license." In 1681 another use of the term emerged. To *empower* meant "to enable or permit." According to the first definition, some person or formal body with power approves or sanctions the transmission of power to another person or formal body. In the second definition, a person or authorizing body provides an opportunity for another to develop power. The idea of direct transmission is deemphasized and the implication is that responsibility for empowerment is shared by both parties.

The difference in these two definitions appears to be subtle, yet the distinguishing features are significant for contemporary use in education. In the first meaning, someone empowers someone else, generally by imparting specific knowledge and skills that allow that person to work within the existing social system. Sears and Marshall (1990) call this *empowerment-by-authorization*. People are empowered to work within the limited framework provided by those who do the empowering. In the second definition, *empowerment-as-enablement*, educators become empowered or enabled in different ways. Their power is created or realized by them—not received from or bestowed by others. In this conception, according to Sears and Marshall, "empowerment is a deeply personal process of meaning-making within particular historical, cultural, and economic contexts" (p. 17). The intent of empowering people is to enable them to recognize, create, and channel their own power, not merely to share limited institutional power.

As a political concept, "empowerment" surfaced in the late 1960s within the rhetoric of the civil rights movement. "Taking control of your own life—refusing to let external authority tell you how to be" was a rallying cry from blacks and feminists during the consciousness-raising phase of their movements. Those involved in social welfare activities began to question the basis on which they treated their clients. The New Hampshire State Department of Education, for instance, published a document entitled *Empowerment vs. Delivery of Services* (Fried, 1980). In his position paper, Fried points out:

> Delivery of service creates a false dichotomy between the "deliverers" and their recipients. Throughout the contemporary range of human services, responding to rich and poor, young and old and in-betweens, we find one rank of people ("service deliverers") who have been trained and hired to treat the rest. They diagnose our problems, assess our needs, and then provide us with anything from a prescription to an entire program in order to fix what's lacking, or leaking, in us.

While establishing (and usually monopolizing) ever greater resources for the teaching, healing, counseling and caring of other people, professional "service-deliverers" leave the rest of the population to view itself, and to be viewed as "unfit," "uneducated," "unlicensed," "unmotivated," or otherwise unable to care, teach, heal, or counsel themselves, their families, friends, or neighbors. (p. 5)

The alternative, according to Fried, is empowerment of those who are being served. "Simply stated, " says Fried, "'empowerment' means helping people take charge of their lives, people who have been restrained by social or political forces, from assuming such control heretofore" (p. 8).

In what has been called the second wave of the school reform movement, however, teachers were viewed as the group needing empowerment, who had been restrained by institutional bureaucracy and needed to take charge of their professional lives (Maeroff, 1988). A political call for teacher autonomy came from the Carnegie Forum on Education and the Economy (1986) when Marc Tucker, its director, released a policy report called *A Nation Prepared: Teachers for the 21st Century*. The Carnegie Report was typical of some 16 other documents that came from national reform commissions composed of distinguished citizens (many from the business world) and prestigious experts (mainly from outside education). *A Nation Prepared* was launched into the public domain through a large press conference at which Tucker announced its recommendations to representatives of large newspapers and the wire services. We mention this to remind ourselves that the reform movement in education is being orchestrated by highly visible policy makers with deliberate strategies to further particular initiatives. The Carnegie Report presented a number of recommendations for "professionalizing teaching," including the creation of a National Board for Professional Teaching Standards and, eventually, "board certified teachers"; the restructuring of schools to provide a freer environment for teachers; teacher accountability for student progress; raising of teacher salaries; and substantial changes in teacher education. A key proposal of the Carnegie Report focusing on a recommendation for creating a new level of teacher, known as lead teacher, was stated as follows: "Restructure the teaching force, and introduce a new category of Lead Teachers with the proven ability to provide active leadership in the redesign of schools and in helping their colleagues to uphold high standards of learning and teaching" (p. 55). The notion of lead teacher enabled educators such as Berry and Ginsberg (1990) to make the connection to teacher empowerment. They state that "second wave reformers call for fifth-year professional degrees, national certification and testing and the identification and empowerment of lead teachers" (p. 618). Thus evidence of the empowerment movement is manifest in the concept of lead teacher and begins to be played out in the Lead Teacher Programs through state departments of education.

The empowerment movement, of course, is much larger than the Lead Teacher Programs. The concept has been a rallying one for scholars and practitioners who propose radical changes in the power structures of schools as well as those who would foster personal empowerment within the ranks of all teachers (Smyth, 1988). The politicization of the concept has been both a part of its use and a problem to those who espouse some form of empowerment for teachers. When he was Secretary of Education, William Bennett announced his view of teacher empowerment as a union power play. He called the advocates "peddlers of the union-hijack reform philosophy" (cited in Hechinger, 1989, p. 24). Gene Geisert, a former school superintendent and presently professor and author, also stated that he "opposed the drive toward teacher empowerment as a union juggernaut intended to put unions in the driver's seat and take away the principal's authority" (cited in Hechinger, 1989, p. 24).

Ironically, as pointed out earlier, the term *empowerment* was used in the 1960s as a rally for those liberals in the civil rights movement. In the early 1990s, empowerment has been co-opted by the previous Bush administration, most notably Jack Kemp, the conservative Housing Secretary who pushed Bush to become the "empowerment president" (DeParle, 1991). Kemp advocated at the U.S. Conference of Mayors that they should "empower poor people" to have more control over their own lives, adding that "welfare programs had become a trap, not a springboard" ("Kemp Tells Mayors . . . ," 1991, p. B3). Many political analysts read this empowerment message as a justification by the federal administration for cutting the budget on welfare programs.

TEACHER EMPOWERMENT INITIATIVES

In the first half of the 1980s governors, legislators, and business leaders initiated what has come to be called "the first wave" of teacher reform. Between 1983 and 1986, for example, 46 states considered some kind of performance-based compensation system for teachers, such as merit pay, career ladders, or mentor teacher plans. In addition to compensation systems, many states initiated schoolwide accountability programs (e.g., Madeline Hunter's *Elements of Instruction*, Effective Schools Instructional Leadership, etc.) aimed at improving instruction through administrative supervision. The financial costs as well as the technical and political problems have limited the effectiveness of the early reforms associated with teacher compensation (Berry & Ginsberg, 1990). The teacher accountability programs (although still flourishing) were criticized for, among other things, their top-down managerial style in which teachers were cast as recipients of mandated staff development programs. In other words, some of these reform efforts were seen as "disempowering" teachers, since administrators were in charge of their improvement. One might suggest that the "second wave," which included the empowerment movement, grew, in part, as a reaction to the previous reform efforts. In any case, it became clear to many educators and reformers that not much would happen to change schools if teachers were not committed to the idea of reform, at both the classroom and school levels. This second wave effort was heralded as "restructuring." A headline in the *Providence Sunday Journal*, on February 18, 1990, signaled, "Exit School Reform, Enter Restructuring of U.S. Education." In it, Frank Newman, president of the Education commission of the States said, "To improve our schools we need a total redesign of our educational system." Marc Tucker called it a "cultural transformation." He described the difficulties of radically changing people's roles and likened it to the Soviet Union. "Gorbachev is trying to mobilize masses of people who have never had much control of their lives and aren't sure how to handle it when given the opportunity. The same thing has to occur in our schools. They call it perestroika. We call it restructuring" (cited in Fiske, 1990, p. B8). Initiatives were underway as teacher participation schemes, such as site-based management, teacher decision making, mentors, and lead teachers, appeared in the name of teacher empowerment.

THE PENNSYLVANIA LEAD TEACHER PROGRAM

When the Carnegie Task Force first recommended the category of lead teacher, they intended to create a career path so that as teachers acquire greater skill and experience, they are rewarded with more responsibility and pay (Tucker, 1988). These senior professionals would be expected to be the most competent and well-respected teachers who would take on the most difficult problems in the school. The career path, as well as bringing increased responsibility, would also bring increasing pay. For example, the 1991 teacher contract in Rochester, New York, permitted lead teachers, those at the top of the level of responsibility in the system, to earn annual salaries of $70,000. Not surprisingly, the impediment to this plan is the teachers' concerns about the criteria used to determine who advances along the career path and how this might happen. Needless to say, teachers express skepticism about how administrators would go about making these kinds of decisions. The Carnegie Report recommended that teachers would have the opportunity to be certified by the National Board of Professional Teaching Standards by taking a series of assessments to give evidence of their *accomplished practice* (an official term used by the director of the National Board). This board certification would be a prerequisite for becoming a lead teacher. Unfortunately, the National Board has several years of work ahead of it to get the assessment process operating, a massive undertaking that has a multimillion dollar price tag. Meanwhile, Lead Teacher Programs are proliferating throughout the country and the issue of selection of lead teachers remains a major concern. There are, however, other issues that need to be examined.

In Pennsylvania the Lead Teacher Program was an initiative of the governor, Robert Casey, who in February 1988 proclaimed his support for empowerment through the Lead Teacher Program (Pennsylvania Department of Education, 1990). He charged the Secretary of Education to establish a 46-member committee, and in November of that year the committee issued a document. At present there are nine centers throughout the state funded by the Pennsylvania State Department of Education and 250 school districts who have some form of Lead Teacher Program. The state document (Pennsylvania Department of Education, 1989) describes the lead teacher as "one who works with other teachers in classrooms, where they observe, demonstrate, guide, suggest, critique, and applaud" (p. 12). The document emphasizes that "the approach of Lead Teacher Programs in Pennsylvania has been to encourage collegiality . . . and to focus on the improvement of instruction" (p. 12). The nine Lead Teacher Centers were established to provide teachers with leadership training, which, in some cases, includes a heavy dose of the state's version of clinical supervision.

STUDY OF PENNSYLVANIA LEAD TEACHERS

In 1990 we began a study of lead teachers in Pennsylvania. Our intent was to find out what was happening in schools in which lead teachers had been designated. Our decision to initiate the study was prompted by an interesting session at a local conference at which four lead teachers had made a presentation about their programs. One lead teacher described her own feelings of empowerment as follows:

> For the first time in my life I was learning about teaching in a very different way. I was learning how to do observations, as teachers, how to give conferences. We were given a great sense of authority in our role— authority over the people with whom we worked as well as students.

We were able to foster different relationships with the teachers. I really felt empowered by the training and the job.

To hear a teacher talk with such honesty and enthusiasm about the feelings of empowerment she gained, in part as a result of the authority she had over other teachers, was quite significant. Empowerment to her apparently depended on her "power" over others. This stimulated the following questions, which began to frame the study:

1. With empowerment efforts such as the Lead Teacher Program, can there be genuine collegiality, or is this yet another hierarchy?
2. Does empowerment mean developing skills such as clinical supervision so that one can claim legitimacy over the language used to control others?

We really wanted to find instances of genuine collaboration and collegiality in the schools we visited. So we talked with lead teachers and those involved with lead teachers in order to search out a sense of the current state of affairs.

Thus far the reviews are mixed. The Pennsylvania State Education Association (PSEA) has described their position on the Lead Teacher Program as one of "cautious interest." Cordell Affeldt, director of professional programs for PSEA, asserts:

The reason we took that position is that the concept of Lead Teacher sounds intriguingly positive, but we are experienced enough in the affairs of public schools to know that good ideas can often be ruined on their way to implementation in the real world. And because we so frequently hear stories from teachers who have experienced the most negative interpretation or misapplication of an idea on a local level, it would be inappropriate for us at the outset to say this is wonderful because so many of our members would not experience it that way. And indeed, experience with this program has borne that out. (Ceroni, telephone interview, 1991)

In talking with teachers throughout the state we found that conditions for selection in schools varied. In some a committee of teachers elect the lead teachers, often choosing colleagues on the basis of personality traits. Commenting on her election by peers, one lead teacher said, "Well, I think they all felt that I'm not the type of person that is judgmental. That's why they liked the idea of me taking the position. I'm not a threat to them. I'm younger than a lot of them. I'm not the type that would gossip." In other schools, lead teachers are appointed by the principal because, as one former lead teacher put it, "Nobody really wanted the job. It was new and people didn't know if it was something they really wanted. A lot of people knew it would be risky and that it might turn out to be a job where everybody hated you." In some districts, potential candidates must possess certain credentials such as a specified number of years of teaching experience and a master's degree. They then write a formal letter of application, and the number of slots filled is based on available funding. In most schools and districts the program was mandated by the administration. Despite this, there are pockets of enthusiastic faculty who have found the collaborative efforts worthwhile. One lead teacher told us:

> I've grown professionally because I've learned from my peers a lot
> and that has helped my kids. And in doing that, I also think that we've
> been able to help other teachers who are interested in trying new things
> and encouraging them and in effect we've touched more kids. I think
> that's how I try to view it, you know, that's how I try to think about it.

Money did not seem to be an issue with most teachers we interviewed. Many did not even know how much they were making in addition to their salary. Some were not receiving additional pay and felt no regret about their lack of monetary compensation.

All lead teachers remarked about the amount of time required of them. One said, "The biggest disadvantage is not having enough time to help teachers and students as much as I'd like to and should." Others indicated that the time they put into their work was often not appreciated by teachers or principals. Though much of the time invested occurred during evening hours, a considerable amount was used during the school day to attend training sessions, conduct staff development programs and building meetings, and work with colleagues in a quasi-supervisory role or as a peer coach. Lead teachers spoke with anguish about having to give up classroom time with their students to attend to the additional duties assigned to them. One frankly stated, "I hated the time out of my classroom. It was just horrible." Another said, "The hard thing for me is being away from my classes and learning to let go."

Clearly these teachers experienced confusion and pain when taken out of the familiar world of their classroom, where they felt confident in their teaching abilities and gained personal satisfaction from their interaction with students. This confusion and pain was compounded in those districts where lead teachers were assigned to perform quasi-administrative duties. Indicating a clear sense of role ambiguity, one lead teacher said, "You're constantly changing hats. Sometimes you're a teacher and sometimes you're doing administrative duties." In this quasi-administrative capacity the lead teacher no longer holds membership in the community of teachers within the building. She becomes, as one non–lead teacher describes it, "cut-off from her colleagues." Talking about their duties in quasi-supervisory terms, many teachers suggested they were doing what principals usually do. In fact, some found that they were asked to take on some of the principal's office responsibilities, which were not related to instruction. One described it as the role of the "principal's helper," saying:

> Some principals just use lead teachers for clerical duties. Some principals don't want to give lead teachers power. So they say, 'O.K. you're empowered, now go run off these dittos.' Each principal in our district has his own interpretation of what he wants to use lead teachers for. Some give 'em bows and arrows and tell them to go get people, shoot 'em, bring 'em back, drag 'em in. But in other schools some principals don't even care what they do. One I know didn't even bother with the lead teachers. He just let them go, he didn't have time for all that; he just wanted to retire.

Another concern voiced by all the teachers we interviewed was a sense of distrust with regard to the role of the lead teacher. One said, "I feel I was helping teachers but I feel that sometimes teachers thought I was helping the principal. If I would go to him and say I don't want to have a meeting this week, there's nothing to talk about, they might say, 'Oh, she's in there talking to *him* again.'" Another said, "Some teachers are suspicious of what we are. Some of their questions are justified because we are still under constrictions in developing what we want to be; therefore, it can be confusing to outsiders." When asked what she perceived as a disadvantage of being a lead teacher, the teacher responded, "Perceptions of *some* other faculty members towards lead teachers. Possibly, a lead teacher should be called by something other than a 'lead teacher.' It has administrative overtones."

In the Pittsburgh public schools the lead teachers perform a function not found in the other schools we visited. There the lead teachers (called Instructional Team Leaders) told us they actually do observations based on the school's supervisory model and collect data that principals can then use for personnel evaluation. The teacher's union (American Federation of Teachers) agreed that lead teachers could engage in this kind of data sharing. Not surprisingly, this has become problematic in the system. This is illustrated by a teacher who stated that she "started hating it when they came up with lead teachers and used them to help target teachers," and by the comment about lead teachers: "You mean the teachers who are spies."

Lead teachers commented on the difficulty of their role in working with seasoned teachers. One remarked, "I'd say we did a lot of arguing, a lot of arguing. Every time I gave in to save peace—except in one sense I was sort of mad at myself for giving in because I really did not agree with what he was saying." Another said:

> I was torn. I didn't want to baby anyone on our team. I just wanted to look at everybody as being a real professional person and they really are. They're very professional; they do a dynamite job. But I think because it was such a new process maybe some more babying was needed with these people that I didn't give them because, in some respects, I gave them too much credit. That's the only thing I can think of. I was just really surprised by their reactions.

One lead teacher who left the program remarked:

> I'm much happier now. I have all this time in my classroom and I've made a lot of changes in my room and I'm happier with what I'm doing professionally after my experience. I don't have stress at all anymore. I really felt stressed out last year and I didn't need people whining and crying and bitching. I don't need that from other adults . . . there was a lack of compassion. You become sort of an enemy, not you personally, but the role you were in.

The role these particular lead teachers found themselves enacting was not one of their own design but rather one that was imposed on them in a top-down bureaucratic manner. Teachers are trained at the teacher centers in the Hunter Clinical Supervisory Model. Their duties, as described by a Pittsburgh lead teacher, "are to hold different kinds of meetings and the other thing is on conferencing with our teachers. We are to go in and do different kinds of conferences with them, reinforcement, refinement, and repertoire." When asked if she was invited into other teachers' classrooms or sent there, she responded, "What I do is say, 'You know guys, I *have* to come in. What's a good time for you?'" Therefore, these lead teachers receive training in specific supervisory skills and are then charged with the duty of patrolling the classrooms of their colleagues to ensure that the official teaching model is being implemented.

One Pittsburgh trainer of lead teachers, concerned about the negative consequences of the training and the analogous duties required of the lead teacher, commented:

I think it's based on the wrong model first of all. It should be a collegial model. It should be something that is horizontal instead of vertical. It's a formula. There's no life to it, no vitality, and nothing happens. Change doesn't happen; growth doesn't happen; and pretty soon resentment does happen.

Indeed, most Pittsburgh lead teachers talked about the resistance they felt when they approached teachers about observing in classrooms and having conferences. One lead teacher expressed a typical view when she said:

What the program was supposed to do, I think, was to bring teachers together and get rid of isolation, reduce it. What, in fact, I see it has done is create bigger rifts and isolation, magnify the isolation. I think we should have gone back to team teaching. Then once you worked with other teachers, you'd be more willing to take risks.

This teacher's comments are indicative of most of the lead teachers in that she felt she had gained a great deal in the program in spite of the conflict. One lead teacher summed up the advantages of being a lead teacher as follows: "The training I had was invaluable. I couldn't have gotten this, I mean I've done graduate work, but I couldn't have gotten this supervisory hands-on training in preparation for the meetings and staff development. It was totally invaluable." The comments that we reported thus far are quite typical of at least 80% of the people we talked to.

The good news is that we found schools in which there is genuine support for the lead teachers by the rest of the faculty. Programs seem to be working and enthusiasm is high. What seems to be a distinguishing characteristic of the programs in place in these schools is that the assumptions driving them are based on agendas designed by teachers rather than those designed by administrators. In these districts, lead teachers create their own training programs, which often consist of communication skills, problem-solving skills, and what one lead teacher called "affirming skills." The focus of the training is on developing a sense of group unity and team support as distinct from leadership training or training in a specific supervisory model. In these districts there was no activity around classroom observations and formal conferences. Descriptions by lead teachers as well as others seemed to tell of collaborative projects, helping to get materials, sharing techniques, writing proposals, and, in some cases, sharing feelings. One teacher commented, "At the beginning of this school year I decided to do a working project in my management class and I asked one lead teacher in our school questions that really helped me get the project off the ground." Another said, "I have received lots of articles on cooperative learning and whole language (at my request). I also was lucky enough to have a lead teacher come into my room and teach a complete trade book, about 10 reading lessons." Another talked about a wide range of collaborative activities she had worked on with a lead teacher, one of which included co-authoring an educational article.

Without top-down management strategies imposed on them, these lead teachers were free to design their own roles, roles they were comfortable with. One commented:

> I think first the kinds of roles that I have taken are in terms of what my background is. I have a process writing background. I have a reading background and I have a background in cooperative learning, so that I would try those things within my own classroom. I started with people who are my friends and I said, "Hey, I'm trying this and if you're interested, come in and watch." Then they'd come in and watch and we'd talk about what we saw and then some of them asked me specifically to come in. . . . I had a student teacher so I was able to go in and try out some things I did in my class with my friend's class and she picked up the ball on that and she began to talk to another grade-level person who said, "You know, this is pretty interesting" . . . and it began to catch on like that. So it wasn't like the lead teacher was in to help me. We pretty much steer clear of the term lead teacher altogether and there might be some people around who would not even make the connection that this is a lead teacher doing this. . . . What we've tried to do is establish a relationship by working with people and teaming with teachers and collaborating with people as peers.

Peer coaching was mentioned a number of times, but the hierarchic-like supervision was not part of these programs.

Lead teachers in these districts, however, are quick to add that progress is slow and some staff members are resentful and suspicious of the lead teacher role. Others are concerned about administrators' perceptions of the program and their degree of involvement with the program. A coordinator of a Lead Teacher Center believes: "The biggest problem is that of administrative involvement. What's happened, unfortunately, in the bureaucracy that schools have created (I'm not gonna' change it; you're not gonna' change it) is that they have become gatekeepers."

OBSERVATIONS

Our research indicates that a crucial factor in how Lead Teacher Programs enhance or detract from collegial network building depends, in large part, on who assumes authority for shaping the role. In those districts where administrative agendas define the role, the lead teachers often feel forced to function in ways that may contradict their own beliefs about teacher development. Additionally, they feel a lack of ownership in the role since they have little or no personal investment in its design. It becomes yet another "job" added to their often already overburdened teaching responsibilities. Initially, many who take on the role do so because they believe it will foster their own professional growth and that of their colleagues. When the Lead Teacher Program is mandated by the district, some take on the job because "someone has to do it." Hargreaves (1991) makes the distinction between the dominant cultural perspective of our understandings of collaboration and collegiality and the micropolitical perspective. He tells us:

> In the more dominant cultural perspective, collaborative cultures express and emerge from a process of consensus building that is facilitated by a largely benevolent and skilled educational management. In the micropolitical perspective, collegiality results from the exercise of organizational power by control-conscious administrators. In these cases, collegiality is either an unwanted managerial imposition from the point of view of teachers subjected to it, or more usually, a way of coopting teachers to fulfilling administrative purposes and the implementation of external mandates. From the micropolitical perspective, collegiality is often bound up with either direct administrative constraint or the indirect management of consent. (p. 51)

When administrators generate lead teacher job descriptions, designated duties often take on a managerial, hierarchic-like structure, as in the Pittsburgh experience. The skill-specific training is regimented in a top-down bureaucratic manner, and the potential lead teachers are monitored as they progress through a series of incremental learning stages. If they successfully complete the training, the teachers are then officially certified. This factor further promotes the notion that lead teachers perform functions analogous to those of supervisors, that they are trained to act as support for principals rather than for teachers. From the vantage point of non–lead teachers, the role translates into one of power and, hence, can be perceived with distrust (Lieberman, 1988). Thus, instead of fostering collegiality, the role has the potential to create fragmentation and dissension among peers, negating its intent.

If, on the other hand, lead teachers are given freedom to create their own role definitions and to function in those roles with discretion and choice, the circumstances begin to exist for the role to serve the interests of the specific culture of teachers in a specific school environment. Moreover, since it is a self-generated role, the lead teacher seems more likely to feel committed to it and to have some ownership of it. In the schools where the administration avoided imposing a role definition for lead teachers and provided them with the support to design their own, the training tended to be more interpersonally oriented, that is, these teachers chose to enhance their communication, problem-solving, and interpersonal relationship skills. The learning focused on modeling behavior that invited rather than inhibited peer participation. They experimented with new teaching techniques in their own classrooms and opened their doors to colleagues who chose to visit. By being in a position to model risk taking and by inviting rather than coercing colleagues, they were better able to assume a sharing stance instead of an authoritarian one. In the best of circumstances, the collegial connections made with different colleagues seemed to increase over time. And, in some instances, lead teachers found themselves being invited into other teachers' classrooms.

The stance assumed by the building principal in the schools where Lead Teacher Programs are in place appears to affect dramatically the perception of the program by both lead teachers and non–lead teachers. If the principal did not support the program, commitment to it from all parties involved tended to be perfunctory. Teachers tended to resist or accommodate depending on the degree of possible negative consequences associated with their action. Conversely, if the principal provided a moral, financial, and organizational framework within which teachers could construct the role of lead teacher, the outcomes were very different. The crucial role that the principal plays in the current restructuring movement has been amply documented (Bacharach, Bauer, & Shedd, 1986; Fuller & Izu, 1986; Lieberman, 1988; Little, 1982).

Our study revealed a variety of roles that principals with lead teachers in their charge tended to assume. Teachers reported that their principals chose to avoid as much as possible the existence of the lead teachers. The reason teachers most often gave for such behavior was that the principals were close to retirement and wanted to avoid any additional responsibilities and/or conflict. This seemed to be the case even in those districts where the lead teacher role was clearly defined and, thus, the responsibilities of the principal in relation to the lead teacher were mandated. Whereas some principals tended to avoid working with lead teachers, others, according to teachers in our study, chose to use them as personal aides, thereby reducing some of their own workload. In such instances teachers reported that these principals used lead teachers to perform a range of activities, including clerical duties. It is possible that in such cases the principal may have been reluctant to relinquish control (Lieberman, 1988). In some cases, as was evidenced by the data collected from Pittsburgh teachers, principals used lead teachers to perform supervisory functions mandated by the district. Some teachers believed that the principals who delegated their supervision duties essentially insulated themselves against criticism from teachers by allowing the lead teachers to do their "dirty work." Even in those districts in which the Lead Teacher Program appeared to have a more positive effect on teacher collegiality and decision making, the role the principal assumed tended to be more laissez-faire. In the data we gathered, we noticed an absence of the active participation and involvement of the principal in developing collegial networks through reciprocity called for in the restructuring literature (Lieberman & Miller, 1990).

Teachers in our study consistently referred to the problem of not having adequate time to perform their role as lead teachers. This lack of time created stress and conflict for some lead teachers as they struggled to fulfill their dual responsibilities of being a classroom teacher and a lead teacher. Without sufficient time to establish collegial relationships, efforts in that direction are sure to fail (Tuthill, 1990).

In districts in which some time was provided during the school day, it tended to be very controlled time. That is, the use of the time was predetermined by district policy. For instance, if lead teachers were required to conduct weekly team meetings, the meetings had to take place regardless of whether a need existed for a meeting. The meetings, therefore, became contrived in format and nature. One non–lead teacher told us that the teachers' concerns were solicited at the end of each meeting while the meeting itself was used for transferring information, usually procedural in content, from the building principal to the teachers via the lead teacher. Conversely, the lead teacher functioned as a liaison from the teachers to the building principal. The content of this exchange usually related to requests for materials and supplies, concerns about the safety conditions of the building as children moved from room to room, or concerns about disciplinary problems. Thus the time allotted appeared to be used for the imparting of information. The controlled agendas of the meetings did not promote conversation about sharing craft and strategies, the kind of dialogue that fosters professional growth. Some of the teachers we interviewed actually resented having to attend the meeting, preferring instead to use the time for planning their own classroom activities. Thus we found that, although time for interactions was allotted, teachers perceived that the substance of the interaction was often not relevant to their needs. Given this, their commitment to the endeavor eroded. This was similar to the findings of Little's 1982 study. Such interaction also appears to illustrate what Hargreaves (1991) labels "contrived collegiality." In his study of how elementary teachers use scheduled time for collaboration, he realized that in contrived collegiality, "collaboration among teachers was compulsory, not voluntary; was bounded and fixed in time and space; was implementation oriented rather than development oriented; and was meant to be predictable rather than unpredictable in its outcomes" (p. 68). In those districts in which no additional school time was set aside for lead teacher activities, those who desired interaction with peers found ways to do so by utilizing time before students arrived or after they departed. Often these lead teachers would use prep period time, but that particular time slot may not have been satisfactory for the teacher requesting a classroom visit. Although the teachers were encouraged to talk and experiment together with teaching strategies, in reality no resources were given to such efforts. Thus principals often conveyed on the surface that they supported collegiality, but their refusal to provide teachers with ample time to engage with one another seemed to contradict what they espoused. This raised questions about the seriousness of their commitment to teacher empowerment through collegial network building. Because the structure of the work day did not promote collegial activities, those teachers who desired professional interaction experienced feelings of frustration and helplessness. Much energy, peer support, and school resources were needed to keep levels of enthusiasm high. Over time, however, as Rosenholtz (1987) concluded, working under conditions that do not permit people to feel efficacious in their work causes feelings of professional disempowerment and lack of commitment. Given this, many teachers in our study had deeply held misgivings about the Lead Teacher Program, causing them to approach it with understandable caution.

The Lead Teacher Programs tend to create a hierarchy. Lead teachers express, overwhelmingly, their own feelings of empowerment by being part of the program and getting the training for the role. When we asked other teachers if they felt empowered because of their work with lead teachers, their responses were primarily negative, even in the schools where the programs seem to be working well. It appears that empowerment for one group may be at the expense of another group. Lead teachers' sense of empowerment often depended on their "power" over others —the authority embedded in the notion of "lead teacher" itself.

OBSTACLES

The voices of the teachers involved in the Lead Teacher Program in Pennsylvania express a sense of disillusionment and frustration. This disillusionment and frustration indicates certain obstacles, such as (1) the cultural flatness of the career of teaching, (2) the paradox of hierarchy versus empowerment, and (3) the residual effects of promised innovations, which come and go in education. These conditions exacerbate efforts to solve existing problems in the schools by piecemeal programs like the Lead Teacher Program and create barriers to genuine school reform.

Cultural Flatness of the Teaching Career

In the professional life cycle of the teacher, Huberman (1989) identifies trends in his subsample of older teachers as a tendency toward gradual "disengagement from investments in one's work to other engagements" (p. 32) and attributed it to frustrated ambitions, to an early "plateauing" in the profession. Plateauing (Milstein, 1988, 1989) occurs in teaching when there is a long period of stability and/or when there is a perception that little progress is likely. Within the context of work, individuals who are "plateaued" will have a sense of intrinsic loss and feel that fulfillment is no longer possible. Teaching is often called a "dead-end position," or as Lortie (1975) describes it, a "front loaded" occupation. Working conditions, including professional privileges and advantages, are not likely to improve noticeably over time. In other words, there is no cultural way for teachers to advance their careers (except to become administrators). In the Carnegie Report, the intent of the lead teacher role was to address this plateauing situation:

> We do not envision Lead Teachers as assistant principals. It will do no good to slim down the bureaucracy at the central office only to replace it with a new one in the school. Lead Teachers must create communities, not additional layers of bureaucracy to clog the system and frustrate their fellow teachers. Lead Teachers would derive their authority primarily from the respect of their professional colleagues. (Carnegie Forum on Education and the Economy, p. 58)

The intent, although noble, does not take into account the existing conditions of the career itself. At present there is no cultural way for teachers to *earn* distinction among their colleagues. The profession in public school does not provide for promotion to a higher rank of teacher through a clearly designated professional ritual and sanction (as, for instance, in higher education, where faculty can advance in rank through a process of peer review). The Lead Teacher Program is ironic, having become another bureaucratic mandate from the administration.

The Paradox of Hierarchy Versus Empowerment

It is clear that the educational establishment supports hierarchical structures. Since there is no cultural way for teachers to earn additional status, it must be designated through the hierarchical structure of authority.

Within this structure there are "superordinates" (leaders) and "subordinates" (followers), and although these designations are not popular in educational literature, they are mentioned in selected writing in supervision (Alfonso, Firth, & Neville, 1981). In a supervisory position, there are such lines of authority. Thayer (1981) describes the pitfalls of hierarchy in terms of authority. "If authority is needed to get things done, genetic endowment becomes an explanation for the 'natural superiority' of leaders, and the 'natural inferiority' of subordinates" (p. 195). Thayer contends that the unadorned ethic of individualism and hierarchy

> legitimizes the repression of some citizens by other citizens. It presumes that those designated "superior" by virtue of talent, organizationally assigned roles, or wealth are turned loose to dominate others. Those who cling to the ethic often forget that the game they play cannot be defined other than in terms of "winners" and "losers." The success of one individual can be described only by the failure of others. (p. 195).

When teachers take on the role of leader of other teachers, the pitfalls of hierarchy prevail. As we found in our interviews, lead teachers reported feelings of empowerment as they took on quasi-supervisory activities such as classroom observation and conference meetings. In many cases, empowerment did depend on one group of teachers having authority over another group. Without a clear understanding of the notion of "earned distinction among colleagues," this sense of empowerment through repression is a predictable consequence.

Residual Effects of Promised Innovations: The "Come-and-Go" Syndrome

Innovative programs have been part of the educational scene for the past century. Little attention has been given, however, to the cumulative effects on school personnel of their investment in these programs, which they often see come and go. It is clear that we hear the effects of the "come-and-go" syndrome on teacher attitudes, yet we know very little about the residual effect over time of these programs, often seen by the teachers as administrative broken promises. Teachers manifest feelings of anger and resistance and/or cynicism and hopelessness. One teacher spoke poignantly about her overriding sense of betrayal. She had participated in an innovative program with enthusiasm and commitment, trusting that such involvement would result in increased professional autonomy. She, like others, invested much time, energy, and hope in the program, becoming an advocate even against many of her "jaded" colleagues. As she said, "I was zealously promoting it as an avenue for professional growth." Within the bureaucratic structure of the school, however, the intention of the program became distorted as it played out in the daily lives of teachers. She felt she had been "sold out," betrayed in the eyes of her older colleagues who could say, "I told you so." Each time this situation occurs, teachers become less willing to give their professional attention and loyalty to educational innovation.

The lessons we have learned highlight the complexity of altering the entrenched structure of school systems and the predefined roles of the professionals who work within those systems. Sarason (1990), in *The Predictable Failure of Educational Reform*, demonstrates how longstanding educational structures, coupled with the need of various groups to defend their self-interests and preserve their power, stifle reform efforts. He argues that reformers have a superficial understanding of the power relationships between and among administrators, parents, teachers, unions, and governing boards and that reform efforts fail because they do not change these relationships. Altering the status of a group of teachers addresses only one of the features of the loci of power and amounts to little more than tinkering at the margins with a longstanding educational structure whose history, tradition, overlearned attitudes, and unrealistic time perspectives ensure turmoil.

CONCLUSION

The lead teacher concept was created to address some of the relentless ills of the teaching profession: isolation from one's colleagues in teaching, lack of career advancement, the need to accommodate or resist bureaucratic controls, the feelings of betrayal when one's commitments are diminished—all these everyday concerns that keep teachers disempowered. The intent, then, was to empower teachers. However, we must recognize the pitfalls of putting people into positions of responsibility with little sensitivity to prevailing conditions and little understanding of what it takes to create genuine collegiality. When we act in such ways, our attempts at empowering teachers only succeed in establishing another layer in the hierarchy that ultimately prevents genuine collegiality from emerging.

NOTE

1. Funding for this project was provided by the Buhl Foundation, Pittsburgh, Pennsylvania.

REFERENCES

Alfonso, R., Firth, G., & Neville, R. (1981). *Instructional supervision: A behavior system.* Boston: Allyn & Bacon.

Bacharach, S. B., Bauer, S. D., & Shedd, J. B. (1986). The work environment and school reform. *Teachers College Record, 88*(2), 241–256.

Berry, B., & Ginsberg, R. (1990). Creating lead teachers: From policy to implementation. *Phi Delta Kappan, 71*(8), 616–621.

Carnegie Forum on Education and the Economy. (1986). *A nation prepared: Teachers for the 21st century.* Washington, DC: Author.

Ceroni, K. (1991, March 19). Telephone interview with Cordell Affelot, Director of Professional Programs for the Pennsylvania State Education Association, Harrisburg, PA.

Cuban, L. (1990). Reforming again, again, and again. *Educational Researcher, 19*(1), 3–13.

DeParle, J. (1991, February 3). Bush blurred message on home front. *New York Times,* p. B3.

Exit school reform, enter restructuring of U.S. education. (1990, February 18). *Providence Sunday Journal,* p. E13.

Fiske, E. (1990, February 14). Finding a way to define the buzzword of American education: How about perestroika? *New York Times,* p. B8.

Fried, R. (1980). *Empowerment vs. delivery of services.* Concord, NH: State Department of Education.

Fuller, B., & Izu, J. A. (1986). Explaining school cohesion: What shapes the organizational beliefs of teachers. *American Journal of Education, 94*(4), 501–535.

Gibbonney, E. (1991). The killing fields of school reform. *Phi Delta Kappan, 72,* 682–688.

Hargreaves, A. (1991). Contrived collegiality: The micropolitics of teacher collaboration. In J. Blase (Ed.), *The politics of life in schools* (pp. 46–72). Newbury Park, CA: Sage.

Hechinger, F. (1989, November 8). More power for teachers: Is it a "union juggernaut" or a path to better schools? *New York Times,* p. 24.

Huberman, M. (1989). The professional life cycle of teachers. *Teachers College Record, 91*(1), 31–57.

Kemp tells mayors he will help them "empower" poor people. (1991, January 24). *New York Times,* p. B3.

Lieberman, A. (1988). Teachers and principals: Turf, tension, and new tasks. *Phi Delta Kappan, 69*(9), 648–653.

Lieberman, A., & Miller, L. (1990). Restructuring schools: What matters and what works. *Phi Delta Kappan, 71*(10), 759–764.

Little, J. W. (1982). Norms of collegiality and experimentation: Workplace conditions of school success. *American Educational Research Journal, 19*(3), 325–340.

Lortie, D. (1975). *Schoolteacher: A sociological study.* Chicago: University of Chicago Press.

Maeroff, G. (1988). *The empowerment of teachers: Overcoming the crisis of confidence.* New York: Teachers College Press.

Milstein, M. (1988, April). *Plateauing and its consequences for educators and educational organizations.* Paper presented at the annual meeting of the American Educational Research Association, New Orleans.

Milstein, M. (1989, March). *Plateauing as an occupational phenomenon among teachers and administrators.* Paper presented at the annual meeting of the American Educational Research Association, San Francisco.

Pennsylvania Department of Education. (1989). *The profession of teaching in Pennsylvania: A report on lead teachers.* Pennsylvania Department of Education, Harrisburg, PA.

Pennsylvania Department of Education. (1990, March). *Lead teachers and lead teacher training centers: Concept paper.* Pennsylvania Department of Education, Harrisburg, PA.

Rosenholtz, S. J. (1987). Educational reform strategies: Will they increase teacher commitment? *American Journal of Education, 95*(4), 534–562.

Sarason, S. (1990). *The predictable failure of educational reform.* San Francisco: Jossey-Bass.

Sears, J., & Marshall, D. (1990). An evolutionary and metaphorical journey into teaching and thinking about curriculum. In J. Sears & D. Marshall (Eds.), *Teaching and thinking about curriculum* (pp. 10–17). New York: Teachers College Press.

Smyth, J. (1988). A critical perspective for clinical supervision. *Journal of Curriculum and Supervision, 3*(2),136–156.

Thayer, I. C. (1981). *An end to hierarchy & competition: Administration in the post-affluent world* (2nd ed.). New York: New Viewpoints/Franklin Watts.

Tucker, M. (1988). Peter Drucker: Knowledge, work, and the structure of schools. *Educational Leadership, 45*(2), 44–46.

Tuthill, D. (1990). Expanding the union contract: One teacher's perspective. *Phi Delta Kappan, 71*(10), 775–780.

PART III

AUTHENTIC DEVELOPMENT: SOME POSSIBILITIES

For new ideas to impact on practice with all the richness of their promise to redefine learning for both students and teachers, we need two conditions: time and a hospitable context. Finding ways of giving good ideas time to mature (when resources are dwindling) in contexts that are conducive to growth may be the most pressing challenge of teacher development.

MacKinnon and Grunau document an attempt to build such a context within an exploratory, school-based preparation program for prospective elementary teachers. Their intent is for the ideas of science to mature pedagogically within the social structure of a "community of learners" through carefully planned experiences that encourage student teachers to learn from one another as well as from their university instructors. They focus on the relationships between and among the participants in this community as the foundation for a number of forums of action and discourse, in which the knowledge base of teaching gradually and continually develops through supported reflection. Inspired by the social theory of George Herbert Mead, they explain how they now think of reflection among beginning teachers as a function of community and discourse, sustained in relation to these multiple forums. Their position is that these shared experiences and discourse within these forums enable teachers to develop their professional "self" by coming to appreciate their classroom practice in new and different ways. They further claim that this represents, for them, the essence of teacher development.

Egan also focuses on a context in which the ideas contained in the content of teaching can mature pedagogically. But his context is not a social community; rather, it resides in the minds of every teacher who attempts to bring alive such content in imaginative ways. The imaginative mind is a context most conducive to connecting the content of the curriculum with the minds of the learners. Egan's purpose is to explore some features of students' imaginations and derive practical tools for enhancing imagination in teaching. He limits his discussion to stories as a source of observations about imaginative engagements. His interest lies in how the communicative power and engaging force of stories can yield tools and techniques that can be used in teaching science, math, social studies, and other subjects. Because students' imaginations change over time, Egan proposes different kinds of tools and techniques for children of different ages. For children under the age of 8, he suggests that content becomes imaginatively engaging when it is built on powerful binary abstract concepts, for example, good versus evil, which students then use affectively to explore and organize their world and experience by mediating between them. For children aged from about 8 to 15, he suggests that students' imaginations are engaged when they explore in exhaustive detail content that is framed around extremes of human experience (e.g., transcendent human qualities, human lives and emotions, with which students can associate) and of the natural world. For Egan, these matters are vital if teacher development is to lead to a redefinition of classroom practice, not according to efficiency in teaching, but according to imaginative engagement in learning.

Egan thus adds another dimension to the social context that MacKinnon and Grunau emphasize, that of a fine, imaginative mind. When fine, imaginative minds struggle together around solid and strong ideas in mutually supportive learning communities, authentic development takes place.

CHAPTER 8

Teacher Development through Reflection, Community, and Discourse

ALLAN M. MACKINNON
HAROLD GRUNAU

> *I remember seeing Roberta at the end of the year during her last week of practicum. She had been working in a kindergarten classroom for almost three weeks. When I arrived at the school she quickly skirted me off to the staff room to tell me how appalled she was at the morning's events. Her associate teacher had taught a lesson on opposites, and she had asked the children what the opposite of work is. Evidently, several of the children said that home is the opposite of work. To this, the teacher had said, "No, the opposite of work is play." Roberta told me that this single event had left her feeling cold—that it stood against everything she and her peers had worked toward all year. (Notes to file, April 11, 1990)*

In science education, perhaps more so than in any other subject area, we have witnessed massive curriculum reform, development, and implementation of projects from the 1960s onward. Yet it is widely known in the international science education community that teachers struggle with many barriers when it comes to the teaching of science, especially in the elementary school. There is a striking similarity in the way these barriers have been characterized by researchers. They generally fall into four categories: lack of time, lack of equipment and support, lack of confidence in knowledge of the subject matter, and lack of familiarity with science teaching methodologies (Johns, 1984; Martin, 1987; Schoenberger & Russell, 1986; St. John & Knapp, 1988; Stake & Easley, 1978; Stronk, 1986; Weiss, 1978, 1987; Wier, 1987; Zeitler, 1984). Recent position statements advocating the "renewal" of science education at all levels continue to argue for the need to promote a "high-technological society," a "scientifically literate citizenry" capable of making informed judgments on science and environmentally related social issues, and an economy that is sustainable in the world market, notwithstanding the need to provide opportunities for children as learners (American Association for the Advancement of Science, 1989; British Columbia Ministry of Education, 1989, 1990; National Center for Improving Science Education, 1989, 1990; Roth, 1989; Science Council of Canada, 1984; Sullivan, 1988). Further, the importance of teacher education has recently been acknowledged as a critical component in any considerations of educational reform and improvement (Fullan & Connelly, 1987; Holmes Group, 1986; Newton, Fullan, & MacDonald, 1987). As a result of this recognition of the important role played by teachers in providing educational services, there has been a phenomenal increase of interest in teacher education and professional development. Yet there is little documented work available on organizational structures that provide some coherence and continuity for the classroom teacher who takes seriously a sustained professional development in the teaching of science-related themes. The main intent of our project, then, is to create and investigate one form of organizational structure designed specifically to support teachers at several stages of professional growth during a time of rapid and extensive curriculum reform.

The purpose of this chapter is to discuss a rather significant shift in our recent thinking about teacher development. Through our involvement in an exploratory, school-based program for prospective elementary teachers, we have begun to conceptualize the matter of teacher education in somewhat different and, we think, useful ways. One of the ideas we wish to examine is implicit in the opening quote, in which a student teacher referred to a perspective on education that "she and her peers" in a faculty of education came to stand for. We aim to explore the notion that a teacher education program has a great deal to do with the social structure among the various participants. We focus on the relationships between and among these participants as the foundation for a number of "forums of action and discourse," in which knowledge and ability in the practice of teaching gradually and continually develop. By "forum of action," we mean a social structure in which students of education and experienced teachers work together with pupils in classrooms. The significance of the word *forum* is that it implies a group of individuals working together; the idea of a "forum of action" is different from a "practicum," for example, which usually suggests a situation in which one student teacher works in a classroom with one supervising teacher. The word *action* draws attention to the behaviors, mannerisms, and gestures that are available in the practice setting for observation by all members of this social structure and that, we feel, are acquired in action. Thus a "forum of action" is a social structure in which the behavior of individuals is shaped by that of other members of a group, as they work together in the practice setting. A "forum of discourse" refers to the social unit in which the criticism and discussion of that practice occurs.

Inspired by the social theory of Mead (1932, 1934), as explicated by Cinnamond and Zimpher (1990), we are beginning to think of reflection among beginning teachers as a function of their community and discourse, sustained in relation to these multiple forums. We wish to argue that shared experiences and discourse within these forums enable prospective teachers to come to "see" their classroom experiences in new ways. We would further argue that this is one way in which they develop into professional teachers.

"Relationship" and "community" among those involved in teacher education occur at many levels. We might speak of the relationships students of education experience with their professors, with their associate classroom teachers and school administrators, or with the children in their practice teaching classrooms. In this chapter, our main concern is with the relationship and community among students of education themselves. We draw on our experiences working in a school-based program in which the candidates developed a strong sense of community within their peer group. We begin by developing a conceptualization for drawing attention to the phenomena of interest, namely, students of education learning from one another by engaging together in the practice of teaching and the critical discourse surrounding their experiences. We then illustrate these phenomena by drawing from some of the case material we have collected over the year of our involvement in this program.

At the outset of communicating our perspective to other teacher educators, it is necessary to make some brief introductory comments regarding the assumptions we make about the knowledge base required for competent teaching practice and how this knowledge is acquired. Following Dewey (1929), we do not believe that such knowledge reduces easily to technical description or rules for practice. We do not hold, for example, that a teacher education curriculum ought to be conceived primarily as a set of courses in which the principles of teaching can be transferred, in any straightforward way, from the minds of teacher educators to the minds of prospective teachers. We prefer to think that knowledge of teaching is actively constructed by practitioners themselves, inextricably linked to their experiences and inquiries in actual situations of practice. We think such experiences and inquiries are sustained through communities that enable ongoing action and discourse. Thus we have come to view the teacher education program as a number of forums in which we might nurture and develop students' own expertise in taking on the role of the teacher, in large part by prompting the development of their sense of action and criticism of practice through interaction with others.

CONCEPTUALIZING THE PRACTICUM
IN INDIVIDUALISTIC TERMS

It is not uncommon to begin to think about teacher education in terms of students of education learning from the masters—professors at the university and associate teachers in schools from whom novices learn in a practicum. It is useful to illustrate this sort of thinking by drawing from MacKinnon's (1989) conceptualization of the dynamics of practicum. This conceptualization is intended to point out, among other things, that student teachers and supervising teachers often "see" classroom events differently. MacKinnon stresses that classroom events are subject to examination by both the supervisor and the student teacher and that, ideally, these ought to serve as the focus of their discussions. He assumes that the supervisor and the student teacher experience these phenomena in rather different ways, at least initially, by virtue of the fact that the student teacher is generally seen to be in the position of learning the practice of the supervisor. According to this conceptualization, the student teacher gradually learns to perceive teaching events as the supervisor perceives them.

The experienced teacher has a rather extensive repertoire of ways to apprehend and represent the phenomena under consideration. Drawing from Schön (1983, 1987), MacKinnon describes this repertoire as being composed of a variety of "frames" and "appreciative systems" that allow the supervisor to attend to certain features of practice situations and not to others. Those frames that the supervisor is able to articulate are derived from "pedagogical language" and give rise to "thematic experience," which consists of specialized ways of perceiving events. For example, a novice may witness a seasoned teacher refusing to excuse from class a student who claims to need the washroom. In fact, the novice may interpret this act as unnecessarily harsh and restrictive—inhumane, even. The seasoned teacher understands that the student is testing her limits, and she knows from experience that by excusing him she may set off a chain reaction: As soon as he returns from the washroom, another hand will go up to make a similar request, and so on, until there is a veritable parade of students filing in and out of the room, up and down the hallway. The seasoned teacher frames her response to the request as a gentle but firm act of managing the classroom; her ability to interpret the situation in this way is part and parcel of her appreciative system: She understands adolescents to require a firm, yet fair and friendly, hand, and she knows that she is perfectly able to detect the genuine request when, game playing aside, a student really does need to be excused from the classroom. When questioned by the novice, the seasoned teacher uses phrases such as "firm, friendly, and

fair" or "they need to test out the situation to find the bottom-line"—
phrases emanating from her pedagogical perspective, which, in principle,
function as much in the way of determining her experiences as they do in
describing them.

According to this conceptualization, the student teacher does not initially have command of the supervisor's ways of representing the phenomena under consideration; these things must be learned. In the beginning
stages of practicum, therefore, and perhaps throughout the practicum in
some cases, the student teacher experiences the phenomena under consideration in an ordinary manner, as illustrated in the example above by
the novice's interpreting the seasoned teacher's actions as unnecessarily
harsh and restrictive. As the practicum proceeds, however, the student
teacher gradually learns to "see" teaching in the way the supervisor does,
thus becoming more familiar with the frames and appreciative systems the
supervisor uses to represent and interpret classroom events.

MacKinnon (1989) uses individualistic terms to portray the way in
which supervising teachers and student teachers experience classroom
events: A student teacher learns to "see" phenomena as an experienced
teacher does, in part, by learning the significance of the experienced
teacher's language. Individualistic terms are also used to represent the form
of communication that takes place between student and supervising teachers. MacKinnon's conceptualization of this communication draws from
more of the work of Schön (1987), as described below.

Schön's ideas about learning in the professions are focused on the component processes of telling and listening, and demonstrating and imitat-
ing. The supervisor must at first try to discern what the student understands, what he or she already knows how to do, and where the difficulties
lie. These things must be discovered in the student's initial performances.
In response, the supervisor can demonstrate a particular technique that he
or she thinks the student needs to learn, or, with questions, advice, criticism, and instructions, describe various features of practice. In short, the
supervisor can show or tell pedagogical knowledge. Thus the supervisor
models actions to be imitated and experiments with communication, testing with each intervention both the diagnosis of the student's understandings and problems, and the effectiveness of his or her own strategies of
communication. In return, the student tries to make sense of the supervisor's demonstrations and descriptions, testing the meanings that have
been constructed by applying them to further attempts to display skillful
practice. In this way, the student reveals the sense he or she has made of
the supervisor's practice, and through imitation—a highly creative process—the meaning of the supervisor's practice is formulated in the context of the student's own practice.

One aspect of this conceptualization of the dynamics of practicum that we feel is important has to do with a central premise—the idea that not all of teaching can be characterized and communicated with words alone. Following Ryle (1949), Polanyi (1962), and Schön (1983, 1987), we believe (1) that at least a portion of professional knowledge resides in the actions of practitioners ("knowing how" as opposed to "knowing that"); (2) that there are some things practitioners know tacitly (things that are communicated through actions and gestures more than language); and (3) that the meaning of certain features of practice is learned largely through imitation—a highly creative and constructive process in the practice setting itself.

MOVING AWAY FROM INDIVIDUALISTIC TERMS

These ideas were paramount in conceiving a school-based elementary teacher education program at the Faculty of Education, University of Toronto (FEUT), in partnership with the Toronto Board of Education. In one sense, the program as a whole was seen to be a practicum. Thirty-four student teachers from FEUT were placed in a large elementary school for at least four days each week for three six-week trimesters (interspersed with three blocks of practicum when the candidates were placed in other schools for their student teaching). During the eighteen weeks of work at the school, professors from FEUT joined associate classroom teachers at the school, where methods courses were taught in classrooms with children. (See Sydor & Hunt, 1990, for an extended description of the administrative structure of this program.)

The intent of our work together in the Toronto program was to focus on student teachers' developing competencies in and knowledge of teaching (in terms of both their practice and their criticism of practice), their views on teaching and learning, and, especially, their intellectual empathy toward children. By *intellectual empathy*, we mean the capacity of teachers to put themselves in the place of pupils, intellectually. As our main curriculum interest was in the area of science education, we decided to concentrate on providing a setting in which children could engage in scientific inquiry under the direction of student teachers. At the beginning of the year (September, October), we videotaped lessons we taught to pupils, and we used these tapes as the basis for exploring and critiquing pedagogy with the student teachers. In this manner, we felt that we could monitor and document both the pupils' understandings of science and the student teachers' understandings of teaching. As the year progressed, the student teachers took over more responsibility for teaching the children themselves. They were typically placed in groups of five or six in a classroom of

25 to 30 pupils. Lessons taught by the student teachers were videotaped and later analyzed and critiqued by the groups.

As the program continued, we became aware that many things were being learned in the student–student forum. Student teachers would plan lessons and units of instruction together, watch one another teaching in classrooms, videotape one another in front of children, and critique one another's methods and techniques during the discussion sessions. Because we could see much of our own teaching styles, both in the student teachers' performances in the classroom and in their sense of criticism, it was clear that they were also learning a great deal from the instructional staff (associate teachers and professors). But the seriousness with which they took their own forum was striking. What they learned by watching and listening to one another was extremely important to them. As one student commented to us after the year was complete, "By the end of the year, we were learning more from each other than we were from you. Their [my peers'] outlook is different; it makes you think. At first we listened to ourselves. Each of us has our own boundaries—our own 'blinders.' As others' ideas and viewpoints were heard, your own boundaries would crumble and eventually change."

As a result of these experiences we have seen the need to extend our ideas about teacher education from individualistic terms to a conceptualization that views learning to teach in terms of social dynamics among participants. Mead's (1932, 1934) social psychology has been very informative in this regard.

Mead (1934) posited that a sense of self arises out of social behavior, which involves the dynamics of communication within a social structure or community. Cinnamond and Zimpher (1990) have begun to elaborate this idea in the context of how student teachers might learn to function in multiple communities within schools. We agree with their conjecture that

> the process of socialization is more complex than simply acquiring knowledge about teaching. The student teacher, while still a member of the community of college students, comes into contact with the communities of teachers, administrators, students, parents of students, university professors, and student-teaching supervisors. Not only must teaching candidates gain access to the communities of the school, they must also learn to function well within these communities. (p. 58)

Interaction in these communities means that exchange, discourse, and development will occur both for the existing members and for the individuals moving into the community. Reflective action is seen by Cinnamond and Zimpher as a fundamental process in attaining a sense of self and community—in short, reflective action brings about the capacity to cope with the impending changes brought about by the socialization process.

But there is much more to the idea that student teachers develop according to their sense of community and their notion of the "generalized other" (Mead, 1934) in these multiple forums. Mead's thesis is that the organized community or social group influences the way in which the individual constructs his or her own identity. In this respect, the attitude of the generalized other is the attitude of the whole community. As Mead (1934) writes:

> The self-conscious human individual, then, takes or assumes the organized social attitudes of the given social group or community (or of some one section thereof) to which he belongs, toward the social problems of various kinds which confront that group or community at any given time, and which arise in connection with correspondingly different social projects or organized co-operative enterprises in which that group or community as such is engaged; and as an individual participant in these social projects or co-operative enterprises, he governs his own conduct accordingly. (pp. 156–157)

Cinnamond and Zimpher stress that the process of socialization into multiple school communities is facilitated among student teachers through the process of reflection. While we would agree with this point, we would submit that reflection itself is dependent on the student–student forum, especially in situations where two or three prospective teachers work together in practicum, or, even more so, in situations where larger groups of candidates are placed together in a school-based teacher education program. We believe that the way in which beginning teachers learn to teach in such programs is actually dependent on the way in which they view their community. We think that the way student teachers understand teaching depends on how they regard the generalized other—the characterizing features of the good teacher that emerge from their discussions; the substantive qualities of teaching that are important to them as a group; their growing sense of criticism for one another's practice; and the manner in which they witness their peers enter the role of teaching.

On the basis of Mead's early ideas, one can capture a whole new understanding of teacher development. This understanding is steeped in social processes and gives a much more optimistic view of socialization in the profession of teaching. For example, one can think of the development of a teacher in terms of the perceived attitudes of others toward the individual and the generalized attitudes of others toward one another in the context of specific social acts. We will attempt to elaborate and illustrate these notions below. For now, it is sufficient to note that we see merit in expanding our view of practicum from individualistic terms to a view of teacher education curriculum that takes into consideration the manner in which student teachers learn to make sense of practice together through their shared experiences and relationships. As noted above, this shift from the individual to the community became evident to us throughout our work in the Toronto program. As a result of that experience, we would alter MacKinnon's (1989) conceptualization of the dynamics of practicum in ways that recognize (1) that beginning teachers' development of competence in teaching and in the analysis of teaching is more social than individualistic in character, and (2) that through multiple forums of interaction in school communities, student teachers begin to conceptualize teaching in terms of the generalized other. Indeed, the generalized other can be extended to include not only other student teachers in the student–student forum, but also student teachers at an earlier stage in their own lives—as elementary school children, for example. While these changes may seem to be a trivial adjustment at first glance, we think they represent a very profound difference. This difference essentially attributes the development of identity as a teacher to idealized images that are formed and reified through participation in the social fabric of particular groups, rather than to individualized processes that remain precariously subject to the contrived pushes and pulls of the traditional practicum. Further, in the case of school-based teacher education programs, we believe this is a more optimistic theoretical stance about teacher socialization than those views that are common in the research literature pertaining to teacher education (e.g., the view that teacher socialization into existing school structures and practices results in more routinization than reflection, together with the more dogmatic teaching approaches associated with prevailing conservatism in some school cultures).

   The development of our perspective is in its early stages. Not only is our idea extremely difficult to put to paper in a way that might make sense to the reader, it is unfortunately complex to consider the kind of evidence required to convince others why we think it is the case that teacher development is more social than individual. The possibility seems remote that we could argue convincingly, on empirical grounds, that teachers' cognitions are influenced by their images of the generalized other, which, in turn, are derived from social processes in teacher education programs. Yet as a result of our joint experiences in the Toronto program, we are left with that impression. The task remaining is to attempt to illustrate this conceptualization with case material collected over the course of this program. A narrative account of our experiences in forensic science follows.

FORENSIC SCIENCE

Our general plan for the science component of the student teaching program was first to have teachers model some teaching with children, with student teachers also involved, then to have student teachers develop and teach elementary school children a series of experiences around the topic of forensic science.

The forensic science unit was an important vehicle by which a variety of program goals—including those of collaboration, action research, and reflection—as well as those of the science education component could be met. In short, we believed through the experience of planning, implementation, and reflection, all participants would develop in appropriate ways. A key component of these experiences was for student teachers to view videotaped episodes of their own and others' teaching and then discuss what "they found interesting, curious, problematic, and so on" (program outline/assignment materials distributed to students, September 1989).

For our purposes in this chapter, the program experience on November 3, 1989, is a convenient entry point, even though the program had been running since mid-September. On the first day of a forensic science sequence of activities, we arranged to teach a lesson to a class of sixth-grade students with all 34 student teachers present, first as observers, but then helping students in small groups. The activity consisted of first learning how to use paper chromatography to detect different colors in a sample of ink as a way of identifying the writer of a note, in this case of a note authorizing a Friday afternoon off school for sixth-grade students! The note had apparently been forged over the signature of the vice-principal, and pupils were to help identify the culprit. Children worked through the chromatography exercise with the help of student teachers and participated eagerly in events throughout the morning, including a mock trial (including a vigorous defense and a serious jury) and, eventually, the "conviction" of the offender—who just happened to be one of the teachers for the day, the first author (MacKinnon). Cowed and in handcuffs, the offender was led off "to the office" for suitable punishment by the vice-principal himself. As things turned out, only four students took full advantage of the scenario and went home for the afternoon (parents of two of them called the school to find out what was going on). In this way, we would argue as designers of this program, student teachers were introduced to some varied dimensions of teaching and, by and large, could see the possibilities for learning and fun.

In early December, we received seven letters responding to our open-ended, noncompulsory request for some feedback about how the program was working out for the student teachers (from the standpoint of their learning about the teaching of science). Significantly, their detailed accounts all began the week when they began to teach groups of children according to their plans.

The remarks of several student teachers, selected from letters they submitted, will be introduced by summaries of the assignments for the five forensic science activities described below.[1]

November 10—Fingerprinting

The forensic science theme continued with an activity on fingerprinting. This activity is significant because it represents a shift from modeling teaching for the student teachers to engaging them in the role of teaching themselves. The activity description was as follows:

- Conduct the fingerprinting activity in groups of five or six children and three or four student teachers.
- Use pencils to shade areas of white paper large enough for the children to press each of their fingers on the shaded area.
- When the children's fingertips are darkened with pencil lead, use a small piece of cellophane tape to lift an imprint from each fingertip. Arrange the pieces of tape on a second piece of paper (yellow), sticking them to an outline of the child's hand so the fingerprints can be examined with a magnifying lens.
- Help the children identify and categorize their fingerprints as "loop," "arch," "whorl," or "composite" (a combination of the first three categories). See the examples of each type of fingerprint in the teachers' manual.
- When the children are dismissed for recess, you will be briefed on upcoming activities. Look at the kit material and prepare for November 17 (i.e., you are free to go off in groups and plan).

With 34 student teachers and two classes of children (one grade 4 and one grade 6), student teachers, with their children in tow, spread themselves around the cafeteria and proceeded to engage the children in the fingerprinting activity. Comments from Joan, a sixth-grade teacher, follow:

> The lesson was reasonably straightforward, as materials were supplied and the manual presented the method. We, the student teachers, helped the younger students and discovered ourselves how to look at our own fingerprints and identify types. It was after the grade 6 students had gone and we had to work together on the next week's lesson that I discovered how different people's approaches are to a problem. We each took a sec-

tion of the manual and some were interested in presenting paperwork, one in stirring up the imagination, and another in assuming a more auxiliary role. We were still a group, working a little independently but seeking advice and opinion from peers, working together so that everyone felt they had made a valuable contribution and listening carefully to each other's thoughts.

Joan's comments include reference to the early stages of working collaboratively. Mead's (1934) writing on the development of self through social interaction illuminates the group process in which Joan and her peers seem to be engaged. Mead (1934) described the development of the individual's relationship with mind, the self, and society as a continual process of construction and internalization of the social environment and knowledge into the self. The self is constructed through an ongoing process that will continue throughout the life of the person and the community. It is not merely the process of becoming aware of one's self that is social—the self one becomes aware of in this manner is itself social. One is aware of one's self as a social phenomenon, or as a part of dynamic social process, or as an agent.

The self is an individual who organizes his or her own responses in accordance with the tendencies on the part of others to respond to his or her actions.

> The self is always preceded by the other. This other is generalized. Thus, the generalized other is a part of every self. It is only because of the generalized other that thinking or creative reflection can occur. The key component of this process is the dialogue that occurs between the I and the organized attitudes of others. *The self becomes unified through social activity, and as a result it does not maintain itself as an individual self. It is always linked to the social communities that help give it definition. Consequently, when individuals act, they take into account the behaviours, values, and orientations of their community.* (Cinnamond & Zimpher, 1990, p. 58; emphasis added)

Here, then, is an analysis of the social development of self that teacher educators might use as an ideal for understanding and supporting social and critical forums among student teachers in which they "work together —and listen to each other's thoughts" (to paraphrase Joan, above).

Roberta, another student teacher, adds in her letter:

> At first I found this series of Friday mornings frustrating. The teaching sessions seemed unnatural, with four student teachers per four pupils. I felt at times that we were hounding these poor students—we didn't know each other's teaching styles yet, we were all eager to develop our own

ideas, and there was a lot of individualistic dueling. This itself, and the observations to be made, were valuable to us, but I worried that, at best, they were of no use to the grade 6's. As we've carried on, though, I feel much more comfortable with the setup. I view it now as a really neat opportunity to try things out that could be done with a whole class, only in the more easily controlled situations of a small group. Perhaps my first feeling was that we were more "tutoring."

November 17—Lifting Fingerprints

The next activity in the forensic science sequence introduced the use of videotape to record lessons for subsequent viewing and analysis. For the purposes of our research, we also began videotaping the sessions during which student teachers viewed and critiqued their lessons with the children. The activity was described as follows:

- Work in the same groups as last week. Begin by reviewing the types of fingerprints that the children can identify on their hand (cellophane-taped prints on yellow sheet).
- Have the children rub their hands in their hair to get their fingers oily. Let them handle the plastic drinking glasses and metal objects, and then examine the objects for fingerprints.
- When the children have found a fingerprint, help them gently "dust" the print with a paint brush dipped in the graphite powder. Tape over the dusted print with a piece of cellophane tape and press the tape firmly in place.
- Carefully remove the tape (which should take the fingerprint with it) from the object and retape it to a sheet of paper. Compare the fingerprint with the example from last week (yellow paper) to see if a match can be made, indicating which finger the print came from.
- If time remains, have children exchange their yellow sheets and lifted prints to check one another's identifications.
- Videotape five groups.
- At recess, gather in auditorium to watch videos (those groups not videotaped watch the others').
- At 11:15 move to the cafeteria to show excerpts of videos that are interesting, curious, problematic, and so on.

Beth, a fourth-grade teacher, commented:

The children generally enjoyed this activity. They were enthusiastic, but had trouble using the self-discipline required to take it step-by-step. When we used the graphite it was the worst mess in the world. They continued to blow it off, even when asked not to do so. (It was so bad we had to move to another table!) We kept the activity very simple and it fit well within the time frame available. Some students got confused about the order of activities and were difficult to convince that they should try another tactic for success—they were enjoying themselves so much, that accuracy really didn't seem to be important to them.

Joan made the following comment:

November 17 went smoothly. The children enjoyed trying to "find" the culprit by means of brushing for fingerprints. Afterwards we were not only able to observe ourselves, our group (in real life), but see how other student teachers had approached the subject and how they had taught it, via videotape. I, myself, silently praised some of the approaches and was critical of others (but didn't want to say anything for fear of hurting anyone).

Thus, immediately after the November 17 teaching sequence, video playback machines were used to review and reflect on the teaching efforts. The reflective sessions were underway and the student teachers were engaged. A videotaped sequence shown to the group of student teachers was discussed as follows (the instructor is one of the authors—Allan MacKinnon):

PAM: We had originally planted [my prints] on that card, but we all [the student teachers] had played with the cards and we should have used a new deck.
ALLAN: So someone, a child, said, "You're the guilty one."
PAM: (from the videotape) *I'm a detective; I couldn't commit a crime.*
ALLAN: I really liked what you did. You're asking them to challenge you.
DONNA: She didn't confirm or deny. It keeps the mood up, keeps motivation up.
ALLAN: I'd like to make a general comment here. Sometimes when kids come to conclusions I like to explore their reasoning—"What makes you say that?"
GARY: I'd say, if they had good reasons, it is acceptable.

Here, Donna and Gary offer interesting insights into the teaching episode under discussion. Donna focuses on the need to keep discussion going in this context, while Gary is quite definite about judging students' conclusions on the adequacy of their reasons.

There was a positive feeling in the room during this analysis session. The weekly patterns (of teaching followed by such sessions) were developing, as was trust in this supportive community. The instructional staff made a point of being supportive and positive, for example, with regard to the prints on the cards (above): "I really liked what you did."

When questioning came up in discussion, Allan suggested that experience might result in different personal rules of practice:

ALLAN: Do you remember what you did when you wanted to know, that is, how you indicated that you had a question?

GAIL: "Put your hand up if you didn't understand."

GRACE: If you just ask if they understand, they may not [commit themselves to a lack of understanding].

TERRI: I think you should avoid asking yes or no questions.

By November 21, we had a general sense that the plan was working, that students were taking responsibility, were working together, and learning in new ways despite some frustration about scheduling, room assignment, and a few other problems. Pat, for example, notes the tension: "The anxiety level is growing. I can just feel the tension rising. When I do something wrong . . . I'm sort of concerned . . . especially now when we are being videotaped and "big people" at the faculty might be looking at us" (Notes to file, November 21, 1989). Roberta, too, had some concerns about videotaping:

> I have some kind of visceral, negative feelings about this whole idea. I would find it more valuable . . . to share . . . verbally. . . . Thus, a look at what worked in their lesson and what didn't, what would have improved it, what would have solved a problem they'd run into. . . . For me, videotape is too distancing and diverting—it doesn't easily capture the feeling or the spirit of the experience. Someone in a group I met with today (December 1) said how much they liked the videotapes because they really slow up things like unplanned lessons. But I feel that's something a teacher really needs to be able to feel—we have to recognize the feeling when something isn't going well, and be able then to analyze why, what would have changed that, etc.

Here, Roberta recognizes the possibility that videotape analysis can become contrived and reductionist. She thinks about her thinking itself, coming to terms (literally) with feeling the problem and considering subsequent action. These comments about feeling and spirit touch on the contextual, holistic, and personal nature of the work, yet they do not relinquish the need for more deliberate analysis to identify problems and alternative courses of action.

November 24—Integrating Language Arts

The third in the sequence of five forensic science sessions was a little different in that integrating language arts activities into the theme was prominent. In this session, students had much more latitude and artistic license for their planning. The assignment for student teachers was as follows:

- Work with children in the same groups.
- Use your own ideas to integrate language arts into forensic science. Try to be creative and playful with the children.
- At recess, in groups, begin planning for December 1 and 7.
- Take about 45 minutes to plan for December 1 (in five "expert groups" of seven members each). Then "jig-saw" the groups and begin to plan a crime center for December 7. This means that there will be 7 "crime center groups," each of which will have five experts in different forensic areas.
- In your crime center group, design a crime center (scene) that includes evidence for children to find in each of the five forensic areas.

Beth's group (grade 4) used the language arts activities of November 24 to prepare the children for eventually solving a fully blown mock crime later in December. She commented about the language arts activities as follows:

> First we described a crime (someone stealing Santa's candy canes) and asked them to respond to a police request for a description of the thief. Next we chose one adult in the room, and all of the children made a "wanted poster" of that person—the idea was to compare them at the end and show how everyone can have a slightly different view of the same person. (Therefore, police work can be difficult at times.) Finally they made up a crime. They really enjoyed the wanted posters and took the exercise very seriously. All the students except one contributed to the story; the one that refused was unable to come up with any ideas, even after gentle suggestions were made. They were quite intrigued with the differences in their wanted posters—I asked if I could photocopy them, and permission was given only after assurances that they would receive them back right after recess. It fit well within the time frame.

Beth's comments suggest that the fourth-grade students were enjoying the work, were themselves reflecting—"they were quite intrigued with the differences in their wanted posters"—and they were pleased with their work (permission to photocopy given only after assurances that they would receive them back after recess). Except for the child who "refused" to contribute, there was no mention of technical difficulty this time. Beth, or perhaps some other student teachers in her group, sensed it was important for all to contribute, and, presumably by "reflecting-in-action" (Schön, 1983), devised and attempted a strategy—"gentle suggestions were made" —to include all the students.

Joan commented:

> During the following week, our group of four met to discuss how we would approach the idea of integrating language arts into the forensic science theme. A suggestion of playing *Clue* was brought forward and enthusiastically endorsed by two. But I was reluctant. My fellow students were kind and contributed new ideas. We had the children answer a 911 call and make reports on two different incidents. After approximately 40 minutes, they played *Clue* and they loved it. I helped Gordie, a boy having trouble with English, and he caught on quickly. He is not very popular either, but all these barriers were dropped in the excitement of the game. They played through recess and, with permission, for half an hour afterwards. Friends joined. They were learning and loving it. What I thought was a cop-out turned out to be a good experience for them and for me. I am glad they did the interviews, but the game gave them a chance to relax and not worry about what they were learning.

Joan's comment—"My fellow students were kind and contributed new ideas"—focuses on planning and group process and indicates the sensitivity of group members to one another and their commitment to work together. The ideas of Mead (1934) help to illuminate Joan's interactions with her peers and the pupils in her group.

> The group advances from old standards toward another standard; and what is important from the standpoint of morality is that this advancement takes place through the individual—one who conceives himself as individuals have not conceived themselves in the past. (p. 386)

Joan's reluctance to use *Clue*, followed by her later change in attitude on seeing the results of the game in practice, and finally sharing her thoughts—"What I thought was a cop-out turned out to be a good experience for them and for me"—in a letter represent not only direct evidence of her change in a "value," but also that the major goals of collaboration, reflection, and a commitment to discourse are being met in the practice setting. Another student's comment, "much of learning is . . . in sharing," also brings Mead's ideas to mind.

In the discussion of November 24, we asked Natasha about her reactions to the activities she had done with her student teaching peers and small groups of children. "Seeing it makes a big difference; it's useful. Howard and I were talking earlier. I found myself thinking about how I would do these activities with a [large] group. . . . You play it more in the back of your mind." Here, Natasha seems to be involved in a kind of "exploratory experiment," in which she imagines her actions in a probing and playful way, as Schön (1983) says, to help get a feel for things.

Sonia, too, considered the problem of adapting the activities to an entire class:

> The only problem that I can foresee is incorporating this unit in an ordinary classroom situation. It is easy to teach six kids when there are four of you to work with them. I think that it is a whole new ball game when there is only one of you and maybe 25 of them. However, I like the unit so much that I wouldn't let this stop me. All that is needed is planning and organization.

Sonia's reflection may be slightly more focused, yet very similar to Natasha's. Notably, she is convinced that some "moves" (planning and organization) will overcome the obstacles. This "move-testing," albeit imaginary at this time, fits well with Schön's (1983) ideas about experiment in action.

One group of student teachers discussed a situation in which they decided to stage a "scene" in front of the children in which one of their number accused another of stealing a wallet:

> We wanted to focus on their observation skills. The kids really bought it. One kid said to another, "A teacher stole another's wallet." Some thought Carla was innocent, others not. There was confusion. Their emotions were confused with observations. We said, "O.K., start writing now." The kids wanted to write—the creative flow was there. When we asked, "How did you feel?" they said, "Weird; frightened; my stomach hurt." (Jennifer)

Later, in a discussion about the crime scenarios, ethical questions regarding the use of deception with this particular scene were raised by student teachers Gary and Roberta. Others did not seem to understand the importance of the issue, and Gary, especially, was bothered by this for several months to come.

During the November 24 analysis session we tried to provoke discussion of interesting or troubling situations, especially in terms of how the children were understanding the forensic science activities. Some of the student teachers were quite surprised by the interest shown by the pupils, and there was general excitement about the possibility of coming to understand more about how and why students were learning. It was noticed, for example, that there were differences in the way grade 4 and 6 students were able to lift, classify, and identify fingerprints. One group of student teachers reported that the grade 4 children had difficulty sorting the prints into the categories loop, whorl, and arch, whereas the grade 6 children were beginning to identify prints on the basis of ridge characteristics.

ALLAN: Anything else?
WENDY: There is no generality. We have to deal with individuals and not generalities.
ALLAN: Yet we do have some understanding of the general.

Throughout the session we tried to be encouraging. The mood was supportive, and our mutual trust seemed to be growing. We acknowledged how much work the student teachers had put into the forensic science activities.

We asked that student teachers write down their reactions for next week—how children see phenomena; how they respond and learn; how the student teachers interpret children's responses. The request was not forced. Such responses were encouraged throughout, but students did not, by and large, see them as obligatory assignments. Nevertheless, a number of letters and reactions were handed in a week later. By December 1, Roberta's comments show a great deal of insight, maturity and growth:

> That we learn by doing has long been a truth for me. . . . On the other hand, we cannot be empirical. Experience alone leads to narrow-mindedness and hasty conclusions. One of the qualities I most appreciate in people is thoughtfulness—not the "be kind to others" version, but the ability to consider things at different levels, and from many sides. For this reason, the emphasis on "reflectiveness" at Dunkin [the name of the school] is of great value. . . . Another reason why this "thoughtfulness," or "reflectiveness," is so important is that education should be an ongoing part of everyone's life. There is something to be learned from every experience. . . . One of the interesting things about this year is the parallels that can be drawn between the students and teachers at Dunkin, and the students and teachers [from the university]. One would hope that this would aid us in developing our understanding.

Roberta went on to comment more specifically on the science experiences:

> I believe that some really vital issues have come out of our science experi-
> ences. For myself, fundamental questions of respect, power, attitudes
> towards children, trust (and violation of) . . . so it has been a valuable
> way of learning. I guess that I could say the whole program is engaging—
> of the intellect, the emotions, the spirit—so that, along with all the other
> pulls on my life, I feel drained. But I'd rather be doing this than anything
> else (almost).

It is interesting to note that many students remarked on being surprised on discovering through their experience that children learn most
from hands-on experience, that teachers need to listen carefully to student
discoveries and build on what they see, "as they often notice things that
we don't" (Roberta). More importantly, the overall insight and scope of
Roberta's remarks are striking: ". . . education should be an ongoing part
of everyone's life . . . something to be learned from every experience . . .
parallels that can be drawn between the students and teachers . . ." In the
latter comment, Roberta seems to be referring to the collaborative, inquiring stance that we advocated for pupils, teachers, and children generally,
but that we also tried to model in our own interactions with one another.
Finally, Roberta's mention of "fundamental questions of respect, power,
attitudes toward children, trust (and violation of)" suggest that she is coming to understand schooling in critical ways as well. The difficulties (especially at first) and the benefits (especially as time went on) of having three
or four student teachers work with four or five students were noted in one
way or another by several students.

December 1—Expert Groups

The December 1 lessons and discussion revealed important considerations
in our growing experience and understanding. By this time, student teachers had taught the same children three times in varied settings (making and
lifting fingerprints and incorporating language arts into the theme) and
were comfortable with the routines. Moreover, they had had some time
to work together preparing lessons in their original groups.
  The assignment for December 1:

- Prepare five centers/lessons for each of the grade 4 and grade 6 children.
- Centers/lessons should relate to chromatography, soil, hair, footprints, and cloth analysis.

- Videotape student teacher groups that were not taped on the 17th.
- At recess, view one another's teaching in the auditorium (as on the 24th).
- At 11:15, meet other student teachers in the cafeteria to show and discuss excerpts of the videotaped centers/lessons.

Beth commented:

> The activity started out well with a review of last week's theft of the canes and a shoe with soil stuck to its sole—they understood that we were attempting to match that soil to one of the samples. At first they paid attention to the techniques of soil testing, but soon began to enjoy testing litmus paper in all sorts of solutions. They had to almost be forced to pay attention to the charting of results (we had to clear the table in order to get them to focus on the charts). We succeeded in finishing the program only by forcing the issue. The time frame was insufficient—two periods would have been preferable—one for the comprehension of base, acid, and neutral, and another for the actual test. Overall, they enjoyed it, but the pressure to accomplish the task in order for them to be an "expert" the next week was not a realistic expectation.

Joan's comments are particularly interesting to us for reasons that will become obvious. We have selected a lengthy excerpt from her writings to illustrate her thoughtfulness.

> December 1 was the day we videoed ourselves teaching. I got to see what I physically look like and have decided on some changes. But it was when we were all looking at the snippets of four or five groups of student teachers teaching that some real revelations concerning students and teachers came forth. The inhibitions which I had displayed two weeks prior were dropped by everyone. We noted actions and reactions of students and teachers and were able to discuss them freely and openly. The ability of students to learn from each other, the importance of listening to the child, the concept of Kounin's "withitness," the importance of concrete materials, the idea of process over product—all were introduced by us for us.
>
> The four science classes to date have made me look into myself and analyze what I am doing and why I am doing it; have made me criticize myself; have made me think of the student and not the teacher. They have made me realize the tremendous value of the ideas and opinions of my peers. I thought this course would rest totally on my own shoulders— a course in which I researched, I wrote, I succeeded. Instead, in the true spirit of cooperative learning, I find myself learning against a vat of poten-

tial knowledge, beside which I abandon some of my "me and me alone temperment" and become a willing group learning tippler.

I will listen and listen well to everyone. I look forward to each and every day from my STEP [Student Teaching Experience Program] days in the classroom, through the talks by informed people, to the interaction with my peers. "The Faculty" is no longer an intellectual exercise. It is a vibrant, moving force in my life, something of which I don't want to miss a minute. I can only leave you with the hope, my hope, that when (and if) I graduate, I can return in five or ten years and thank you for all you did for me that year at Dunkin.

As the analysis session began, we asked small teaching groups to show segments of videotape about which they wished to comment to the whole group.

Beth's group: One student teacher commented on the "really hyper kids." Beth said that all were interested, trying things, and enjoying themselves. Another student teacher commented on how the children's interest changed during the lesson (. . . not interested in the charts at first—but later they were).

Jennifer's group: Carla talked about trying to get a student to name the parts of a hair (under a microscope) but said she felt uncomfortable while doing so: "The reason I did that [name the parts of a hair] was because it was in the manual, but you pick out what works with your group. You don't have to follow it [the manual]."

Chantelle's group: What happened was we were looking at soil . . . and the problem we had was that one child's filter didn't work at all, and another's came through dirty.

Discussion led to appropriate hypothetical responses to pupils' questions by the student teachers, including different ways of handling technical difficulties. The following excerpt from the discussion illustrates the concern for the understanding of children.

ALLAN: Do kids give wrong answers?
ANNA: No, you're trying to encourage them to express whatever they think.
ROBERTA: And to trust . . . [their answers] . . . take risks, believe in themselves, not always give pat answers. For example, you could just ask, "Do you want to think about it?"
ALLAN: Kids do not give wrong answers? Any thing else? I really like your

technique of having them make a prediction because I think when you do, it gives you access to what they know and gives you material to work on.

STELLA: The process of predicting helped. I'm always surprised when they make predictions, and I [always] think they know more than they do.

TANA: I know it is important to introduce vocabulary, but it should be natural.

GARY: I found it difficult to get grade 1's to estimate. They would always erase their estimates after they did it.

December 8—Crime Day

December 8 was "Crime Day." Each of the groups was to design and present a "crime center." The assignment was as follows:

• Crime Day will involve a double "jig-saw" of the group structure. You will have done part of this already in your planning groups on the 24th, in which each group had an expert student teacher in forensic techniques with cloth, an expert on soil, and so on for chromatography, hair, and footprints.

• Present your crime center to the students, including the clues that the children will need to find out "who-done-it." Jig-saw the children's groups as well, so there will be at least one child whose expertise lies in the area of cloth, soil, and so on.

• The point is that these are "cooperative groups"—the children will have to cooperate at their center in order to solve the crime.

• But this is only the basic outline. The rest is up to the creativity and imagination of all. Avoid competing for the best crime center, enjoy one another's work and ideas, and a very good time will be had by all.

This assignment is worth examining carefully. In the "jig-saw" we tried to ensure that children and student teachers would cooperate, although, at times, such an arrangement can become contrived. We also tried to emphasize the opportunities for creativity and spontaneity among the student teachers. Finally, we encouraged students to enjoy one another's work and ideas (i.e., to share the joy of work and fun). Throughout all the forensic science activities, Allan's directions and advice to students reinforced the general objectives of the program, as presented to the students at the first of the year. The latter part of the December 8 assignment (above) is a particularly good example of that consistency.

The crime centers were videotaped and later analyzed in the last discussion session before Christmas break. Indeed, the centers showed a great deal of creativity, and the videos generally portrayed student teachers who appeared remarkably confident and competent, considering they had been in the teacher education program for only a little over three months. Examples of the students' competence in the teaching of science were many. At several crime centers, student teachers realized the children were interpreting evidence in ways that were quite unexpected, sometimes contrary to the intended solution or conclusion that might be reached if all interpretation went according to the plan. In these cases, the student teachers seemed at ease, as, in stride, they readily adapted the scenarios in order to accommodate the children's interpretations. In our judgment, this observation suggests the student teachers were developing their sense of intellectual empathy toward the children. We observed one of the student teachers carefully instructing a child in what to look for while viewing a hair through the microscope; clearly, she knew that the child needed direction in order to make the pertinent observation. Both capacities—intellectual empathy and knowing how to direct a child's observations—are essential to the teaching of science.

The student teachers' capacity for critical analysis in the discussion session showed similar growth, and it was clear that most had moved beyond the initial fear of hurting one another's feelings. Students watched one another's videos intently and made very insightful observations and comments. In previous analysis sessions we had the sense that, as instructors, our analyses and comments had directed the sessions. Throughout this last analysis session of the term, it became clear to us that the students' insights and comments were taking precedence over our own. This was extremely rewarding, for, in our judgment, the quality of the session was excellent.

Before closing the session, a few general comments were made about the work of the term. The following have been selected for their pertinence to the theme of the chapter:

> Through getting to know [my peers], I began to understand what I was being taught. (Donna)

> Whatever we did, we did together; whatever we learned we learned together. (Linda)

> I know myself better through listening to and watching others. (Joan)

CONCLUSION

This case has illustrated several program planning initiatives that emphasized collaboration among participants, inquiry into practice, and reflection. Our account and documentation of the forensic science theme has been constructed in a manner that embellishes the theoretical framework proposed in this chapter. We submit that Mead's ideas provide a rather edifying way of thinking about the education of teachers. As we moved from one teaching experience to the next throughout the year, we had many discussions that were equally rich. A three-week block of student teaching, for example, would lead to other groupings of student teachers and further opportunities for meaningful discourse. We believe the perspective advanced in this chapter serves as a useful beginning in, as we say, making sense of the social fabric lying behind the development of individual student teachers' understanding of self. In our case, our aim was to direct most of our attention to the student–student forum in which we believe much of this development occurs.

It is not surprising that a model developed to illuminate many important features of teacher development can be proposed and, indeed, be useful in interpreting the events that transpired. We would hope that this case and its analysis is sufficiently convincing to begin to conceptualize teacher education programs in ways that allow the kinds of forums and opportunities that have been described. Forensic science, of course, is only one of countless themes that might be explored, yet it did seem to be effective in the circumstances. The particular arrangement of small groups of student teachers assigned to teach small groups of children, or a class of some 34 teachers critiquing one another using videos, can also be modified. Again, we are advocating the nurturing of appropriate forums in which community and relationship are valued, and reflection and discourse encouraged in large part simply by living the experience.

Providing for and carefully nurturing appropriate forums in which community, reflection, and discourse come together in the development of teachers is no easy accomplishment, however. Our interpretation of events in the course of a year would reinforce this view. At the end of the year, for example, several students recalled their reaction to the emphasis described in the program handbook, as they remembered it from the beginning of the year. As Beth put it—"What a hoot! We [student teachers] laughed about it. At the time it didn't mean a thing." Only through living the model did the intended results appear to come about. Indeed, it was Beth who was to say, "By the end of the program we were learning more from each other than we were from you."

Relatively few examples of nonverbal discourse have been provided and identified in this chapter. Neither has the discourse that individuals have within themselves been explored in depth. Each of these, it is hypothesized, can also be accounted for by the perspective that has been advanced. For example, Donna had had considerable experience as an actress before entering the FEUT teacher education program. She moved so easily into a candid role as a teacher during the forensic science activities that we were all suitably impressed. In the analysis session when we viewed her video, comments were made about how uplifting her countenance had been. We believe that most of us in the forum—instructors and students alike—came to see ourselves in new and exciting ways as a result of this experience, not only in terms of the manner in which we could represent ourselves as teachers, but also in terms of coming to recognize and manage the socially formed perceptions of ourselves that are available to others. Indeed, many of the student teachers exhibited a much more candid and relaxed manner in their teaching after the experience of watching Donna.

Finally, while there are inevitable obstacles to overcome in working out the ideas presented in this chapter, we believe strongly that the view we have presented, together with the kinds of enabling conditions we believe we have described, represent for many a new way of "seeing" teacher development. Our hope is that Mead's analyses and our experiences in the Toronto program will at least provide a refreshing perspective and new hopes for teacher development at the preservice level.

NOTE

1. The student teachers and pupils who are mentioned have been given pseudonyms.

REFERENCES

American Association for the Advancement of Science. (1989). *Science for all Americans: A project 2061 report on literacy goals in science, mathematics, and technology*. Washington, DC: Author.

British Columbia Ministry of Education. (1989). *Year 2000: A curriculum and assessment framework for the future*. Victoria, BC: Queen's Printer.

British Columbia Ministry of Education. (1990). *Year 2000: A framework for learning*. Victoria, BC: Queen's Printer.

Cinnamond, J. H., & Zimpher, N. L. (1990). Reflectivity as a function of community. In R. T. Clift, W. R. Houston, & M. C. Pugach (Eds.), *Encouraging reflective practice in education: An analysis of issues and programs* (pp. 57–72). New York: Teachers College Press.

Dewey, J. (1929). *The sources of a science of education*. New York: Horace Liveright.

Fullan, M., & Connelly, F. M. (1987). *Teacher education in Ontario: Current practice and options for the future*. Toronto: Ontario Ministry of Education/Ministry of Colleges and Universities.

Holmes Group. (1986). *Tomorrow's teachers*. East Lansing, MI: Author.

Johns, K. W. (1984). Wanted: Money and time for science. *School Science and Mathematics, 84,* 271–276.

MacKinnon, A. M. (1989). Conceptualizing a "hall of mirrors" in a science-teaching practicum. *Journal of Curriculum and Supervision, 5*(1), 41–59.

Martin, D. R. (1987). Project support: Teachers helping teachers to improve elementary science. *Teacher Education Quarterly, 14,* 41–49.

Mead, G. H. (1932). *The philosophy of the present.* Chicago: University of Chicago Press.

Mead, G. H. (1934). *Mind, self, and society.* Chicago: University of Chicago Press.

National Center for Improving Science Education. (1989). *Developing and supporting teachers for elementary school science education.* Washington, DC: The Biological Sciences Curriculum Study / The Network.

National Center for Improving Science Education. (1990). *Developing and supporting teachers for middle school science education.* Washington, DC: The Biological Sciences Curriculum Study / The Network.

Newton, L. J., Fullan, M., & MacDonald, J. W. (Eds.) (1987). *Re-thinking teacher education: Exploring the link between research, practice and policy.* Toronto: Joint Council on Education, the University of Toronto and the Ontario Institute for Studies in Education.

Polanyi, M. (1962). *Personal knowledge.* Chicago: University of Chicago Press.

Roth, K. (1989). *Conceptual understanding and higher level thinking in the elementary science curriculum: Three perspectives.* East Lansing, MI: Center for the Learning and Teaching of Elementary Subjects, Institute for Research on Teaching.

Ryle, G. (1949). *The concept of mind.* London: Hutchinson.

Schoenberger, M., & Russell, T. L. (1986). Elementary science as a little added frill: A report of two case studies. *Science Education, 70*(5), 519–538.

Schön, D.A. (1983). *The reflective practitioner: How professionals think-in-action.* New York: Basic Books.

Schön, D.A. (1987). *Educating the reflective practitioner: Toward a new design for teaching and learning in the professions.* San Francisco: Jossey-Bass.

Science Council of Canada. (1984). *Science for every student: Educating Canadians for tomorrow's world* (Report 36). Ottawa: Science Council of Canada.

St. John, M., & Knapp, M. S. (1988, April). *Developing teacher leaders and advocates of elementary science education.* Paper presented at the annual meeting of the American Educational Research Association, New Orleans.

Stake, R. E., & Easley, J. A. (1978). *Case studies in science education.* Urbana: Center for Instructional Research and Curriculum Evaluation, University of Illinois.

Stronk, D. R. (1986). Trends in teachers' recommendations for changing elementary and junior-high school science programs. *Journal of Research in Science Teaching, 23,* 201–207.

Sullivan, B. M. (1988). *A legacy for learners: The report of the Royal Commission on Education.* Victoria, BC: Queen's Printer.

Sydor, S., & Hunt, G. (1990, June). *A field-based partnership in teacher education: Administrative issues.* Paper presented at the annual meeting of the Canadian Society for the Study of Education, Victoria, BC.

Weiss, I. R. (1978). *Report of the 1977 National Survey of Science, Mathematics, and Social Studies Education.* Research Triangle Park, NC: Center for Educational Research and Evaluation.

Weiss, I. R. (1987). *1986–87 National Survey of Science and Math Education.* Research Triangle Park, NC: Research Triangle Institute.

Wier, E. (1987, April). *Primary teachers' perceptions of barriers to teaching science.* Paper presented at the annual meeting of the National Association for Research in Science Teaching, Washington, DC.

Zeitler, W. R. (1984). Science backgrounds, conceptions of purposes, and concerns of preservice teachers about teaching children science. *Science Education, 68,* 505–520.

CHAPTER 9

Tools for Enhancing Imagination in Teaching

KIERAN EGAN

Mention of tools and imagination in the same phrase perhaps suggests a confusion of rhetoric at least, and perhaps even a confusion of ideology. Words such as *tools* have been associated with mechanistic approaches to teaching, approaches that have drawn on conceptions of efficiency derived from factories or industrial management (Callahan, 1962). Such approaches have introduced us to studies of "effective teaching," which never mention imagination. If one looks at reviews of research on "effective" teaching, such as O'Neil (1988), one may see as many as 20 "research factors" discussed, but imagination does not appear anywhere among them. Similarly, Porter and Brophy's (1988) review and synthesis of research on "good teaching" also ignores imagination. This is odd, because one of the commonest commendations we hear about good teaching or good teachers is that they are "imaginative."

Clearly the research methods that are currently dominant in education have difficulty dealing with something as complex as the imagination, but it would be a pity if its virtual absence in empirical research on teaching should encourage us to focus on the behavioral repertoires prominent in that research and ignore something so obviously central to good teaching as imagination. Also, it is important to remember the great practical value of tools and techniques. To leave a concern with tools and techniques only to those who draw on mechanistic metaphors in thinking about education is a little like leaving the devil with all the best tunes. What I want to do in this chapter, then, is explore, in perhaps a somewhat preliminary way, some features of students' imaginations and try to infer from them some practical tools that might assist us in teaching.

And how might one go about this? We might focus on activities in which we see students very readily engaged imaginatively, observe some of the prominent features of what engages them, and try to infer some tools or techniques that we might be able to apply in our everyday teaching. This seems quite straightforward, and one would expect that in doing something like this one must have a fairly well-beaten path to follow. But looking for footmarks around the topic of imagination in education is not that encouraging, and one searches for the path from there in the direction of tools and techniques with some bewilderment.

It comes as less surprising, then, that some of the inferences to be made from observations in this area suggest some unusual tools and techniques for teaching. Some seem to conflict rather starkly with those that are currently prominent, inferred as they have been from educational research that has paid attention almost exclusively to a limited set of logical cognitive skills and has attended hardly at all to the cognitive capacities connected with imagination.

Given the limitations of space and time in a chapter, I shall restrict myself here to focusing on stories as the source of observations about imaginative engagements. My aim is not at all to make inferences about how to use fictional stories in teaching. Rather I am interested in how the communicative power and engaging force of stories can yield tools and techniques that can be used in teaching science, math, social studies, and so forth. Also, as it is clear that the kinds of stories that engage students' imaginations change over time, we will sensibly expect different kinds of tools and techniques to emerge for different ages. So here I shall just make a crude distinction, dealing first with tools or techniques we might derive from stories that commonly engage students under about 8 years of age, and then some that engage students from about 8 to 15 years of age.

In each case I shall discuss characteristics of stories, and also some other evidently imaginatively engaging materials. I shall then follow what seem fairly straightforward lines of inference and see what tools or techniques seem implied by each inference. At the conclusion of the two main sections I shall draw the set of tools together into a model or framework that could be used in planning a lesson or unit.

STORIES AND TOOLS FOR TEACHING YOUNG CHILDREN

If we look for stories that consistently engage young children's imaginations, we might settle on the classic fairy tales as worthy of investigation. What is it about these stories that so readily engages young children, and can we infer principles that will lead to tools for imaginative teaching from our observations? Let us begin by considering a few characteristics of the classic fairy tales, and then exploring how we might turn our observations into practical benefits for teaching.

One of the most obvious structural features of the classic fairy stories is that they are based on powerful conflicts between security and danger, courage and cowardice, cleverness and stupidity, hope and despair, and, ultimately, good and evil. This feature of these stories has been observed often and is commonly taken as a reflection of the "manner in which the child can bring order into [the] world . . . by dividing everything into opposites" (Bettelheim, 1976, p. 74).

We can observe, then, that the stories are made up of characters and events that embody the conflict between these powerful underlying forces. Two features of these forces are evident. First, they are abstract, and, second, they are affective.

For the stories to make sense, children must in some form be familiar with concepts of security/danger, courage/cowardice, cleverness/stupidity, hope/despair, and good/evil. They need not, of course, be able to articulate, or define, such terms explicitly in order to be able to use them. It seems reasonable to say that these abstract binary concepts are what children use constantly to make sense of the world and their experience; they know such concepts most profoundly.

We are familiar with claims that young children are "concrete" thinkers. Perhaps if one focuses on a particular range of their logical skills, this is the case. But focusing on their imaginative engagements brings out vividly that young children's cognition also involves abstract thinking. Indeed, it seems that the most powerful organizing concepts they use are among the most abstract we ever learn. The typical young child is evidently deploying profound abstract concepts in order to make concrete content meaningful. And, from observation of fairy tales, it seems that it is the underlying abstraction that provides access, and meaning, to the concrete content.

Inference 1: If we want to make concrete content accessible, meaningful, and imaginatively engaging to children, we should build it on powerful binary abstract concepts.

Inference 2: We can make any content meaningful and engaging to young children if we build it on the kind of powerful binary abstract concepts that they use to explore and organize the world and experience.

This second inference might seem to be going beyond anything that our observation can sustain. But I think not. Certainly it runs counter to a prevailing presupposition that forms a part of the conventional wisdom of teaching and even of the structure of the curriculum. That is, it is conventionally presupposed that children's knowledge expands "from the known to the unknown," and this unobjectionable truism is generally taken to lead to the principle that you must connect the knowledge students are to acquire to something they already are familiar with, and this in turn is taken to mean some content that forms a part of their everyday environment or their secured store of knowledge. The second inference above is drawn from the observation that the kind of knowledge that children seem to use most effectively in going "from the known to the unknown" is their knowledge of courage/cowardice, security/danger, good/evil, and so forth. That is, if we keep in mind that these powerful binary abstractions are a part of what children know, we may see a different way of interpreting the truism about moving from the known to the unknown than has been common.

Consider the following observation: "The sort of familiarity which a child demands in a story is often a social one, a doing of things which the child expects to have done. Thus *Peter Rabbit* is a manageable story for Carol at two years eight months because of its familiar family setting" (Applebee, 1978, p. 75). But if knowledge based on familiar features of the child's environment is the key to making the story accessible and manageable, one must wonder why Peter is a rabbit. One might also wonder about the wild wood, which is safe, and the cultivated garden, which is dangerous, and the closeness of death, and so on. One might say that knowledge of security/danger can make any content that is built to embody that conflict accessible and manageable to children. If it is familiarity, one must wonder why *Star Wars* and stories about talking rabbits and bears are so readily accessible and imaginatively engaging to young children.

Now I do not mean that no other considerations besides embodying binary abstractions is important. What I want to emphasize, counter to the currently dominant interpretation of the truism that we work from the known to the unknown, and counter to the principle of "expanding horizons" on which the social studies curriculum is built, is that children can have direct access to all kinds of "concrete" content, as long as that content can be built on the kinds of powerful, abstract concepts that children deploy so readily in making sense of the world and experience.

The other part of the observation about these binary abstract concepts is that they are typically *affective*. They all seem to have a strong emotional component. That is, these paradigms of children's imaginative engagements suggest that a very significant part of children's initial grasp on the world and experience is affective. Early in our lives we seem to deploy emotion-laden categories to make sense of things.

Inference 3: *The abstract binary concepts we use to organize knowledge so that children will find it accessible, meaningful, and imaginatively engaging should be affective.*

The intellectual tool or technique that we have for organizing content affectively is, of course, the story. So the implication of inference 3 is that we should shape our lessons and units in a more story-like fashion than is common. If we begin to think of our lessons less as sets of objectives to be attained and more as good stories to be told, we will begin to get a sense of what this implies. Our lessons and units will be made up of true stories, of course, the great stories of our mathematics, and science, and social studies, and so on.

Now we will obviously not want to teach children that the world is made up of binary opposites. What we are doing, rather, is aiming to cohere with the tools and techniques children seem spontaneously to use in making sense of stories. And, of course, we see the deployment of these abstract, affective binary concepts ubiquitously in children's language and sense-making (Paley, 1981, 1984, 1990). The kind of expansion of knowledge from such binary concepts seems to proceed very commonly by mediation between the binary pair. So in our teaching we will want to use the binary concepts to provide access to our topic and perhaps seek ways of extending understanding by leading toward a mediating concept. Indeed, mediation will often be the point of the lesson.

Take the temperature continuum, for example. Typically we learn first the concepts of "hot" and "cold." "Hot" means hotter than my body's temperature and "cold" means colder than my body's temperature. We then mediate, or coalesce, those concepts, generating or learning the appropriate application of the concept "warm." So in teaching we need not stay with our original binary concepts but can, where appropriate, seek their mediation or coalescence. This process can be extended considerably. For example, in conceptually grasping the temperature continuum, we can next mediate between "warm" and "cold" and grasp the concept "cool," and between "cool" and "warm" and get "lukewarm," and so forth.

Consider for a moment what happens when you seek mediation between concepts like "life" and "death" or "nature" and "culture." These are concepts that have no real mediation; they are discrete. But as children we have found this binary discrimination and mediation procedure very useful for expanding our conceptual grasp over a whole range of phenomenal matters—temperature, size, speed, plants, animals, and so forth. What do you get when you apply this successful procedure to "life" and "death"? Well, you get things such as ghosts. That is, ghosts are both alive and dead in the same way that warm is both hot and cold. If you mediate between "nature" and "culture," you get creatures like Peter Rabbit; Peter is a rabbit but he also talks, wears a jacket, and drinks chamomile tea. That is, the stuff of the fantasy stories of children is composed of attempted mediations between discrete conceptual categories. This observation is intended to suggest that the procedure that is identified above is not something casual or insignificant, but seems fundamental to our early thinking.

Inference 4: We can expand understanding by seeking mediation between the abstract, affective binary concepts we use to provide access to content.

Let me try to draw these inferences in the direction of a tool-set that can be used in planning teaching. It tries to draw on the above inferences from children's imaginative engagement by stories in the way the currently dominant objectives models drew on inferences from the efficiency of the assembly line. (In building a car, for instance, one first designed the objective in great detail, then one organized the materials needed, then these were put together using appropriate methods, and one evaluated at the end of the assembly line to see that the car worked properly. This led to the familiar objectives/content/methods/evaluation schemes.) Here is a planning tool that incorporates the above inferences. (For examples of applying a framework such as this one to topics in mathematics, science, social studies, and language arts, see Egan, 1986, 1988.)

1. Affective engagement. Identify what is the source of potential affective engagement in any given topic. What is there about it that a child could find emotionally engaging?
2. Binary concepts. What are the most powerful abstract, affective binary concepts that can be identified to express and articulate the content?
3. Story structure. What content from the topic best embodies the binary concepts? For access to the content, the most dramatic embodiment of the concepts should be chosen, then the rest will articulate the topic into a developing story form.
4. Conclusion. What is the best way of resolving the dramatic conflict or tension created by the binary concepts? What degree of mediation between those concepts is it appropriate to seek?
5. Evaluation. What allows us to see whether the topic has been learned and understood?

What we have here is an attempt to develop some tools or techniques for teaching derived from observations about children's imaginative engagements. Let us be clear about what we have here. This framework rests on nothing other than some fairly general observations and what may be tendentious inferences from them. The value of the resulting planning tool must be determined by experience, not by the above kind of inferences. The inferences are informal at best, but they serve a heuristic purpose in moving in the direction of educational practice.

IMAGINATIVE ENGAGEMENTS OF OLDER CHILDREN

When we tell a typical 5-year-old the story of Cinderella we do not expect to be asked where the Fairy Godmother lives when she isn't present or what means of locomotion she uses. Such fantastic features are typically accepted without question. If we tell a typical 10-year-old the story of Superman, we anticipate all kinds of questions by explaining his great powers with an account of his birth on the planet Krypton, his journey through space to Earth, the different molecular structure of our sun, and so forth, and so forth. We feel obliged to provide what philosophers call an etiology, a causal account of a possible world in which the fantastic elements of the story are given a kind of plausibility, however flimsy.

Put in its most general terms, what we see entering children's stories after about age 7 or 8 is what we might call a reality principle. And indeed we may see the development of a particular, distinctive imaginative engagement with reality becoming increasingly urgent during the period after about age 7 or 8. We may see one of its more prominent features in students' engagement in the more extreme and exotic aspects of the world and of human experience. Consider having two lessons prepared, either one of which you could take in to a seventh-grade class you have been asked to take for a sick colleague. You want to engage their interest for this final 50 minutes on a Friday afternoon—so do you take in "The structure of your neighborhood" or "Torture instruments through the ages"? (This does not reflect a curriculum recommendation!—just a point about students' engagements.)

What we recognize in this example is students' easy engagement by the extreme or exotic, by things distant from their everyday experience. Consider what provides the most engaging kind of reading or television show for students in these years. Reading *The Guinness Book of Records* or watching bizarre feats and near-incredible achievements exemplify something vitally engaging to such students. What is it about such activities, which we observe so commonly, that so interests students? Well, it seems rather straightforward—these things all serve to inform students about the limits of reality and of human experience. Students clearly are eager to learn who were the biggest and smallest people who ever lived, who was the hairiest, the fastest talker, the most daring tightrope walker, and on and on. Similarly they are avid to know about extreme features of the natural world—the oldest and the tallest tree, the biggest animal, the smallest, the hottest and coldest places on earth, and on and on.

Inference 1: Students' imaginations are most readily engaged with knowledge about the extremes of human experience and of the natural world.

We tend to have elevated to an unassailable principle of teaching that content should be made "relevant" to students. And, again, this truism is most commonly interpreted to mean that if we want students to be engaged by something and to find it meaningful, we should connect it with the content of their everyday experience. But of what "relevance" to students is knowledge about who is or was the fastest talker? That is, the kind of material we can observe as most easily and intensely engaging students' intellectual interests seems not at all to fit the common interpretation of the "relevance" principle. The problem seems to follow from attending too little to students' imaginations. What is most "relevant" to their imaginative lives seems to have little to do with their everyday experience, except in the sense that it provides an understanding of the context within which their everyday experience becomes meaningful.

We may also observe commonly during the 8- to 15-year-old range an engagement by what I will call "the heroic." I do not mean by this simply male heroes using violence to achieve some supposedly noble aim, though this particular stereotype has been common and continues to be so. The heroic refers to the way students very commonly associate with someone or something that transcends the threats or the routines or the boredom of the everyday world in which the student is immersed. This "association with the transcendent" is observable in the engagement with a film star or pop singer or football player or some heroic person like Mother Teresa or Martin Luther King, and so forth. The association is with the human quality exemplified by the heroic figure that transcends the everyday experience of the student.

As I have argued elsewhere (Egan, 1990), everything has some kind of transcendent quality if only we consider it in the appropriate light. One further tool or technique for engaging students' imaginations, then, is to bring out whatever transcendent qualities are embodied in the topic to be taught; such qualities as self-sacrifice, power, courage, compassion, persistence, ingenuity, and so forth, can form a basis for our lessons and units. We can make whatever content we wish students to be engaged by "relevant" by enabling them to make a transcendent association with it.

Inference 2: *Students are imaginatively engaged by knowledge that embodies transcendent human qualities with which they can associate.*

Another observation we may routinely make concerns the development of students' imaginative engagement in hobbies or collections during these years. The typical profile of these involves their becoming more systematic at about age 7 or 8, reaching their greatest intensity around age 11 or 12, and fading gradually till they commonly disappear around age 15 or 16. Why do students become such collectors? Why do these hobbies come and go? While providing explanations is not always necessary for us to be able to draw pragmatic inferences, it does seem that a plausible hypothesis might help us along here. The observation above about the interest in the extremes of reality and experience perhaps contains a clue. If indeed we may see this layer of development in terms of exploring the limits of reality, which can guide us toward a proportionate understanding of our experience and everyday environment, the development of hobbies or collections can be seen as another feature of this same exploration of the limits of reality. By discovering everything about something, as we can do within the constraints of our hobby or collection, we gain first the security that reality is not limitless. By exhaustively exploring something, we also get some sense of the scale of reality, or some part of it.

Whatever the explanation for the collecting or hobbies, we can see that commercial interests have been energetic in exploiting implications of this phenomenon. The injunction to "collect the set!" reflects the recognition that students during these years experience an engagement of a kind that seeks to discover the extent of *something* exhaustively. The near universality of this kind of activity suggests that what we are concerned with here is not some casual or peculiar interest. We would be sensible to reflect on how we might engage this drive to discover something exhaustively with topics in science, mathematics, social studies, and so forth.

Inference 3: Provision should be made in teaching any topic to allow students to explore some part of it in exhaustive detail.

We can observe, finally, how readily students respond to stories or anecdotes that highlight individuals' hopes, fears, intentions, or other emotions. All knowledge is human knowledge. In its discovery or invention, in its elaboration or use, it has been involved with human beings and their emotions. This is as true of mathematics and science as it is of social studies and literature. It would seem to follow that if we can introduce the knowledge to students through the emotions of those who invented, discovered, elaborated, or used it, we have another tool for potentially engaging their imaginations with that knowledge. This is far from a novel observation and inference and has often been discussed under the name of "humanizing" the curriculum. The suggestion implied by that term is that our concern with the logical structuring of curriculum content has led us to disembed the knowledge, particularly of mathematics and science, from its human sources. The educational task is to re-embed algebra, geometry, science, and so forth, in the context of the human hopes, fears, intentions, and passions that gave rise to them in the first place.

Inference 4: *Knowledge can be made imaginatively engaging if it is embedded in the human lives, and their emotions, out of which it originally came.*

Let me take these inferences and again construct a framework that might be used in planning lessons or units for students between approximately ages 8 and 15. (For examples of applying a framework such as this one to topics in mathematics, science, social studies, and language arts, see Egan, 1990, 1992.)

1. Identify transcendent qualities. What transcendent human qualities can be seen and felt as central to any given topic?
2. Organizing the content
   * Initial access. What content, distinct from students' everyday experience, best embodies the transcendent qualities most central to the topic? What extreme or limit of reality can this expose within the topic?
   * Humanizing the content. How can the content be shown in terms of human hopes, fears, intentions, or other emotions?
   * Pursuing details. What content best allows students to pursue some aspect of the topic in exhaustive detail?
3. Concluding. How can one best bring the topic to satisfactory closure? How can the students *feel* this satisfaction?
4. Evaluation. How can one know whether the topic has been understood and has engaged and stimulated students' imaginations?

CONCLUSION

This preliminary attempt to move from students' imaginations in the direction of tools to help teaching is avowedly exploratory. But while emphasizing the tentative nature of this kind of activity, it is perhaps worthwhile also to note that it is not merely idle speculation or flimsy theorizing. The observations are of a solid, empirical kind. Indeed the basis from which I have moved is so firmly empirical that I think, in most cases, the observations are quite uncontentious. It would be interesting to do some careful empirical research to discover more about young children's use of binary opposite concepts, but one would hardly do empirical research to discover if children do use them. That they are very common in children's thinking, and that they are abstract, is incontrovertible. Similarly we might indeed conduct empirical research to discover more about older students' engagement by the limits of human experience and the natural world, but we hardly need such research to tell us that such engagements are very common in students' intellectual lives. The observations about their existence are indisputable.

Contention might arise when we move from the observations to the inferences. Yet even here, and even though some of them clash significantly with deep-rooted principles current in teaching, it is hard to see on what grounds they can be easily dismissed. That young children routinely use powerful abstract concepts and deal with content that is far removed from their everyday experience, seems again uncontentious. It would seem, then, that it is only sensible in teaching to take advantage of these features that play so powerful a part in children's imaginative activities. Similarly if we note that older children find it easier to engage imaginatively certain kinds of knowledge if they have access to it through human emotions or by making associations with transcendent human qualities, we would be shortsighted to teach about, say, Pythagoras' theorum while ignoring Pythagoras and why he thought the theorum so important.

I hope I am not alone in finding the above steps from observation to inference to teaching tools worthwhile, worth further exploration and research. It might be noted that the materials used in this research activity are those most readily available to the classroom teacher. Observation of students, inference, and the construction of practically useful tools require no complex research procedures and sophisticated statistical treatments. Teachers as researchers in their own classrooms can adapt this straightforward procedure to their own practical purposes. They could even test some of the tools suggested above, refine or elaborate them, discard some and develop others, and so forth.

Perhaps when we see future reports on "teaching effectiveness" or attend workshops on "effective teaching," we will wonder aloud about why the imagination has been ignored. It seems clear, even if the above observations and inferences are somehow faulty, that attending to students' imagination leads us to principles and tools for teaching that are different from those we are encouraged to use if we focus more or less exclusively on students' logico-mathematical capacities. It can help us redefine classroom practice, not according to efficiency in teaching, but according to imaginative engagement in student learning.

REFERENCES

Applebee, A. N. (1978). *The child's concept of story.* Chicago: University of Chicago Press.

Bettelheim, B. (1976). *The uses of enchantment.* New York: Knopf.

Callahan, R. (1962). *Education and the cult of efficiency.* Chicago: University of Chicago Press.

Egan, K. (1986). *Teaching as story telling.* London, Ontario: Althouse Press (Chicago: University of Chicago Press, 1988; London: Routledge, 1988).

Egan, K. (1988). *Primary understanding: Education in early childhood.* New York and London: Routledge.

Egan, K. (1990). *Romantic understanding: The development of rationality and imagination, ages 8–15.* New York and London: Routledge.

Egan, K. (1992). *Imagination in teaching and learning: The middle school years.* Chicago: University of Chicago Press (London: Routledge; London, Ontario: Althouse Press).

O'Neil, P. G. (1988). Teaching effectiveness: A review of the research. *Canadian Journal of Education, 13*(1), 162–185.

Paley, V. G. (1981). *Wally's stories.* Cambridge, MA: Harvard University Press.

Paley, V. G. (1984). *Boys and girls: Superheroes in the doll corner.* Chicago: University of Chicago Press.

Paley, V. G. (1990). *The boy who would be a helicopter.* Cambridge, MA: Harvard University Press.

Porter, A. C., & Brophy, J. (1988). Synthesis of research on good teaching. *Educational Leadership, 45,* 74–85.

The Authenticity for Struggle

JONATHAN NEUFELD
PETER P. GRIMMETT

The challenge in compiling this edited collection was to explore what we could identify as patterns of theoretical coherence in an emerging field of study, which, we have argued, is comparatively young in its own development. We attempted to accomplish this by selecting representative pieces by 11 authors, all of whom have established reputations as leading scholars in the field of teacher development. We were surprised to conclude at the end of our project that, while the field itself is relatively young, the concepts and theoretical foundations on which it draws are very mature indeed.

We chose to plan our exploration with the assistance of three categories: settings, conditions, and criteria of teacher development. We did this on the assumption that theoretical and practical settings function within varied layers of macro-level social and economic conditions that influence, but are not always conducive to, the derivation of criteria for teacher development. We believe that these macro-level conditions form part of a complex but taken-for-granted reality for most of us, for there is a mode of vital experience—experience of space and time, of the self and others, of life's possibilities and perils—that is shared in our culture. In chorus with many others, we call this mode of experience "modernity." To be modern is to find ourselves in an environment that promises growth, power, joy, and adventure—and that, at the same time, threatens to destroy everything we are, everything we know, and everything we have. Our contemporary culture seems at times to be hurled into a maelstrom of perpetual renewal and disintegration, of agreement and contradiction, of serenity and anxiety.

The tension of living the modern experience emerges from negotiating between these dualities of contemporary life, and the search for a modern identity can be characterized as struggling with seemingly endless contradictions. While, on the one hand, we may inwardly believe that we have the potential for limitless growth and knowledge, it is the very consequences and inherent contradictions of this belief that threaten to destroy what we become and know. But this struggle toward a modern identity, when understood as a movement toward the ultimate ideal of authentic individualism (see Taylor, 1989, 1991), promises hopeful possibilities of growth and adventure.

Taylor (1989, 1991) responds to three perennial criticisms, which some contemporary social theorists—in particular, Lasch (1979) and Bloom (1987)—have leveled concerning the destructive and disintegrative aspects of modernity. He names these concerns as: (1) an anomic individualism manifested in a "loss of meaning" when interacting with others in our culture; (2) the predominance of instrumental reason, as an "eclipse of ends," that fosters the formation of instrumental, temporary relationships with others; and (3) the increasing restriction of choices in our society, which has led to a perceived loss of freedom in conducting our daily affairs. It is possible to argue that the authors in this edited collection are responding to a perceived anomic individualism manifested in a "loss of meaning" in the teacher culture combined with an increasing restriction of choices in that occupational culture. These developments, in consequence, have led to a perceived loss of teachers' freedom when conducting their daily affairs. It might also be argued that teacher development researchers, in response to these trends, are engaged in a theoretical project of reviving a sense of meaning in the experience of teaching; of building supportive relationships and rebuilding opportunities of choice for teachers; and of restoring a sense of freedom for teachers in schools, where it is observed that freedom is eroding. In this conclusion, we shall draw on Taylor's analysis of the origins of the European philosophical ideal of authentic individualism and argue that many of the concepts and theoretical foundations of the emerging field of teacher development are consistent with a philosophical lineage dating back possibly as far as Augustine. We shall refer to the authors located in our edited selection specifically and cite parallel sources in the broader field more generally.

THE MODERN CONCEPT OF IDENTITY

The modern concept of identity as formed within a referential community evolved out of a premodern concept of social order based on rank within social strata. In premodern European society, the concept and design of "community" was divinely ordered and enduring. Individuality was God-given and one was assigned a station within the social order at birth only to remain there throughout one's ensuing biography. Given the importance placed on hierarchy in premodern European society, deference and respect were accorded to individuals in view of their relative social rank and moral questions were determined with reference to codified laws, which were divinely decreed by an omnipotent force. The measure of respect that everyone claimed—proportional to their rank in the hierarchy—was based on a sense of honor or on one's hierarchical relation to the omnipotent figure. The greatest personal curse to be experienced in the community was shame; hence, the popularity of publicly witnessed punishment for crimes committed against the community or dishonorable banishment from the community itself.

During our modern period the social conception of order by rank has been transformed into a conception of order based on the dignity of the individual in which democratic and egalitarian claims are declared and defended. Modern individuals conceive of themselves as autonomous and self-directed and are taught to uphold standards of self-evident, inherent rights. We have come to believe that our identity may be inherently discovered and developed by "looking inward," and we have accepted a faith in an almost limitless potential for growth through reflection on ordinary experience (Taylor, 1989). The greatest personal curse one can experience in our modern society is not public shame, but instilled private guilt (see Hargreaves & Tucker, 1991), and punishment is meted out through incarceration in institutions that restrict access to the community where authentic individualism may be proclaimed and cultivated.

This ideal of authenticity is partly rooted in the disengaged rationality of Déscartes (Taylor, 1989, 1991) under which autonomous individuals are called on to think responsibly for themselves in their interaction with others. Within this tradition, individuals are conceived of as being endowed with an inner moral sense or an intuitive voice from within. An increasing ability to be in touch with this guiding "inner voice" is something we may gain as we become whole and unified human beings. Rousseau appears to be the archetypal mouthpiece for this idea, since he made reference to the source of our moral sense as a voice of nature within us (Rousseau, 1966/1979). Rousseau was also the first philosopher to use the word *moderniste* to describe a way of being that would characterize our nineteenth- and twentieth-century identity. According to Taylor (1991), however, progress toward an authentic individualism through a connection with an inner source was also heralded by Augustine's neo-Platonic theology; by Kant's concept of moral autonomy; by Locke's notion of political individualism; and by Herder's advocacy of creative originality wherein each person possesses his or her own measure of existence and inner grasp of what it means to be human (Taylor, 1989).

The ideal of authenticity, according to these successive European philosophical interpretations, evolved out of a shift in perspective that moved the center of moral gravity from a place external to the body and in the cosmos to a place conceived as being within the body (Taylor, 1989). From a modern perspective, our authentic, inner qualities of unity and wholeness are not assigned but are designed by us and nurtured through dialogue with others in the community. It is through dialogue that we attain a sense of personal identity and subsequently come to comprehend our human agency; and it is through recognition by "significant others" in the community with whom we interact that we confirm a personal and collective but unified solidarity as individuals in groups. The dialogic community also establishes recognized standards of moral significance, defines moral questions and issues of value, and fixes parameters within which moral decisions are made.

The modern struggle for authenticity is, in summary, the struggle of growth toward a self-directed, autonomous agency accompanied by an acute knowledge of one's inner moral self. This is, in one way, a solitary quest, for responsible agents must take control of their own struggle; in another way, it is fundamentally communal, for it is accomplished through dialogue within a community that reflects on ordinary experience and negotiates the criteria of authenticity using a common moral language. To possess a modern identity, therefore, is to know objectively where one stands in relation to a metaphorical "field" of self-governing discipline; it is to draw on a "body" of knowledge and to speak and act from those moral spaces with a confidence that is rooted in a conscious, collective understanding.

The thesis of this conclusion about teacher development theory generally and the edited selections specifically is that the struggle of teacher development in a constantly changing educational context is congruent with the modern struggle for an authentic identity as it is understood in our contemporary society. We argue that the image of teacher-as-professional who stands in the field of teacher development is synonymous with the modern philosophical image of the autonomous, self-directed agent. Briefly stated, *to be* professional *and to function* professionally *is to possess* an authentic identity.

TEACHER DEVELOPMENT AS A STRUGGLE
FOR AUTHENTIC IDENTITY

We shall proceed by examining the central theoretical components of Lieberman's and McLaughlin's contributions as a dyad. We shall then examine Hargreaves's chapter separately, with the intention of adding some clarification to the notion of "voice" as a concept in teacher development theory. The contributions by Woods, Chard, and Siskin will be treated as a group. They provide diverse accounts of settings in which conditions have not proven to be conducive to the derivation of criteria for the forms of teacher development theorized by Lieberman, McLaughlin, and Hargreaves. Ceroni and Garman's chapter about empowerment is somewhat unique in this section, as it provides a partial response to the previous six authors in the book. Ceroni and Garman show us the difficulty of implementing a program that is supposed to "empower" teachers when prevailing conditions of the educational setting are not conducive for teachers to *feel* empowered in the first place. Their statement then enters into the third section of the book, which responds to the second section and incorporates the theoretical perspectives illuminated by Lieberman, McLaughlin, and Hargreaves.

MacKinnon and Grunau provide a detailed account of a highly successful but experimental teacher education program in which preservice teachers were prepared for their practical setting under conditions that allowed them to construct authentic criteria of teacher development through discourse and mutual interaction. Central to this process was a conscious shift away from education along individualistic lines toward one which pivoted on a view of "self" arising from social interaction and connection within a community of diverse but sharing individuals. Egan's discussion of imagination in teaching appears, at first glance, to be somewhat unusual, considering the focus of the other chapters. A second glance, however, helps us see that many unexpected possibilities arise if we take seriously the assumption that all of us never stop being "learners," engaged in a journey toward an authentic identity.

Emerging Theoretical Patterns

To begin, we shall presuppose that there is a measure of respect in our society that all of us—teachers, most certainly—have claim to, and that this measure sits as the foundation of our social order. We characterize this measure as *human dignity*. We might expect to discover emancipatory projects that seek to instill this fundamental sense of human dignity when conditions do not nurture it in modern social settings. Numerous examples of emancipatory projects currently exist in the modern world, a world that seems at times to be saturated with situations of oppression and inequality. Recent representations of teachers adopt emancipatory perspectives by conceptualizing them as "perpetual learners" (Fullan & Hargreaves, 1991) who should be central figures in their own development (Lieberman

& Miller, 1991) and who should be treated as "total persons" (Fullan & Hargreaves, 1992) possessing a unity and wholeness.

In this collection, Lieberman confers the label of "learners" on teachers who think deeply and who accordingly should be viewed as "scholars" and "visionaries," deserving the right of equal participation in their own development. Lieberman proclaims that teachers have a "leadership destiny," and she is supported by McLaughlin, who declares that teachers should not be infantalized or treated as automotons but treated fairly, with all that the dignified social status of "professional" entails. The measure of dignity they deserve merits a collective autonomy from forms of professional control that mandate or dictate the ways in which teachers would educate students under their care. It also merits a personal autonomy, with the assumption that teachers exercise discretion and are self-directed, having the right to decide the specific direction of their own professional development.

It is assumed in teacher development theory that growth toward a developed professional state (which we name as an autonomous, self-directed agency) can take place through reflection on the ordinary, day-to-day experience of instructing students in classrooms. This assumption elevates the activity of instruction from the level of mundane drudgery to one that has the potential to educate practitioners, thereby changing and improving their practice. For Lieberman, this assumption is visible in her reference to teachers as "reflective practitioners," a term popularized by Schön (1983, 1987, 1988) that has become common currency in teacher development theory (see Clift, Houston, & Pugach, 1990; Grimmett & Erickson, 1988; Grimmett, MacKinnon, Erickson, & Riecken, 1990). The reflective practitioner, as an autonomous self-directed thinker, is described as continually inquiring into the practice of instruction. Self-examination through the practical medium of instruction is more vividly articulated by McLaughlin, who writes of self-development as arising from typical teachers' classrooms and day-to-day responsibilities. This development is ongoing, embedded in current practice and rooted in dailiness. Professionally relevant pedagogical knowledge is constructed, therefore, by the self-directed teacher objectively examining "self-as-practitioner," engaged in the everydayness of instruction in the classroom. We find similar assumptions in recent North American studies by Hargreaves and Fullan (1991) and Lieberman and Miller (1991), but the most thorough elaborations of the concept of the teacher's "self" are from the United Kingdom (Nias, 1989) and Switzerland (Huberman,1993).[1]

In the modern tradition, our "self" has been conceived as being inside our bodies (Taylor, 1989). The assumption that teachers have a self that can be developed is consistent with the modern conception of the individual who has the capacity to "go inside" and construct an autonomous notion of agency and who then ventures into the world to construct relevant knowledge through reflection on ordinary experience. In 1991, Fullan and Hargreaves recommended that teachers attend to the sound of their "inner voices." This concept of the inner self is largely absent in the chapters contained in this collection. While Lieberman does refer to "habits of mind," she does not directly refer to any inner source to which teachers appeal when reflecting on their experience. McLaughlin speaks of empowerment in a "fundamental sense," which might allude to the possession of an inner self having the capacity to be awakened and empowered. This absence may be less curious when we observe that great attention is paid to dignity, self-directed autonomy, continuous growth, and reflection on ordinary experience, all in combination with what seems, so far, to be an intellectual quest for understanding in teacher development. We would suggest that the intellectual merely serves to rationalize another realm of teachers' development for us and that the developing teacher is not so much inclined to refine habits of the mind as to move in directions that explore ways of being having to do with habits of the heart.[2] This suggestion is partly based on the polyphony of references in the texts that discuss beliefs arising from attaining identity through community and the preoccupation with values and norms of sharing and collegiality (see this also in Fullan & Hargreaves, 1991, 1992; Grimmett & Crehan, 1992; Hargreaves & Fullan, 1991; Lieberman & Miller, 1991; Little & McLaughlin, 1993). Beliefs, values, and norms may require rational articulation for their communication and implementation, but they are often inspired by nonrational sources such as feelings (Hargreaves & Tucker, 1991) or, as Hargreaves suggests in Chapter 3, by concepts as complex and elusive as truth or beauty.

Inspired by the work of Little (1986) and of Rosenholtz (1989), Lieberman writes that teachers socially construct their belief structure and that they rethink values and practice in concert with others. Means of social construction seem to have adopted central importance in teacher development theory, but the recurrent argument that the criteria for teachers' development are understood within ideological and valuative realms may represent a gradual shift in perspective away from a conception of growth and development as merely social or largely cognitive. As Lieberman indicates, growth in teacher development is related to (socially constructed belief-) structures, which are inspired by norms of teachers' work. The composition and form of these structures are prelegitimated through a communal dialogue (as distinct from being provided by an authority external to the community) and would be thought of (socially constructed) and thought about (inquired into) in a collaborative cultural setting.

Following a presumption that all human beings deserve to be treated with dignity trails the modern assumption that each human being has the capacity to be in control of his or her own individual development as a self-directed agent. Our conception of agency as one criterion of teachers' continuous educational development may be traced to a period when it was not assumed that teachers held the potential to direct their own professional destinies. The archetypal impotence of the teacher in the field may have been partly inspired by Waller's (1932) somewhat pessimistic book, succeeded in scope by Lortie's (1975) landmark sociological study, which introduced the three banes of "individualism, presentism, and conservatism" into the teacher's inherent makeup, characteristics that seem persistently to haunt our impression of the archetypal teacher (Little, 1990). During the 10 years leading up to Lortie's work, teachers were generally interpreted as sometimes shadowy—and even as villainous—figures on the educational landscape who impersonally processed students through the school system (Goodson, 1991a). During the late 1970s the archetype underwent a reformulation in the literature from sinister villain to impotent victim, even a "dupe" of the bureaucratic "iron cage" in which they worked (Goodson, 1991b). As is evident in this collection, the archetypal teacher of teacher development theory is portrayed as a complex, powerful figure: an activist-agent making contact with and constructing his or her own professional biography while interacting with a sometimes hostile social system. We are witness to a story of elevated self-concept in the teacher development literature. But it is interesting to note that the emancipation of teachers as proclaimed in teacher development theory is rarely advocated by means of a teacher revolution that would place the control of schooling in teachers' hands—it is not a radically *restructured* perspective, in the sense that restructuring power relationships alone might guarantee the formation of communities of learners. Rather, it is better understood as radically *destructured* in its perspective, recommending the elimination of encumbering structures as they now stand and transforming only those whose presence would enable the potential for development toward an authentic identity. The urgency of restructuring power relationships is clearly in evidence, but it is commonly advanced along with and in support of higher priorities, which include processes of self-actualization through personal and collective educational development. It is not the mission of the archetypal teachers-as-agents to gain control of the school system; it is their mission to demand settings and conditions that permit their continuous educational development. It is this emancipatory tone of professional development that exerts overt and subtle influence on the changing role and function of educational administration.

Pedagogical practice also undergoes successive alterations when scanned alongside this history of elevated self-concept. Where practice may once have been debased as a mundane chore or an oppressive conspiracy, it is now elevated to the level of being a self-actualizing medium. Significant characteristics are adopted with this elevated status. Teachers are described as reflecting on their experiences to improve themselves and their practice. This elevated status also confers normative dimensions on practice (i.e., an action of practice may be recognized and judged by the community as being "good"); practice has valuative overtones (i.e., it may conform to negotiated criteria of authenticity); and assumptions about practice are ideologically consistent with collectively established ways of proceeding (i.e., teachers have confidence that their action is rooted in a collective understanding). These dimensions, overtones, and assumptions elevate the specific practice of curriculum planning to levels surpassing skills development and training. In conditions where teachers feel empowered with an authentic agency, curriculum planning has the potential to adopt moral dimensions and can act as a vehicle through which teachers might be able to communicate with students in more connected and meaningful ways.

McLaughlin picks up on the ideas of Lieberman and takes them several steps further. These steps take advantage of extensive research on the context of secondary schools in Michigan and California. She begins by telling us that teachers learn from challenging one another and thereby construct principles (beliefs) together. She employs some similar terms to forward her argument, such as shared challenges and collective responsibility, but supplies us with some clear articulations that align the emerging theory of teacher development with the philosophical ideal of authenticity. This is accomplished through her discussion of three significant foundational concepts: professional identity, discourse communities, and standards and expectations (criteria of authenticity). In close proximity with Lieberman, McLaughlin's study demonstrates strongly that teachers' professional development "of the most meaningful sort" takes place in the context of learning communities and that enabling professional growth is about enabling professional community. Professional identity, in her view, is attained through a normative attachment to a community that shares a common discourse. Situated in that moral field or body of knowledge, the autonomous teacher-as-agent gains the freedom to speak with confidence, since what is being said has been theoretically tested and is grounded in a field of discourse.

McLaughlin names communities of growth and identity as "discourse communities," indicating that growth toward a developed authenticity—an identity—takes place not only through reflection on ordinary experience but through articulation of the knowledge that is attained through that reflection. As we have mentioned, possessing a professional identity in a community is articulated by a shared moral language. It is essential, therefore, that communities of growth toward authentic identity share a common moral discourse of action and speech, and she cites examples of this from her study.

As to moral criteria of authenticity, McLaughlin specifies that teachers in communities of growth establish recognized standards and expectations of teacher development. This is expressed in several instances by the following phrases: norms of sharing bring standards and expectations; successful leadership maintains, enforces, and reinforces norms and beliefs in practice; the district-level community establishes norms, rules, codes of conduct in a culture; teachers are "socialized" into norms, practices, expectations; and cultural authority communicates, reinforces, maintains norms. Teachers have, then, a double challenge on the road to their development: first, to construct a sense of self-as-practitioner based on a sense of identity gained through collegial interaction in community and, second, to construct pedagogical knowledge by reflecting on their experience as practitioners.

To summarize thus far, we might characterize teacher development as a hopeful and optimistic theoretical framework of elevated dignity. As such, it is a modern emancipatory project that justifies and defends the elevation of teachers to "professional" status; that defines the professional being as an autonomous, self-directed agent who has limitless potential for growth and power; and that perceives this growth as attained through interaction within a community that reflects on ordinary experience to improve self and practice. Teachers' ordinary experience is the instruction and initiation of youth and, given the importance of this activity in our society, we could say that teachers' discourse, as a medium toward self-improvement and improvement of practice, might seem to carry along with it certainly moral and possibly spiritual dimensions. We argue that the components of this professional definition are consistent with the modern ideal of the developing "authentic individual" that has evolved in our culture through the successive European philosophies of Augustine, Déscartes, Kant, Rousseau, Locke, and Herder, among many others. Our argument is bolstered by the preoccupation with reflection on ordinary practice as a medium of individual and collective growth in teacher development theory; by the presence of the notion of teachers' "inner selves"; by the importance placed on beliefs, values, and norms of the community; by the archetypal image of teachers as autonomous, self-directed agents; and by a well-articulated conception of the professional community as a space of common discourse that establishes criteria for an authentic professional identity.

Readers should take cautious note, however, that Lieberman and

McLaughlin are not necessarily depicting the prevalent criteria under which teachers' work. They are engaged in a project of emancipation, taking for granted that the present settings and conditions of teachers' work are somewhat derelict. It is assumed theoretically that teachers are not being treated with dignity as professionals in most cases and that this is one of the main reasons that schools are not growth-enhancing places for them or for their students. It is also implied by extension that the emancipation of teachers will transfer into the construction of growth-enhancing environments for students (Barth, 1990). So, as teacher development theorists, we might remember that we have good reason to pause and reflect on our own practice. We have begun to refine a field of study and a body of knowledge that consistently draws from specific ideals of an Enlightenment philosophical tradition and have coherently applied these ideals to a conceptualization of teachers' professional development in schools. In a word, we are looking toward the refined *modernization* of experienced teachers' educational development.

While pausing to reflect, we can mourn the reality that many (if not most) teachers in North America and throughout the world do not enjoy the opportunity to work in settings in which conditions allow them to imagine many forms of professional development. Some specific examples of such settings and conditions in the United Kingdom and the United States are presented in this book. Our calling as teacher educators would then seem to include a commitment not only to advertise the existence of settings in which we observe conditions that encourage the pursuit of criteria of professionalism (as Lieberman and McLaughlin are doing) but, more urgently, to advocate the alteration of present conditions such that teachers are enabled to pursue a self-actualized authenticity; in short, to have the freedom and choice to derive meaning from professional relationships.

Hargreaves's contribution extends the ideas of Lieberman and McLaughlin. His chapter focuses on macro-level conditions and, inspired by an opposition to the derelict characteristics of bureaucratic hierarchy that keep teachers in their "iron cage," basically argues for professional empowerment and agency. Hargreaves explains how the erosion of macro-level social and economic boundaries produces vacuums for smaller marginalized groups to reconstruct meaningful identities of enhanced choice and freedom in micro-level settings.

Hargreaves refines the conceptual notion of "voice" in his particular discussion. The entire notion of "voice" was originally conceptualized as the articulation of moral criteria for development. The metaphor originates in Gilligan's (1982, 1989) studies of women's moral decision making, which successfully challenged Kohlberg's traditional stage theory of moral development. "Voice" is a metonymous term for a complex assembly of verbal, physical, and social communications that arise from a perception of authentic identity in individuals and groups. As Hargreaves helps us to understand in the context of the book, the teacher's voice is the linguistic and social expression of knowledge that is grounded in a moral field or a body of knowledge. This knowledge is orientational in its perspective, as it imposes strong qualitative evaluations on practice that are associated with judgments on how best to proceed. The initiative of sponsoring the teacher's voice is part of a modern tradition of dignifying teachers-as-professionals and of expanding our concept of professionalism to include them. Sponsorship assumes the presence in educational settings of some hostility to teachers' linguistic or social expressions of relevant pedagogical knowledge. As theorists of teacher development, two emancipatory strategies present themselves in this potentially hostile situation. We may choose to defend and sponsor the articulations that arise from teachers' collective interactions (i.e., their criteria for development) in an effort to legitimate them or to integrate them into the ideology of a macrosocial order, which we may assume remains intact. One goal of our defense and sponsorship would be, one hopes, the recognition of teachers' evaluations of practice and criteria of authentic development by the representatives of that order. Alternatively, we may take for granted that that macrosocial and economic order, along with its implicit supporting ideological narratives, is simply on a course of unalterable decline. Our strategy then changes. We may then go about our work refining and facilitating teachers' articulations without a great deal of concern for whether or not the authority of the macrosocial order will recognize, legitimate, or integrate them. Hargreaves seems to embark from the latter position and, whether or not we choose to agree with him, our choice in the matter is dependent on how we see ourselves as being related to the macrosocial and economic order to which we are all connected. In either case, we ally ourselves with the advocacy of articulations of knowledge that are not structurally codified but that are derived through teamwork and cooperation (menus not mandates); through a trust in processes, not in persons; and through a faith in the indeterminate dynamics of lively culture, not only in the supposed predictable control of a centralized structure. "Voice" is the sound of an authentic identity—the articulation of an autonomous, self-directed moral agency in relation to the solidarity of a collective.

A Context of Inauthenticity

Hargreaves's ideas foreshadow the discussions of MacKinnon and Grunau and of Egan. But before looking at how the latter chapters attempt to establish a sense of authenticity, we shall pause to reflect on why the emancipatory theory of teacher development is becoming relevant at this time. We do this by examining the contributions of Woods, Chard, and Siskin, who provide us with vivid descriptions of settings and conditions in which the derivation of criteria for teacher development is hindered and even subverted. They help us understand how complex the construction of settings and conditions can be for the educational development of practicing teachers.

Woods opens this section with an examination of the relationship between manifest conditions for teacher development and the larger social context in which the enterprise takes place. He insists that teacher development must be considered within a framework of economic and political trends and events that, in large part, determine what is possible, what is considered desirable, and that essentially define how it will occur. He describes three models of teaching that have come about in England and Wales as a result of the macropolitical context. Two of these models have seriously constrained teacher development to the extent that the optimistic tones of the first section about restructured roles and responsibilities in professional discourse communities of positive risk and continuous improvement are largely rendered unworkable. The third model is less pessimistic but also less widespread than the other two. Woods uses these three models to characterize three scenarios of conditions for teacher development. Creative teaching occurs when the constraints from the macropolitical context are few and teachers are given many opportunities to teach. When constraints force teachers to modify their teaching according to externally derived instructional practices, however, teacher development consists largely of strategically refining coping skills. When the constraints on teachers are overwhelming and restrict opportunities to teach to a minimum, teachers experience regression and stress. The economic and political trends and events over the last few years in Britain have rendered the latter two scenarios more prevalent than the first. Woods therefore documents how the conditions for teacher development are inextricably linked with the events and policies of the larger social, political, and economic context. Although he describes pockets of teacher subversion leading to possible optimism about a rebounding professionalism, the picture is one of raw political power overwhelming professional teachers and, in the process, creating a sense of cataclysmic dependence in the ranks of practitioners.

Chard continues Woods's discussion with a specific focus on the implementation of the National Curriculum in England and Wales during the political regime of Margaret Thatcher's Conservative government. Her study explains how interventions in the ordinary experience of teachers in classrooms by a centralized government have the potential to impede teachers' educational development and lower their performance. As found in Hargreaves, there is the assumption that an ideological boundary separates the internal space of the micropolitical school and its teachers and the external field of the macropolitical order and its representatives. Citing Pollard (1990), Chard cautions that externally imposed interventions in the setting of the ordinary experience of the teacher will unavoidably be interpreted through criteria, aims, and values that are held at that "point of delivery." The school may be one vortex of the macropolitical order but macro-level standards, aims, and goals instituted by the order's representatives may rarely be congruent with the criteria for educational development that arise from communities of professional teachers. In most cases it would seem that direct interventions from the macrolevel actually subvert teachers' criteria of authenticity and may work in directions that seem to entrench them in debilitating work settings. Chard concludes by advising that one way of fortifying conditions of growth is to foster "self-confidence" and "a sense of perspective" in teachers to express their autonomy and their responsibility. Along with the authors in this book, we have argued that self-confidence, autonomy, and responsibility are all criteria of authentic teacher development that arise at "points of delivery" when specific conditions are present for their realization in educational settings. One burning dilemma that faces us here would seem to be whether a nation's education goals can possibly be congruent with conditions that nurture aspirations of authentic development in teachers (or in students). A nation's goals may address urgent social and economic questions and may mobilize resources toward social order and greater productivity. By contrast, the complex conditions for attaining an authentic professional identity in a work setting seem to address moral questions and would seem to seek resources for self-development, personal exploration, and supportive relationships.

Siskin's contribution is a very interesting companion to Chard's chapter, since she directs her focus directly inside the latter's "point of delivery" during a period of intense stress. She begins with the oblique question of whether the school could be called a professional community at all—one in which increased site-level autonomy could and should be granted and in which shared goals, norms, and objectives can and will be established. This challenge is highly significant in the context of this book since it is sometimes assumed, as Siskin points out, that schools can become settings in which conditions favorable to growth do lead to criteria of authentic development. Some of her conclusions corroborate Chard's, in that macro-level social and economic conditions do influence, and are not always conducive to, the derivation of criteria for teacher development; but she also shows how the school as a setting for community is not necessarily a discrete, unitary body of change.

Siskin observes that teachers retreat to the most basic structural mechanisms under conditions of organizational stress. In this case, stress was exerted by the withdrawal of financial resources that initially supported conditions for innovation toward a "sense of community." The most basic, traditional structural mechanisms identified by Siskin are subject-based departments, which seem highly resilient in the face of organizational stress. We see subject-based departments as traditional in two senses. First, they have long histories as convenient and discrete organizers of knowledge and are very familiar as a result. Second, they are normatively traditional in that the criteria of evaluation they promote are not established through dialogue in a community but originate in ready-made, narrowly defined subject-oriented fields and bodies of knowledge to which teachers can align their practice and from which they can conveniently speak and act.

Narrowly defined subject-based disciplines originate outside local communities of teachers and may allow for the renunciation of a communally based professional responsibility. This renunciation accompanies a reluctance to consider self as an autonomous agent, since the social order of the school is not based on a professional dignity but on conformity to rules that originate outside the community. As more narrowly defined criteria accumulate in importance, teachers may reach a point in their development at which they may be ignorant or forgetful of what constitute conditions or settings of growth toward an authentic professional identity. In some settings and under some conditions, they may choose to embark on quests of identity that are dysfunctional or even harmful to their own or to their students' educational development. Siskin identifies this encumbering, pathological condition as metaphorical "weight," and when weight is a burden it becomes difficult to move one's self. Siskin shows how the teachers of Rancho were reluctant to enter into relationships of collegiality because there was no "payoff" in financial terms, but less tangibly, there was no payoff in "feeling" the experience of authentic identity. "Their hearts were not in their work," she observes, meaning that there was no healthy mix between an inner moral energy and ordinary experience. When ordinary experience is perceived as pain, why reflect on it?

Chard and Siskin show that policy decisions that ignore the complex moral undercurrent of educational settings and the conditions that influence criteria of authenticity have the ability to destroy the will of teachers to view themselves as developing professionals. Vivid terms used by Siskin describing the science teachers as an "endangered swarm" could be taken literally as she describes their reaction to attacks by an externally perceived enemy on their setting, which once had fostered the derivation of criteria for professional identity. We witness a mutation under stressful conditions in the nature of the teachers' interaction from what might be characterized as a life-sustaining creative community to one resembling a marauding battle unit that, out of necessity rather than out of freedom and choice, establishes characteristic criteria of survivalist language and behavior. Contrast this to the mathematics department, which adopted a form of community resembling a conquered people who lament in waiting for a time when previous conditions of choice and freedom will return to their setting. It is worth probing into why a macro-level social or economic structure could institute policies that would seem to subvert conditions in educational settings such that potential criteria for development toward authenticity are replaced by survivalist criteria or practice that is rooted in despair and nurtured only by a glimmer of hope. We can observe that there do exist organizational relationships that do not sustain life-giving communities of learners but have the force to determine standards of derelict development in teachers. Hence, we advocate the design and implementation of educational policy that would facilitate settings favorable to the establishment of criteria that would liberate forms of growth and authentic professional identity in teachers. Sadly, it would almost seem from our discussion thus far that the theoretical ideal of a community of sharing, based on meaningful moral dialogue in which members grow through reflection on ordinary experience, is an illusive luxury.

The Authenticity of Struggle

If the second section of the book demonstrates that conditions of the larger social context infiltrate and, indeed, largely determine what is possible in teacher development, it also shows that using a "teacher development" strategy instrumentally does not counteract the potency of the prevailing conditions. Ceroni and Garman close the second section with a description of an attempt to empower teachers through restructured roles and responsibilities that did not address in any substantial way the power relations that existed between policy makers and teachers. Teachers were given the opportunity to become instructional leaders, but in a manner in which they were controlled by the hierarchy and the particular model of teaching that was imposed. Teacher leadership had not emerged from among the ranks of the professionals; rather, it had been organizationally contrived. Because the initiative was deeply embedded within a political and economic context that militated against a redefinition of learning for teachers and students, it was doomed to fail.

Hargreaves's dualities of bureaucracy and professionalism return for evaluation when reviewing Ceroni and Garman's study of the paradox of hierarchy and empowerment. We are reminded that a bureaucratic hierarchy can confer authority on superordinates over subordinates but that empowerment cannot be conferred. In teacher development theory, to be empowered is to have an identity; it is a perceived knowing where one stands in relation to a field, or body of knowledge, and to speak from those spaces with a confidence rooted in a conscious, collective understanding. Empowerment is felt when one discovers one's self to be in relation with a dialogic community under conditions whereby a "feeling" of power (synonymous with feeling a self-directed agency) is perceived. It arrives by living within a discourse of speaking and acting. Hargreaves introduced this point in his chapter. Ceroni and Garman remind us that no one can empower teachers; we can only designate settings and attempt to organize sufficient conditions whereby people might choose to enter into relationships that empower. They then open the way for MacKinnon and Grunau with these words: "We must recognize the pitfalls of putting people in positions of responsibility with little sensitivity to prevailing conditions and little understanding of what it takes to create genuine collegiality."

MacKinnon and Grunau represent an experimental implementation of the concepts and theoretical perspectives presented by Lieberman, McLaughlin, and Hargreaves; and they respond to the derelict conditions that subvert the derivation of criteria in settings of teacher development described by Woods, Chard, Siskin, and Ceroni and Garman. MacKinnon and Grunau describe how a community of preservice teachers established recognized criteria of authenticity by reflecting on ordinary experience, and how communal sharing allowed for the "seeing" of experience in a new way. Seeing experience in a new way provided clearly articulated spaces toward which teachers were able to imagine moving and growing in their practice. It is movement of this imaginative type, using language and criteria of potential, that we wish to classify as teacher development. According to MacKinnon and Grunau, a "sense" of community is that which is felt when teachers are in a growth environment in which criteria of authenticity are constructed. Similar to McLaughlin, they employ the term "standards of practice," but with this usage they are not referring to "rules of practice" but to agreed-upon images to which one can aspire. They caution that these images are not easily reduced to technical description, nor codified or structured.

MacKinnon and Grunau posit that the typically premodern, traditional master/apprentice relationship, along with individualistic thinking/speaking articulations, is not entirely effective when faced with conditions of rapid curricular change. They also take the view that relevant pedagogical knowledge need not only be articulated or perceived linguistically in rational forms but can equally be shown with the body—connecting their ideas to our earlier suggestions that authentic development is not entirely mindful but inclusively heartful in its source and orientation. Their chapter demonstrates how they employ the language of hope alluded to by Lieberman. It is hopeful because the discourse in which the student teachers live moves toward a potential, but not in directions defined by an identifiable supervisor. The students move in the direction of an image of the "good" teacher, toward which they perceive themselves as moving together. This image exists in discourse, not in form or structure, and it is this difference that allows for spontaneous realignments in teachers' practice under conditions of rapid curricular change. This more flexible educational process is also partially accomplished through a mutual, trusting criticism of one another's practice such that they are able to witness one another enter the role of the imagined "good" teacher, an imagined role that they have constructed based on the context of their immediate experience. Their education thus provides them with opportunities to initiate one another and observe this passage so that their apprenticeship bonds are lateral rather than hierarchically vertical.[3]

Development is conceptualized as movement toward some ultimate state or image of perfection. Conceived metaphorically, the preservice teachers in MacKinnon and Grunau's study look toward a horizon where they see an image of the good, an image they have constructed in discourse. They see their "selves" as moving toward that horizon and that image together. They learn a potential, for they have not arrived in form but experience their education as a passage in the direction of an imagined form. Witnessing entry into the role of the good teacher is the experience of witnessing a brief arrival and return and produces diverse communicative exchanges of what that experience looked like, sounded like, and felt like. Two key theoretical components in the student teachers' initiative entry are the concept of discursive dialogue between the "I" and the "other," along with the theoretical claim that the self is able to attain a unity or wholeness in terms of "an image of their generalized other."[4]

MacKinnon and Grunau transfer these concepts into the claim that self-conscious student teachers need opportunities to develop toward generalized images of mastery that are generated out of social interaction and dialogue. The self-directed student teacher is thus put into a position of invitation into a set of social relations (Hargreaves's menus) that are to a large part determined by the composition of the participants concerned. Accepting mutual invitation and entering into a set of social relations coincides with acceptance of communally established criteria of authentic identity. These criteria are self-governing. They have disciplinary qualities but they assume a perspective of self-direction, not a reliance on the community or on a codified structure of laws.

MacKinnon and Grunau bring us to a further understanding of the concepts introduced by Lieberman and McLaughlin and refined by Hargreaves. We understand that elevating the dignity of teaching children and youth as a valued activity involves something as simple yet as complex as allowing teachers to have full exposure to the ordinary experience of meaningful relationships with one another and with their students. Teachers' "voice" can be seen as articulations that spring from focusing on a valuative image or a "vision" of "the good" (teacher) and that teachers' voices are complex assemblies of verbal, physical, and social communications arising from a group perception of that image or vision. By reflecting on their ordinary experience and by expressing and hearing their own and one anothers' voices, teachers gain a sense of autonomous, self-directed agency. We understand how the moral spaces from which teachers articulate criteria of development can be established through common discourse in an identifiable community. Images, visions, and articulations of discursive knowledge can arise when teachers have opportunities of choice among self-generated menus of "the good" and attraction to these images has great motivational power. MacKinnon and Grunau show what comes about when we put our trust in process and culture, rather than in people and in structure, but they also show that this requires some faith in mystery and some willingness to "pull away" and allow silence or the hum of creation to do its work. Recalling the predicaments put forth by the authors in the second section, trust involves administratively engendering and generously supporting settings and conditions that assume and facilitate processes of discourse and articulation, with far less administrative manipulation of the criteria of teachers' and students' educational development.

Egan portrays the "good teacher" as one who is imaginative, implying that the school should be a safe place in which to dream. He locates the space of imagination for young children (and teachers) as being at points of mediation between such binary opposites as despair vis-à-vis hope or evil vis-à-vis good. We introduced this concluding chapter with the statement that mediation between contradictions characterizes the living out of the modern experience. The struggle for authenticity is a struggle of endless mediation between contradictions that we face in our moral choices. We suggest that relevant knowledge for teacher development occurs at silent or humming points of mediation between such binary opposites as problem versus solution or between what is imagined as bad versus good practice. We are interested in the energy of the *versus*.

One intriguing *versus* consists in the juxtaposition of ordinary vis-à-vis extraordinary experience. Egan argues that knowledge of relevance for adolescents has little to do with their perception of ordinary experience but deals instead in hopes, fears, and passions of extremity. This, it seems, has important implications for teachers or for any of us who, by forging our modern identity, need to risk thinking and feeling the extremes of experience so that we can confidently establish images of the potential good with others. This very recognition, however, raises trenchant questions about the value of reflecting on ordinary experience, which, as we have seen, is central to the derivation of an authentic professional identity. If imaginative thought and action is more likely steeped in extraordinary rather than ordinary experience, then it would seem that teachers' struggle for authenticity in a changing educational context involves a serious grappling with this apparent contradiction.

Students, teachers, and theorists are all learners. In many ways, teacher development theorists have never left the classroom either as students or as teachers. Reflecting on our own ordinary experience as theorists offers us the possibility of moving toward an authenticity of sorts: a concurrent journey with teachers in classrooms, which is only differentiated by the vehicles in which we choose to move. As learners, we can sympathize with our adolescent colleagues in the suspicion that every thing or every experience may have some transcendent quality. What, then, are the transcendent qualities of conceptualizing teachers' and our own educational development? Is it that we have retained an image of the potential good that sits on a moral horizon of significant questions and that we can imagine ourselves as moving toward? Or is it that we, as scions of a modern philosophical tradition, have actually constructed a concept of power that does not reside in the cosmos but that we have imagined as being inside our bodies; and, if we deem this concept to be acceptable, then what curriculum content—what conditions—would facilitate the exploration of this power when we are immersed in a world of ordinary experience? Under what conditions and in what settings could the content of teachers' or of our own continuous educational development be shown in terms of hopes, fears, passions; and how can the satisfaction of viewing the image of the good be felt by living the experience of arrival and return? And finally, what of modernity itself: a mode of experiencing space and time, of the self and others, from which we have drawn these theoretical concepts and foundations; a conceptual mode of experience that had a beginning in space and time and that may some day come to an end (Taylor, 1989).

Egan hopes he is not alone in finding his steps from observation to inference worthwhile, worth further exploration and research. We know that we are not alone in asserting that development of the most meaningful sort for teachers does not focus on skills training provided by topical workshops or discrete, bounded convocations. As advised by Lieberman, teacher development represents a much broader idea, viewing teachers as perpetual learners. As such, we hope that we are not alone in proposing that attendance to teachers' imaginative capacities also leads to principles, tools, norms, values, and criteria that are much broader than those that would encourage training in the formation of skills. We would even like to imagine that there may be room some day in the spatial field of teacher development theory for the nonrational languages of dream, of myth, of passion, and of enchantment. Could this actually be so? Perhaps. For now, we may only be permitted to employ the "language of hope": hope in the potential of mediated reflection on ordinary (and extraordinary) experience as a means whereby we may all struggle toward some authentic identity.

IMPLICATIONS FOR PRACTICE AND RESEARCH

It seems to us that the derivation of criteria of teacher development occurs in those spaces where, within the larger social context, the conditions of the practical and theoretical settings coalesce around teachers' views of what constitutes appropriate learner-focused practice. Within the confines of this volume, three exemplars of micro-level conditions (restructured roles and responsibilities, professional discourse with colleagues in community, and imaginative thought and action) become transformed into criteria of teacher development. It would appear that, when teachers experience and theoreticians hypothesize about and observe these conditions in operation, they also accept them as evidence that development is taking place. Yet these conditions are not in themselves unproblematic.

Restructured roles and responsibilities are a necessary organizational response to constructivist and social constructivist redefinitions of student learning. It is not possible to redefine student learning without first reconceptualizing teachers as leaders and learners. These restructured roles and responsibilities are designed to give greater decision-making power to teachers as a way of "honoring the educative agenda of schools" (Grimmett, 1993, p. 229). But they are also deeply embedded within the macro- and micropolitical contexts. Without organizational support and a strong professional culture in both these contexts, restructured roles and responsibilities for teachers can become little more than token gestures of hope in a world where legitimated authority and power reside elsewhere. There is a need, then, for future research in teacher development to look closely at schools in which restructured roles and responsibilities for teachers translate into an environment defined according to the needs and priorities of teachers and students as learners. There is also a need to look at how widespread such restructuring is. What typically has been the case is that these innovations, few in number, are located in settings where organizational support for the project has been championed by powerful political figures. Future research, then, needs to examine the extent to which these novel arrangements are essentially instituted at the pleasure of political forces, as a way of examining the feasibility of recommending these restructured organizational arrangements to the bureaucratized settings of the majority of schools.

Professional discourse with colleagues in community helps build the professional culture that is so vital to the successful working of restructured roles and responsibilities for teachers. It allows for the collaborative negotiation of purpose and task in teaching and learning and helps teachers transform their classrooms from places of work into centers of learning. It provides the social interaction and dialogue through which teachers derive and construct their identity as autonomous professionals. But most schools are not typically geared to a constructivist or social constructivist view of learning, or to a social interactionist understanding of teacher development. As with restructured roles and responsibilities, future teacher development research needs to study exemplars of professional discourse communities with a view to understanding the extent to which their very existence and nature are determined by the macro- and micropolitical contexts. Only when we have a clearer sense of these sets of complex yet delicate interrelationships will we understand how realistic it is to talk about establishing professional discourse communities for teachers in schools.

Imaginative thought and action both in curriculum planning and in the act of teaching is an undoubtedly appealing criterion of teacher development. Individuals can become extremely creative and take inordinate risks as they attempt to view learning through students' eyes. They can redefine learning and bring concepts alive for students by connecting them with the minds and worlds of children. But the problematic feature here is how to foster this kind of individual expression without reinforcing the "individualism, presentism, conservatism" (Little, 1990, p. 510) of most schools, thereby undermining the potency of the proposed restructured roles and responsibilities for teachers and the establishment of professional discourse communities. Future research, then, needs to study imaginative teachers developing their practice, examining how individual imaginative expression is linked to or separate from professional discourse in community with colleagues who view themselves as instructional leaders and pedagogical learners.

Finally, we would argue that there is a need to refine more rigorously our theoretical understanding of teacher development as a way of making sense of life's phenomena and experience through pedagogy. We would additionally argue that the refinement of our theoretical concepts would greatly serve teachers-as-learners, since it would facilitate our partnership with them as educational theorists and clarify our role in that partnership. This argument is put forward based on the observation that there appears to be at least one emerging sense of incoherence in how teacher development is conceptualized in the expanding literature. We have proposed that teacher development researchers, in response to such perceived trends as widespread disintegration of social and personal relationships in our culture, are engaged in a theoretical project of reviving a sense of meaning in the experience of teaching and of building supportive relationships and rebuilding opportunities of choice for teachers in schools. We have argued that theorists are drawing concepts and theoretical perspectives from a European philosophical tradition that values development toward an authentic identity. Taylor's (1989, 1991) analysis of the modern identity was used to characterize the struggle for authenticity as an exertion that ultimately leads toward an autonomous self-directed agency. But we would also characterize the search for a modern identity as a struggle of negotiating between such contradictions as renewal and disintegration, agreement and contradiction, or serenity and anxiety. In this scenario it is the struggle of negotiation itself that constitutes identity rather than any perceived arrival at an authentic end-state. We observe these two characterizations of development in emerging teacher development theory. The distinction is subtle but important and shows up when terms such as *inner selves* or *professional identity* are used in combination with such terms as *discourse, significant others,* and, especially, *continuous inquiry.* These categorical terms align the rhetoric of teacher development theory with mature philosophical traditions, and they have the potential to carry with them prescriptive implications for the settings and conditions in which teachers work.

In the Preface to this volume we characterized the struggle for authenticity as being marked by "an earnest search for authentic professional development" and added in the Introduction that "the struggle [search] lies in ensuring that the potential for the transformation of practice is, in fact, central to the interests of teachers, students, and their learning." We believe that it is time to ask what coherent theoretical framework and tradition, along with entailed conceptual categories, is central to the interests of teachers. If the primary concern is with issues of the inner self, or an autonomous professional identity, then we may align our thinking with notions of the Cartesian subject and the Kantian self-directed agent. We frame our arguments in terms of potential closure and construe teacher development in terms of a moral quest toward the goal of professional identity. We might also welcome the critique of such figures as Heidegger or Foucault, who sought to redefine our ways of thinking about how we perceive ourselves to be subjects or objects in a struggle for identity. If, on the other hand, we are concerned with growth, or with continuous inquiry into practice, and if growth is accomplished through a discursive, common moral language with significant others, we then align our thinking more closely with such sources as Mead, Habermas, and, to some degree, Wittgenstein. In the latter case, authenticity is felt as an experience of struggle. Here, the struggle is continuous and pursues endless moral questions and reinterpretations rather than seeking the attainment of authentic closure.

These two theoretical interpretations carry implications for settings, conditions, and criteria of teacher development. In the former case, we might advocate the creation of settings that provide sufficient conditions for teachers to develop toward the ultimate criterion of professional autonomy and its authentic identity. We would focus on the teacher's "self," and how the teacher-as-learner attains a self-directed agency. In the latter case, we might advocate the creation of settings that provide conditions for the important criterion of rigorous examination of practice as an ongoing reflective activity intended continually to redefine the relationship of teachers and students as co-learners. Our purpose here is neither to explore nor resolve this sense of incoherence; rather it is to indicate that teachers, educational researchers, teacher educators, and educational administrators are making choices based on existing robust theoretical frameworks, that these frameworks are connected with mature philosophical traditions, and that these choices may have significant implications for what is advocated as valuable settings, conditions, and criteria for teachers' development.

All three criteria mentioned above illustrate to some extent this sense of theoretical incoherence. Restructured roles and responsibilities can be regarded as structures that facilitate or are ultimately indicative of an authentic professional identity. Professional discourse with colleagues in community could be viewed as an essential process to or a particular benchmark of authentic teacher development. And imaginative thought and action could conceivably be a means toward or an end-state of authentic practice. Our suggestion is that teacher development may be ill conceived when it is viewed as struggling to arrive at an authentic end-state of autonomous self-directed agency. We would argue that this book suggests a further important criterion of teacher development, one which makes it clear that the struggle for authenticity in a changing educational context is constituted and continually reconstituted around the negotiation of perplexing dilemmas and vexing contradictions.

Building on the discussion in the Introduction to this volume, Figure Concl. 1 shows how teacher development in a changing educational context can be characterized as a struggle in three different ways. When teachers develop their practice according to what is rewarded by the institutional context, their struggle becomes an exertion toward compliance and "fitting in" with hierarchically and externally derived criteria of teacher development. When teachers develop their practice according to what they find professionally rewarding, their struggle is one of overcoming potentially burdensome drudgery to find what is appealing and satisfying. In so doing, they are defining their own criteria of teacher development but in a manner that is self-referenced rather than learner-focused. Thus these traditional and alternative forms of struggle are still forms of exertion toward a teacher-centered classroom; they do not provide teachers with opportunities to view, redefine, and support learning from the perspective of the learner. As a consequence, they remain struggles for self-preservation and self-consideration, not for authenticity. By contrast, when teachers develop their practice according to what is important and of value to learners, the struggle becomes one of grappling with how to act morally in an uncertain and constantly changing educational context. This moral quest, requiring teachers to transcend traditional and alternative forms of struggle to engage in the pursuit of moral aims in teaching, constitutes the struggle for authenticity. It is exertion, negotiated within the discourse of a community of a common language and shared values, toward the continual grappling with perplexing dilemmas of practice in

Figure Concl 1. Traditional, alternative, and authentic forms of struggle

RULE	MOTIVATION	INVOLVEMENT	STRUGGLE
Traditional What gets rewarded gets done	Extrinsic gain	Calculated	"fit in"
Alternative What is rewarding gets done	Intrinsic gain	Personal	"find what appeals"
Authentic What is good gets done	Moral aim	Moral	"act morally"

From *Moral Leadership* by T. J. Sergiovanni: San Francisco, Jossey-Bass, p. 27. Copyright 1992 by Jossey-Bass. Adapted with permission.

morally appropriate ways. Unlike the struggles for self-preservation and self-consideration, the struggle for authenticity provides an interesting twist. *The more teachers embark on this moral quest, the more they experience the authenticity of struggle.* That is, they come to recognize the value and importance of struggle in teacher development. The authenticity of struggle comes about when teachers value stretching themselves under great difficulty, not because it is generally accepted practice that has its institutional rewards, nor because it is inherently satisfying, but because it is the morally appropriate thing to do, particularly when macro- and micro-level contexts produce conditions unsupportive of a learner-focused orientation in the practical setting of teacher development. This entails negotiating the dualities and seemingly endless contradictions inherent in a changing educational context. It involves grappling with vexing questions and puzzling dilemmas to obtain some form of moral coherence in settings in which dispersion and fragmentation are the prevalent features. Whereas the struggle for authenticity suggests that teachers exert themselves in settings that do not typically have conditions that value and encourage a strenuous wrestling with moral issues and dilemmas, the authenticity of struggle implies that the presence and celebration of struggle per se constitutes one of the primary criteria of teacher development in a changing educational context.

NOTES

1. Nias (1989) explains how the notion of the self is conceptualized in symbolic interactionism, Freudianism, and self-psychology. Her book is important because she claims that not all teachers incorporate an occupational identity into their self-image. She adds that the self shifts in its conception over the span of the teacher's career from a preoccupation with survival and a search for occupational identification to the consolidation and extension of work-related skills and then to a search for greater influence within what becomes a personally-selected profession. Huberman's (1993) significant study chose to construe the teacher's life as a *career*. He and his colleagues concluded that teachers have the tendency to delineate their careers into identifiable stages or phases but that professional career journeys were not linear, predictable, nor certainly identical.

2. We are aware that *Habits of the Heart* is the title of a book in which Bellah and his co-authors (1986) have examined and responded to specific malaises of the modern experience. Taylor (1989) draws on their work to a large degree for his own analysis. He credits them as inspirational in his analysis but adds that their view of the modern predicament is oversimplified.

3. This point is consistent with Habermas (1981), who borrows a great deal from the social psychology of Mead. He also claims that the self-directed agent is constituted by linguistic exchanges between agents. Significant others are not

conceived as external to the agent, therefore, but help to constitute our internalized selfhood (Taylor, 1989).

4. The idea of a generalized other is drawn from the social psychology of George Herbert Mead (1934), who also influenced the pragmatic philosophy of John Dewey. Mead believed the individual could attain a unity, a wholeness, and a coherence of self through a connection with an actual community and by focusing on a commonly generated vision or image of the generalized other. A question worth posing here is whether teachers could ever be construed as arriving at such a unity or wholeness in their careers. The process of development as movement toward a vision or image of the generalized other would seem to continue during the ensuing course of their careers. Conditions, such as the gradual aging of their bodies, and settings, such as surrounding working conditions, would change, but they would continue to live in communal discourse of action and speaking. Imagined criteria of the "good teacher" would remain on the horizon and teacher development toward that image would seem to continue, given that conditions in settings would be consistent with this development.

REFERENCES

Barth, R. S. (1990). *Improving schools from within*. San Francisco: Jossey-Bass.

Bellah, R. N., Madsen, R., Sullivan, W. M., Swidler, A., & Tipton, S. M. (1986). *Habits of the heart: Individualism and commitment in American life*. New York: Harper & Row.

Bloom, A. (1987). *The closing of the American mind*. New York: Simon & Schuster.

Clift, R., Houston, R., & Pugach, M. (Eds.). (1990). *Encouraging reflective practice: An examination of issues and exemplars*. New York: Teachers College Press.

Fullan, M., & Hargreaves, A. (1991). *What's worth fighting for? Working together for your school*. Toronto: Ontario Public School Teachers Federation.

Fullan, M., & Hargreaves, A. (1992). *Teacher development and educational change*. Lewes, UK: Falmer.

Gilligan, C. (1982). *In a different voice*. Cambridge, MA: Harvard University Press.

Gilligan, C. (1989). *Mapping the moral domain*. Cambridge, MA: Harvard University Press.

Goodson, I. (1991a, October). *Exploring the teacher's professional knowledge: Constructing identity and community*. Paper presented at the first Invitational Symposium on Teacher Development (Spencer Hall), London, Ontario.

Goodson, I. (1991b, April). *Studying teachers' lives: Problems and possibilities*. Paper presented at the annual meeting of the American Educational Research Association, Chicago.

Grimmett, P. P. (1993). Teacher research and British Columbia's curricular-instructional experiment: Implications for educational policy. *Journal of Educational Policy, 8*(3), 219–239.

Grimmett, P. P., & Crehan, E. P. (1992). The nature of collegiality in teacher development: The case of clinical supervision. In M. Fullan & A. Hargreaves

(Eds.), *Teacher development and educational change* (pp. 56–85). New York & Philadelphia: Falmer.

Grimmett, P. P., & Erickson, G. L. (Eds.). (1988). *Reflection in teacher education.* New York: Teachers College Press.

Grimmett, P. P., MacKinnon, A. M., Erickson, G. L., & Riecken, T. J. (1990). Reflective practice in teacher education. In R. Clift, R. Houston, & M. Pugach (Eds.), *Encouraging reflective practice: An examination of issues and exemplars* (pp. 20–38). New York: Teachers College Press.

Habermas, J. (1981). *Theorie des kommunikativen Handelns* (2 vols.). Frankfurt: Surkamp.

Hargreaves, A., & Fullan, M. (1991). *Understanding teacher development.* New York: Teachers College Press.

Hargreaves, A., & Tucker, E. (1991). Teaching and guilt. *Teaching and Teacher Education, 7*(5/6), 491–505.

Huberman, M. (1993). *Lives of teachers* (J. Neufeld, Trans.). New York: Teachers College Press.

Lasch, C. (1979). *The culture of narcissism: American life in an age of diminishing expectations.* New York: Norton.

Lieberman, A., & Miller, L. (1991). *Staff development in the '90s: New demands, new realities, new perspectives.* New York: Teachers College Press.

Little, J. W. (1986). Seductive images and organizational realities in professional development. *Teachers' College Record, 86*(1), 84–102.

Little, J. W. (1990). The persistence of privacy: Autonomy and initiative in teachers' professional relations. *Teachers College Record, 91*(4), 509–536.

Little, J. W., & McLaughlin, M. W. (1993). *The school as workplace.* New York: Teachers College Press.

Lortie, D. (1975). *Schoolteacher.* Chicago: University of Chicago Press.

Mead, G. H. (1934). *Mind, self and society from the standpoint of a social behaviorist.* Chicago: University of Chicago Press.

Nias, J. (1989). *Primary teachers talking.* London: Routledge.

Pollard, A. (1990). The aims of primary school teachers. In N. Proctor (Ed.), *The aims of primary education and the National Curriculum* (pp. 63–77). Lewes, UK: Falmer.

Rosenholtz, S. (1989). *Teachers' workplace.* New York: Longman.

Rousseau, J. J. (1979). *Emile* (A. Bloom, Trans.). New York: Basic Books.

Schön, D. A. (1983). *The reflective practitioner: How professionals think in action.* New York: Basic Books.

Schön, D. A. (1987). *Educating the reflective practitioner: Toward a new design for teaching and learning in the professions.* San Francisco: Jossey-Bass.

Schön, D. A. (1988). Coaching reflective practice. In P. Grimmett & G. Erickson (Eds.), *Reflection in teacher education* (pp. 19–29). New York: Teachers College Press.

Taylor, C. (1989). *Sources of the self: The making of the modern identity.* Cambridge, MA: Harvard University Press.

Taylor, C. (1991). *The malaise of modernity.* Toronto: Anansi.

Waller, W. (1932). *The sociology of teaching.* New York: Wiley.

About the Editors and the Contributors

Peter P. Grimmett is Associate Professor of Education in the Faculty of Education at Simon Fraser University. Formerly Director of the Centre for the Study of Teacher Education at the University of British Columbia, he now works in the newly established Institute for Studies in Teacher Education (INSITE) at Simon Fraser University. His research interests focus at the preservice and in-service levels on the relationship between teachers' development of their craft and the processes of reflection, collegial consultation, and classroom-based action research. His recent publications include *Reflection in Teacher Education* (Teachers College Press, 1988, with Gaalen Erickson); *Craft Knowledge and the Education of Teachers* (American Educational Research Association, 1992, with Allan MacKinnon); *The Transformation of Supervision* (Association for Supervision and Curriculum Development, 1992, with Olaf Rostad and Blake Ford); and "Teacher research and British Columbia's curricular-instructional experiment: Implications for educational policy" (*The Journal of Educational Policy*, 1993).

Jonathan Neufeld studied Educational Administration at the Ontario Institute for Studies in Education and is now a doctoral student in Curriculum Theory related to teachers' educational development in the Faculty of Education at Simon Fraser University. He is translator of Michael Huberman's *Lives of Teachers* (Cassell & Teachers College Press, 1993). His work focuses on critically examining the epistemological, historical, and philosophical bases of teacher development as a field of study. He is currently doing research at the University of California at Berkeley.

Kathleen M. Ceroni has taught English at Southmoreland Senior High School, Mt. Pleasant, Pennsylvania, for the past 21 years. As a district staff development facilitator, she has conducted workshops for teachers about current classroom innovations. She has also taught courses in methods of teaching at the University of Pittsburgh. She has made presentations at the American Educational Research Association and the Bergamo Curriculum Conference. She is currently writing her doctoral dissertation, an interpretive study of the lead teacher experience in Pennsylvania. The focus of her research interests is on the effects of reform movements on teachers' professional lives with specific emphasis on the notion of "betrayal" and its relationship to teacher commitment and sense of professionalism.

Sylvia C. Chard is Associate Professor of Early Childhood Education in the Department of Elementary Education in the Faculty of Education at the University of Alberta. Her early teaching experience was at the secondary level and later in preschool and elementary schools in England. She gained her M.Ed. and Ph.D. at the University of Illinois and recently completed a 10-year study of teacher development. She is co-author with Lilian G. Katz of *Engaging Children's Minds: The Project Approach* (Ablex, 1989) and has also produced an in-service package to help teachers develop project work in their own classrooms.

Kieran Egan is Professor of Education in the Faculty of Education at Simon Fraser University. His recent books include: *Teaching as Story Telling* (University of Chicago Press, 1989); *Primary Understanding: Education in Early Childhood* (Routledge, 1988), for which he won the highly prestigious Grawemeyer Award in 1991 for outstanding scholarship in the field of curriculum; *Romantic Understanding: The Development of Rationality and Imagination, Ages 8–15* (Routledge, 1991); and *Imagination in Teaching and Learning* (University of Chicago Press, 1992). Most recently, he has become the first education theorist to be admitted to the Royal Society of Canada.

Noreen B. Garman is Professor of Education in the Administration and Policy Studies department at the University of Pittsburgh. She teaches course and publishes in the fields of instructional supervision and curriculum studies. Her articles have appeared in the *Journal of Curriculum and Supervision*, *Journal of Personnel Evaluation in Education*, *Journal of Curriculum Theorizing*, *Educational Quarterly*, and *Australian Administrator*. She is currently writing a book on clinical supervision from an interpretive perspective and also a co-author of a book on portfolio making in higher education. In 1982 and 1986 she was a visiting professor at Deakin University, Australia, and in 1989 she became a senior Fulbright Scholar for the Philippines.

Harold Grunau is Professor of Education in the Faculty of Education at the University of Manitoba. He received his Ph.D. in Curriculum and Secondary Education with an emphasis in science education at Michigan State University after several years of public school teaching in Ontario. At present he teaches preservice and in-service courses in Curriculum and Instruction in elementary science education. His research and service contributions and publications include those in preservice program development and science assessment. More recently his research efforts have been oriented toward collaborating with students and university colleagues using personal practical knowledge, story, and narrative to explore teacher development in the area of science teaching. Presently he is principal investigator of the project titled "Collaborative Inquiry into the Lives of Science Teacher Educators."

Andy Hargreaves is Professor in Educational Administration at the Ontario Institute for Studies in Education, Toronto. He has published more than a dozen books and monographs on educational change, restructuring, curriculum reform, teacher development, and the culture of the school. His most recent publications include: *Changing Teachers, Changing Times: Teachers' Work and Culture in the Postmodern World* (Cassell & Teachers College Press, 1994); *Understanding Teacher Development* (Cassell & Teachers College Press, 1992, with Michael Fullan); and *Teacher Development and Educational Change* (Falmer, 1992, with Michael Fullan). He is currently one of the two international directors for the eight-country project on "Professional actions and cultures of teaching" (PACT). He consults widely with schools and provincial and state education departments across the world on educational restructuring and reform.

Ann Lieberman is Professor of Education at Teachers College, Columbia University. She is also (with Linda Darling-Hammond) Co-Director of the National Center for Restructuring Education, Schools, and Teaching (NCREST) at Teachers College, Columbia University.

Allan M. MacKinnon is Assistant Professor of Education in the Faculty of Education at Simon Fraser University. He is also a member of the Institute for Studies in Teacher Education (INSITE). He received his Ed.D. in science education at the University of British Columbia. He taught at the elementary school level in Alberta, and subsequently at the University of Calgary and the University of Toronto before moving to Simon Fraser University. His research interests have been primarily directed toward identifying the processes and conditions by which beginning teachers are encouraged to reflect upon their practice. He is principal investigator of a project titled "Investigating the 'Continuum' of Teacher Development in Science Teaching," and co-investigator of an "Analysis of an 'Engineering for Children' program in Elementary Science." He is also coordinating an interactive video link between Simon Fraser University and Cariboo Hill Secondary School in Burnaby, British Columbia. His recent publications include "Conceptualizing a 'Hall of Mirrors' in a Science-Teaching Practicum" (*The Journal of Curriculum and Supervision*, 1989); *Seeing Classrooms in New Ways: On Becoming a Science Teacher* (Teachers College Press, 1991, with Gaalen Erickson); *Craft Knowledge and the Education of Teachers* (American Educational Research Association, 1992 with Peter Grimmett); and "Examining Practice to Address Policy Problems in Teacher Education" (*The Journal of Education Policy*, 1993).

Milbrey Wallin McLaughlin is Professor of Education and Public Policy at Stanford University and Director of the Center for Research on the Context of Secondary School Teaching (CRC). Her research interests include the organizational contexts of teaching and learning, policy implementation, and neighborhood-based organizations for youth. She has written, co-authored, or edited numerous books on these topics, including most recently *Urban Sanctuaries: Neighborhood Organizations in the Lives and Futures of Inner-City Youth* (Jossey-Bass, in press, with Merita Irby and Juliet Langman); *Teaching for Understanding: Challenges for Practice, Policy, and Research* (Jossey-Bass, 1993, with David K. Cohen and Joan E. Talbert); *Identity and Inner-City Youth: Beyond Ethnicity and Gender* (Teachers College Press, 1993, with Shirley Brice Heath; *Teachers' Work: Individuals, Colleagues, and Contexts* (Teachers College Press, 1993, with Judith Warren Little); and *The Contexts of Teaching in Secondary Schools* (Teachers College Press, with Joan E. Talbert and Nina Bascia).

Leslie Santee Siskin is Associate Professor in Educational Leadership and Policy in the School of Education at Hofstra University. Her research focuses on the context of teaching in high schools, and on departmental organization and subject cultures. Her recent publications include: "Departments as Different Worlds: Subject Subcultures in Secondary Schools" (*Educational Administration Quarterly*, 1991) and *Realms of Knowledge: Academic Departments in Secondary Schools* (Falmer, 1994).

Peter Woods is Professor of Education at the Open University, Milton Keynes, England. After graduating from the University of London, he taught for several years in both elementary and secondary schools. His Ph.D. dissertation was published as *The Divided School* (Routledge & Kegan Paul, 1979). At the Open University he was, for a number of years, Director of the Centre for Sociology and Social Research. He has contributed to many courses there, mainly in the areas of the sociology of education and qualitative research methods. His chief research interests are in the field of teacher–student interaction, and he is currently researching how creative teachers are adapting to the National Curriculum. His many publications include an ethnographic research methods text, *Inside Schools* (Falmer, 1984); two companion books on teaching and learning, *Teacher Skills and Strategies* (Falmer, 1990) and *The Happiest Days?* (Falmer, 1990); and, most recently, a study of exceptional educational events, *Critical Events in Teaching and Learning* (Falmer, 1993).

Index